THE BRONTË NOVELS

The
Brontë Novels

W. A. CRAIK

METHUEN & CO LTD
11 NEW FETTER LANE · LONDON EC4

First published 1968 by
Methuen & Co Ltd
11 New Fetter Lane London EC4
Reprinted 1969, 1970 and 1971
© 1968 W. A. Craik
SBN 416 11280 3

First published as a University Paperback 1971
SBN 416 11330 3

Printed in Great Britain by
Latimer Trend, Whitstable

Distributed in the U.S.A. by
Barnes and Noble, Inc.

CONTENTS

to my husband

INTRODUCTION

Historically speaking, there were four Brontës (the family of the Rev. Patrick Brontë, rector of Haworth) – Charlotte, Patrick Branwell, Emily Jane, and Anne; for the student of the English novel, there are three – Charlotte, Emily, and Anne; for the reader of poetry there is only one – Emily. I am concerned only with the second group, and with them only as the authors of their published, complete works, that is, with seven novels: Emily Brontë's *Wuthering Heights*, Charlotte Brontë's *Professor*, *Jane Eyre*, *Shirley*, and *Villette*, and Anne Brontë's *Agnes Grey* and *The Tenant of Wildfell Hall*.

The Brontës have the misfortune of existing as a single entity, as though they wrote in collaboration, or as though what is true of one of them is true of all. The grounds for their doing so are biographical; they were a closely-knit family, four years only separated Charlotte Brontë the eldest from Anne the youngest; they spent much of their lives secluded at Haworth, in a seclusion voluntarily (for Emily at least) made greater than it need have been, restricted further by a chronic shortage of money and by ill-health; they all ventured into teaching in private families and disliked it; and were all cut off by death before reaching middle age. Robert Martin remarks

> It would be an unimaginative mind that was unstirred by the lives of the Brontës, and it would require a heart more steadfast than most of us would care to own to be unmoved by pity for them.[1]

The remark and the response are legitimate, just as they would be with many other writers who suffered great personal loss, poverty,

[1] *The Accents of Persuasion*, Faber & Faber, 1966.

or illness, such as Tennyson, Thackeray, Keats or Swift. Yet these writers do not draw from us a response to themselves and their own lives in the way the Brontës do, which moves us even before reading what they write, and colours our response to the writing itself. The Brontës' biography does them disservice with the reader, and invites him to read them in ways which, while not wrong, may prevent him from seeing properly what are their individual merits, or indeed what are their purposes in writing at all.

It is easy to suppose that their purpose is no more than personal emotional release, either a compensation for a constricting existence for Emily Brontë, or a fantasy reliving of an unsatisfying life for Charlotte and Anne. Charlotte and Anne offer the reader two supports for the idea: they write in the first person, thus inviting him to equate the narrator with the author, and they draw freely upon people and incidents from their own lives, thus inviting him both to belittle the skill that can recognizably render the actual, and to read the novels as autobiography, assuming that because a character or event is based upon a real one, the way the author uses it must tally with life at all points. When put like this it seems that only a naïve reader could be so duped; that so many readers are so constantly duped, notably with Charlotte Brontë, is a measure of her power in making life serve the ends of art.[1] However, to make a critical estimate of the achievement one must recognize what is happening, and examine how it is brought about. I have concentrated on the novels themselves therefore, and on what light they throw on themselves and on each other, have examined the evidence they provide for their own merits, the terms in which they present themselves, how far they adhere to their self-imposed conditions, how far they reveal and carry out their aims; how far these conditions and aims are those of earlier novelists known to the Brontës, or those of their contemporaries, and how in a final estimate the Brontë novels compare with their great coevals in the nineteenth-century novel. A second concern of the book has been to consider

[1] F. R. Leavis who is 'tempt(ed) to retort that there is only one Brontë' recognized her 'remarkable talent that enabled her to do something firsthand and new in the rendering of personal experience, above all in *Villette*'. (*The Great Tradition*, Chatto and Windus, 1948.)

Anne Brontë as seriously and thoroughly as her sisters, on her own terms as a writer, and to assess her place as an independent novelist, not merely as an interesting minor appendage.

I have tried therefore to put personal pity for the authors (if indeed one may presume to pity) on one side, and to draw upon biography only when it serves one of these ends; when, for example, what each writer selects out of their mutual experience, and how she uses it, reveals her purpose in writing. Similarly I have not dealt with the poems[1] or with the various unfinished fragments of stories and of the last novel, *Emma*, by Charlotte Brontë, or with the vast body of the juvenile writings; these things supply very valuable contributory evidence of what goes into the novels, but are not valid as evidence of the stature of the novels themselves.

Since the sisters had written for each other all through childhood, and listened to and commented on each other's work whilst it was in progress, they necessarily learned from and influenced each other, with results plain in the published novels. It would be convenient therefore to discuss them chronologically, in the order in which they were composed. Unfortunately the exact order cannot be certain, some were written concurrently, and (a more serious objection to the method) such an order could cut across the more vital progress of the individual writer. I have adopted a compromise. Emily Brontë's *Wuthering Heights*, one of the earliest, and by the least impressible writer, comes first, followed by Charlotte's novels in the order in which they were written (which is not, unfortunately, that either of importance or interest), and last Anne, in the position she always occupies and – though she is as original as Charlotte and in some ways as unimpressible as Emily – in a last estimate, merits.

In quoting from the novels I have used the text of *The Shakespeare Head Brontë*[2] and all chapter references are to this edition. In the footnotes I have given, at the first mention of all other works, the full bibliographical reference, and thereafter used a short title; the full titles are given in the bibliography. References to secondary sources have been kept to a minimum in the interests of concentrating

[1] Magnificent though many of Emily Brontë's poems are, and necessary though they would be to a study of her as a whole.
[2] Ed. T. J. Wise and J. A. Symington, Oxford, 1931.

3

on the novels. The bibliography itself is a measure of my indebtedness to other scholars.

For the use of their facilities I am indebted to the library staffs of the University of Aberdeen, the British Museum, and the Brontë Parsonage Museum, Haworth; for typing the manuscript, to Miss Lily Hay, Miss Joyce Anderson and Mrs Constance Keith. For invaluable help in discussing and arranging my ideas I am grateful to my colleagues in the English Department at Aberdeen University, to Peter Stein, Professor of Jurisprudence, to my students, and to my husband, without whose constant encouragement I should never have carried out either my inclinations or my contract.

Department of English,
King's College,
Old Aberdeen.
September 1967

I

WUTHERING HEIGHTS

For any one reader who testifies to the greatness of Charlotte Brontë as a novelist, there are dozens who will testify to Emily; and there are almost as many ideas of what constitutes her greatness as there are readers to expound them. It has been common, since the establishing of a reliable text of the poems by G. W. Hatfield,[1] and the invaluable research into them by F. E. Ratchford,[2] demonstrating their essentially dramatic nature, to regard Emily Brontë's poems as the 'way in' to the novel – as being the impressionistic raw materials of situation, attitude, and philosophy out of which the novel sprung.[3] However, such an approach, whose value is indisputable, frequently explains rather than assesses: it is taken for granted that *Wuthering Heights* is a great novel, and what follows is exposition of the elements which are presumed to constitute greatness. While acknowledging that the poems come from the same mind as the novel, and often resemble it closely in situation and in spirit, I want to examine the novel as it stands, to discover what are Emily Brontë's purposes in writing, how she goes to work, what effects she brings about, how original, and, finally, how great is her achievement.

With most novelists, especially those of the nineteenth century, two of the most profitable things to consider are the relationship between the author and his reader, and the author and his material. In Emily Brontë's novel, however, these matters are never explicit.

[1] *The Complete Poems of Emily Brontë*, New York, 1941.
[2] *The Brontës' Web of Childhood*, Columbia, 1941, and *Gondal's Queen*, Austin, Texas, 1955.
[3] One of the most perceptive of such examinations is Mary Visick's *The Genesis of 'Wuthering Heights'*, Oxford, 1959.

Her attitude may be powerfully felt, for it is inseparable from the responses drawn out of the reader, and these are themselves the reader's only means of discovering Emily Brontë's own feelings; her purpose can be conjectured from her choice of topic, and from the movement and selection of her narrative. She is deliberately a dramatic writer: she not only lets her characters speak for themselves, and reveal themselves by what they do, but also presents her narrative through one or other of the characters, mainly Ellen Dean and Lockwood. But this self-effacement is not so thorough as it seems. The two narrators are as much a means of involvement as a means of detachment. Through them, particularly Ellen, Emily Brontë presents a limited range of extreme emotions, all concerned fundamentally with the unity between individual man and man, or man and his natural surroundings, and with what happens when the unity is broken: centrally and primarily the unity between Heathcliff and Catherine, and their relation with Wuthering Heights. She presents them to us essentially for our admiration, for their spiritual and physical power, their courage, inflexibility and capacity for intense feeling, irrespective of whether these qualities are exerted for what is normally regarded as good or bad. Happiness in any normal sense of the word does not interest her as a novelist, but she is not inflexibly solemn. Humour is part of her method, as it is part of Shakespeare's, not only to release tension but to heighten it.

On these emotional concerns most readers agree, and the emphasis on individual scenes confirms our impressions; the great scenes are the emotional ones: Cathy's confession to Ellen of her love for Heathcliff and Edgar Linton; Heathcliff's words and her own at her death; Heathcliff's agony that night in the garden; or his outbursts to Ellen just before he himself dies. While we also recall scenes of violent action – like Hindley's drunken ravings (Chapter 9), or the occasion when he and Isabella attempt to shut Heathcliff out of the Heights (Chapter 17) – these crises of the body do not loom so large in our minds as the crises of the spirit.

Emily Brontë is clearly always concerned to enter utterly into the emotion of the moment, the 'now' of the story, without reservations or withdrawal, but yet with the power to see its relevance not merely to what comes immediately before or after, but to its place in the whole. The story is told in such a way that we either know the result already, or we are prepared to expect a particular outcome. The results of this method are several, and illuminate Emily Brontë's intentions, her attitude, and that she intends for the reader. By telling us the end of her story first, so that we know that the three main moving spirits are dead – Catherine, Edgar Linton and Hindley Earnshaw – she does away with one of a novel's usual main powers, suspense. She is in a way therefore 'realistic', and gives us the feeling of history rather than of fiction; no event is rushed or scamped by the artificial narrative excitement of wondering what is to happen next; nor is the reader racked beyond bearing by the distress of some of the events, as he might well be if suspense or even hope were added to the other emotions he is made to suffer. Emily Brontë the creator, and the reader sharing her knowledge, can be almost godlike, since her characters are clearly acting according to their own wills, and yet, knowing what their future will be, we feel them to be predestined. We can at the same time enter into the agonies and struggles of the characters – any of them, at any moment – yet remain detached from them by knowing their fates. We understand without necessarily sympathizing, and are never given the chance to 'identify' in the usual way with either hero or heroine. Pity of the usual sort for individuals is never elicited, but Ellen, nostalgic for the past, feeling the plight of her fellows and of mankind, without fully understanding it, allows us a sorrow that we partake as well as observe.

These emotions we are offered are all those whose impulse we can readily understand at their beginnings – they are emotions such as any child can feel – but their manifestations become more violent and more extensive than we could imagine. This is even true of Catherine Earnshaw, probably the most difficult person of all: she explains quite simply and clearly to Ellen (Chapter 9) how she is divided between Heathcliff and Edgar Linton and why she must marry Edgar, an unusual but by no means impossible condition. The torments she suffers, and in her suffering inflicts, as a result of tearing herself spiritually in two are beyond anything we expect to encounter, but are rendered intelligible by their simple and

7

intelligible cause. All the emotions felt by characters are, while powerful, essentially static, immutable, and curiously impersonal. Everyone remarks the state in Catherine and Heathcliff, but it is also true of the younger Catherine loving Linton, repellent as he shows himself to be, or of Ellen's ties to Hindley Earnshaw and Hareton, brutalized and degraded though they become. We do not understand these characters by rational effort, but only by accepting what they do and say, by allowing Emily Brontë to build up setting, mood and action gradually, and by entering into the experience she offers. Only then can we look back, analyse, and perceive how she has induced our understanding of the whole. She calls on childhood as the age of spiritual understanding from which the rest of life is either development or falling away. She sees man and his environment as inseparable and even at some points as part of a greater whole. In their unity is peace, and in their breaking the violence of misdirected or frustrated energy.

A pattern can therefore be seen established, a relationship between violence and power, where the greater the outward expression the less real power beneath it suggests. Degrees of violence and cruelty actually relate either to degrees of ineffectuality and impotence or to degrees of frustration. Emily Brontë works with great skill to establish her negative – a difficult task. Linton Heathcliff, the feeblest person, is the most willing to indulge in gratuitous cruelty, and all that prevents him from physical violence is incapacity – the will is there. The two most violent scenes in the book are caused by Hindley and Isabella, two of the characters most lacking in purpose and power. Cathy rages herself into delirium and insanity, not when being ill-treated by Hindley, but when she is helpless under the fate she herself decreed, separated from Heathcliff by being bound to Edgar. Heathcliff, the most powerful figure of all, is for a long time the least violent, and as will later be seen, never initiates action, but only responds to it.

Emily Brontë, then, though committed to revealing passions which must express themselves in fierce and even cruel action, is not herself absorbed by cruelty, nor does she wish her reader to be so. Many brutal or sickening scenes are avoided.[1] Power

[1] Notably Linton Heathcliff's slow dying and Catherine's agonies during it.

rather than violence of feeling absorbs her, and much of this is expressed in imagery in Ellen's analyses or in speech. It is these images quite as much as what is actually done that move us at great moments.[1]

This power rests in Catherine and Heathcliff, and Emily Brontë's attention, like ours, is always upon them. The only events retailed are those which involve Catherine and Heathcliff in their relations with each other either personally or indirectly: they are what shapes the novel and selects the incident. Emily Brontë clearly directs how the reader shall respond to her heroes, even though she is so self-effacing.[2] She regulates the tone by the events and their juxta-position, and by the discrepancy between what we see and how Ellen sees it. Characters are frequently repellent and estimable by turns and in quick succession, and a fine richness of meaning and response is won, while still using quite uncomplicated emotions in the characters. One of the most powerful instances occurs in Chapter 11 where Ellen visits the Heights and hears the young savage Hareton's view of Heathcliff; returns home to see Heathcliff surreptitiously paying court to Isabella, to hear him cry out to Catherine that she has treated him 'infernally'; and then witnesses the quarrel in which Linton attempts to turn Heathcliff out of the house and strikes him, the quarrel in which Catherine throws the key in the fire to deliver to Heathcliff the husband she has just been defending against him. Emily Brontë has in quick succession made a recoil from Heathcliff as the destroyer of peace at the Heights and Thrushcross, and yet recognized his agony at being rejected by Catherine; has recognized Linton's rights and dignity as husband and master of the house, yet despised his physical feebleness; and has, finally, exposed Catherine's ungoverned temper and perver-sity in scolding Heathcliff and scorning Edgar and apparently using her frenzy for her own ends. All these rapidly-produced responses and random incidents culminate in Catherine's last mortal illness, whose justification we feel the more by having responded and

[1] Hence, as many have noted, the easiness with which outsiders like the doctor Kenneth and the servant Zillah accept what is happening.

[2] It is clearly not a matter merely of accepting Ellen's guidance, since the reader is frequently compelled to be both wiser and more responsive than she.

reacted ourselves to the tensions that have caused it. She does not arouse admiration or pity, but rather a horrified recognition, respect and understanding of the power of a passion that can break both mind and body – a passion that Ellen, the only obvious guide, neither recognizes, approves, nor understands at all. The reader is clearly in the hands of an accomplished author who while not dealing in any of the usual forms of structural irony, yet leads him to read and respond differently from what he normally does, and to perceive more than any one character can do. These are Catherine's own words about Heathcliff:

> 'Pray don't imagine that he conceals depths of benevolence and affection beneath a stern exterior! He's not a rough diamond – a pearl-containing oyster of a rustic; he's a fierce, pitiless, wolfish man. I never say to him let this or that enemy alone, because it would be ungenerous or cruel to harm them – I say Let them alone, because I should hate them to be wronged: and he'd crush you, like a sparrow's egg, Isabella, if he found you a troublesome charge. I know he couldn't love a Linton; and yet, he'd be quite capable of marrying your fortune, and expectations. Avarice is growing with him a besetting sin. There's my picture; and I'm his friend – so much so, that had he thought seriously to catch you, I should, perhaps, have held my tongue, and let you fall into his trap.'
>
> Miss Linton regarded her sister-in-law with indignation.
>
> 'For shame! for shame!' she repeated, angrily, 'You are worse than twenty foes, you poisonous friend!'   (Chapter 10)

Plainly this says much more than Isabella perceives, since we believe Catherine is telling the truth, but it also does more than Catherine herself here intends: it presents the conventional as both trivial and enervated – 'a rough diamond', 'a pearl-containing oyster' – and directs us to value the apparently repulsive – 'a fierce, pitiless, wolfish man' – for being neither trivial nor mean. It recalls Catherine's earlier great confession of love to Ellen, and so we feel the enormous truth here of 'I'm his friend'. Isabella's reply, 'You are worse than twenty foes', is indeed about to be proved ironically true, since it is Catherine herself who brings about her own and Heathcliff's great miseries. There is force also in her next remark, 'he has an honourable soul, and a true one, or how could he remember her?', which Catherine does not or cannot answer, since the next speech is Ellen's and changes the topic.

While readers agree on how they respond emotionally to characters, how they judge them is not always so unanimous. Even so, the reader is clearly being directed. Conventional religious and moral standards soon come to feel curiously inadequate. While Ellen often speaks of Catherine and Heathcliff as evil – using words like 'wicked', 'unprincipled', 'diabolical', 'selfish', and 'unchristian' – and while Lockwood soon judges Heathcliff to have 'a bad nature', neither of the protagonists themselves recognizes the relevance of such concepts to their behaviour. As a boy Heathcliff cannot understand the notion of 'envying' Catherine (Chapter 7), he claims the right to revenge on most shakingly convincing grounds, 'God won't have the satisfaction I shall', just as Catherine feels that being able to help Heathcliff will be her best reason for marrying Linton (Chapter 9). Emily Brontë has laid aside Christian morals. God clearly exists in the novel, not a Christian God, but one who while being the source of damnation has no power or right over the characters or what they suffer: even Hindley can declare that far from having mercy on his own soul he will have 'great pleasure in sending it to perdition to punish its Maker' (Chapter 9). Religious references (in contrast to principles) are frequent, because some theory of right and wrong and salvation is clearly being worked out, and Emily Brontë must use the terms at her disposal. But she is merely availing herself of Christian references as a narrative method, without inviting us to postulate a Christian basis for action. She takes her stand on the concepts of personal salvation and damnation, and personal wrongs. The first admission of any kind of sin is Catherine's 'If I have done wrong, I'm dying for it', replying to Heathcliff's declaration, 'Because misery, and degradation, and death, and nothing that God or satan could inflict would have parted us, *you*, of your own will, did it' (Chapter 15), where God and Satan are almost synonymous. The first definition of Heaven is Catherine's also, revealed in her dream that she was in heaven and broke her heart with weeping, 'and the angels were so angry that they flung me out, into the middle of the heath on the top of Wuthering Heights; where I woke sobbing for joy'

(Chapter 9.)We come to feel that nothing is good or bad except as it affects the union of Heathcliff and Catherine, and Heathcliff can at last say, justly, 'I've done no injustice, and I repent of nothing' (Chapter 34). It is never suggested (in any way that we can agree with) that characters ought to control or attempt to change themselves, but only that they should direct their impulses so that they do not cause trouble, suffering, or crime.[1] What *is* required and accepted is that they experience the full consequences of their actions.

This attitude on which Emily Brontë has founded the novel is that of the Brontës' juvenile epics as far as we can know them. While she has clearly purged the vulgarities of the early work, she has not changed the attitude. She has managed to find a setting and a situation which can partake extensively of the stuff of normal life and natural setting, and set aside the social and moral values that would normally accompany it. In a way she has not grown up, or developed as Charlotte Brontë has. One might compare her characters and the assumptions on which they act with those on which Jane Eyre acts as a child before she has learned all that experience of other men can teach her:

> 'You are good to those who are good to you. It is all I ever desire to be. If people were always kind and obedient to those who are cruel and unjust, the wicked people would have it all their own way: they would never feel afraid, and so they would never alter, but would grow worse and worse. When we are struck at without a reason, we should strike back again very hard; I am sure we should – so hard as to teach the person who struck us never to do it again. . . . I must resist those who punish me unjustly. It is as natural as that I should love those who show me affection, or submit to punishment when I feel it is deserved.'   *Jane Eyre* (Chapter 6)

Such are the feelings of all the active characters in *Wuthering Heights*, suggesting that Emily Brontë has created mankind in her

---

[1] They clearly can curb impulses if they wish – Heathcliff delays his revenge for years – but they are not asked to do so – Isabella, a minor, is left free to run away with Heathcliff.

own image, that all her characters are facets of their creator: it is a book rather of mood than of character in the usual sense; hence the novel's enormously concentrated power and unity. With the single exception of Linton Heathcliff, the one thoroughly repellent personality, all characters are passionate, honest and frank, they show little fear, they have a shared elation – even joy – in a natural impulse reaching a natural end, even though it may be a savage one, and they share a sense of the humour of the grotesque and incongruous at moments of stress. Conversely, frustration is always agony – Isabella's ill-founded love, for instance, tries her much more than her subsequent hate – and in general all characters respond similarly to it by obeying an urge to revenge upon the oppressor. All characters are given great freedom from the common social pressures – whether through neglect, like Cathy and Heathcliff, or Hareton; or through spoiling, like the younger Catherine and Linton Heathcliff – so natural tendencies and impulses are not checked, or concealed, by social decorum or personal reticence. Even the natural ties of blood relationship are done away with as far as possible: parents die, brothers and sisters are estranged, the feeling of cousin for cousin soon changes to sexual love. A parent's love for the child – the commonest of causes for return from the dead in folk-lore and ballad – is deliberately set aside as a motive for action: when Hareton is born his mother Frances has 'nothing to keep her [alive]' (Chapter 8) and Edgar is as eager to die and rest with Catherine as to live and take care of his daughter (Chapter 25). The dead do not walk for the child's sake. All the characters are alone and expect no help or understanding in crises, even from those who love them, and do not attempt to give it. Isabella regrets marrying, but does not condemn her unforgiving brother; the younger Catherine, brought up though she has been by Ellen, never looks to her for help. Even Catherine and Heathcliff do not understand themselves or each other in any usual sense of the word, not even when Catherine is dying. They merely accept their fate and react to their suffering. Morality, as obedience to outside standards of right and wrong, does not exercise any influence on any person at any moment of crisis. There is never the least suggestion that they can call to their aid humility, patience in suffering, or Christian resignation.[1] Ellen, the voice of morality, is rejected, and the effect is not to make the reader condemn, but to reach a proper understanding:

'Mr Hindley do take warning (begs Ellen). Have mercy on this unfortunate boy, if you care nothing for yourself!'
'Any one will do better for him, than I shall.'   (Chapter 9)

Hareton's drunken father's reply rings much truer than does what Heathcliff once called Ellen's 'cant'. The ultimate moral paradox is Catherine's, since her one 'unselfish' act – marrying Linton for Heathcliff's sake – is her ruin.

Characters are in fact more like each other than they are unlike – a rare condition in a novel; the one main and great difference is between Catherine and Heathcliff, and all the rest. The violent outbursts of all except Heathcliff are ill-directed and pointless: Hindley in his drunken raving threatens Ellen with the carving knife, Isabella vents her spite on her wedding ring; in crises they despair and degenerate, Hindley to dipsomania, Isabella to sluttishness. By contrast Heathcliff, cut off from Catherine, actually rises in the world and returns two years later as a gentleman; while in his time of greatest agony when, fretted by marriage to Isabella, he has to watch Catherine dying helplessly and at a distance at Thrushcross, he is 'the only thing [at the Heights] that seemed decent' (Chapter 14). We therefore admire him and Catherine for their power and strength, and despise Heathcliff's victims for what is in fact only comparative weakness.

Wuthering Heights on one level is about what Virginia Woolf so admirably expressed, a sentence beginning 'We, the whole human race, and you, the eternal powers';[2] but on a more graspable level it is about, centrally, one thing only, the love of Heathcliff and Catherine. Of these two Catherine Earnshaw is the ruling force, and it is she who, though she dies almost exactly half-way through the novel, dominates the whole. She is the driving force, and after her death Heathcliff is her instrument. Though the reader need not

[1] Isabella's 'love' is the nearest thing to these, and this is clearly romantic, sentimental, and deluded, and we do not respect her for her unreal attempts to keep faith in Heathcliff.
[2] *The Common Reader*, First Series, Hogarth Press, 1925.

like her any more than Ellen Dean does, and certainly never identi-
fies with her – both remarkable conditions for a heroine – it is vital
that he should understand her and feel her power. Hence we see her
first (Chapter 3) in her triple role – Earnshaw, Heathcliff, and Linton
– as the writer of the journal-fragment, and as the child-phantom
of Lockwood's dream: all of which epitomizes, Blake-like, her
'spiritual form'. Her spiritual power is instantly established; her
unity with Heathcliff is strongly felt – physical hardship has moved
her merely to defiance, but separation from him has made her head
ache 'till [she] cannot keep it on the pillow; and still [she] can't give
over [weeping]' (Chapter 3); and while it is natural for Lockwood
to dream of her as a child, his doing so suggests that this child
Catherine at eleven or twelve years old is the true Catherine. The
hopeless child-phantom's tone looks forward to Cathy's at her
death, and the whole lifelike nightmare, beautifully placed just after
the comic and grotesque dream of Jabes Branderham's sermon,
seems so nearly real that when Heathcliff cries out to the phantom
we are shaken and shocked, but not at all inclined to feel him ridiculous or mad. Emily Brontë's greatest victory over the reader's disbelief is thus already won at the end of Chapter 3. The whole of
Ellen's story of the Earnshaw childhood is then read in the light of
this supernatural illumination, which causes us to modify and re-
interpret all that Ellen relates about Cathy and Heathcliff.[1] Ellen
the external observer can emphasize Catherine's perversity, her
charm, and her likeness to her brother, and leave her spiritual state
alone, until it is imperilled by contact with the Lintons. The relationship between Catherine and Heathcliff is clearly a calm thing, not
requiring any kind of expression until it is in danger of being
broken.[2] The first onslaught upon their relationship is made by

[1] One of the most important incidental effects of hearing of Catherine as the
'man Heathcliff's 'heart's darling' (Chapter 3) is that we never think of the
two as brother and sister, even though Catherine 'was much too fond of
Heathcliff' (Chapter 5) from the age of six. Incest is not Emily Brontë's concern
and she takes care it shall not be ours – if we are reading with the proper
responses.
[2] Catherine scorns Hindley and his wife (six years her senior) for 'kissing and
talking nonsense by the hour – foolish palaver that we should be ashamed of'
(Chapter 3), already seeing herself and Heathcliff as potential lovers in their turn.

Hindley's persecuting Heathcliff and neglecting Catherine, but this is not actually the force which breaks them apart, it is merely the circumstance which allows Catherine to follow her mistaken impulses to their fatal end. Catherine suffers, like Jane Austen's Emma, from 'the power of having rather too much her own way' (*Emma*, Chapter 1).

The second key to Catherine is her 'confession' to Ellen in Chapter 9, and this is the key to her actions, just as the journal was the key to her personality, as her delirium will foreshadow the resolution of the dilemma, and as her dying words will indicate the events that are to prelude the resolution. All these revelations are complex, and all by their constantly shifting ideas of time and change set the isolated girl and woman against eternity. This confession is vital to Heathcliff as well as herself, since her reason for marrying Linton is what drives Heathcliff into all he says and does in the rest of the action:

'If the wicked man in there, had not brought Heathcliff so low I shouldn't have thought of it.'   (Chapter 9)

She gives him the impulse to leave, driven away by her rejection, and intensifies the impulse to revenge, by naming Hindley as the cause of separation. We are made to see dramatically the errors of Catherine's reasoning: 'I have only to do with the present' (Chapter 9), she claims, yet her dream of heaven, and her love for Heathcliff which resembles 'the eternal rocks beneath' (ibid.), both reveal, not the present, but deserts of vast eternity. She says, and we believe her on the evidence of all they have done as children,

'I *am* Heathcliff – he's always, always in my mind – not as a pleasure, any more than I am always a pleasure to myself – but, as my own being – so, don't talk of our separation again – it is impracticable.'
(ibid.)

The last clause is the vital one – one of the first instances of the casual remark that is shockingly and literally true, and proved so by the whole of the story. By rejecting Heathcliff, Catherine spiritually tears herself in two. Ellen's shock and reply help to define our own feelings:

'If I can make any sense out of your nonsense, Miss, it only goes to convince me that you are ignorant of the duties you undertake in marrying; or else, that you are a wicked, unprincipled girl.'

(ibid.)

Catherine clearly does understand her 'duties' and is not 'unprincipled'. She does not want Heathcliff as a lover in any usual sense: indeed, the physical attraction she feels is to the comely and eligible young Linton. The reader is driven from his two easiest reactions and forced to see Catherine by her own light:

'Whatever our souls are made of, his and mine are the same, and Linton's is as different as a moonbeam from lightning, or frost from fire.'

(ibid.)

Hereafter, happiness is at an end for Catherine. By accepting Linton, she makes a full life impossible for herself. She, who has been the most living personality, becomes by her own act the embodiment of frustration, and the source of disunion and disaster. Neither she nor Heathcliff can find release from their trouble by revenge, and have only death left to them as an escape. Catherine, up to now 'half-savage and hardy and free' (Chapter 12), suffers such agony that a brain fever at sixteen weakens her health, and another at twenty unseats her reason and kills her.

Emily Brontë makes Catherine a child violent and wilful by nature, because violence and seeming wilfulness are to be the means by which we see her suffering. The violent scene in which she quarrelled with Heathcliff, defied Ellen, and boxed Linton's ears (Chapter 9) is a first witness to her spiritual turmoil, which her confession and later conduct explain. Her rages, which seem to Ellen like ungoverned passion, are really outbursts deflected by intolerable frustration. Sitting all night in her wet clothes and bringing on her first fever is clearly much more than Ellen's word 'naughtiness' (Chapter 9) comprehends. She is doing nothing; because with Heathcliff gone, her motive for doing anything is gone. She is having her first taste of what Heathcliff feels as 'living without

17

your soul' (Chapter 15), and consequently nearly fails to live at all.[1]

Structurally Catherine does not exist until Heathcliff returns.[2] She is restored to life and delight when he comes back, only to be almost immediately re-engaged in the struggle with her fate. She can bear, uneasily, the passive division exemplified by her suggested mode of dining:

'Set two tables here, Ellen; one for your master and Miss Isabella, being gentry; the other for Heathcliff and myself, being of the lower orders.' (Chapter 10)

But open conflict drives her again to distraction. Her frenzy (Chapter 12) is the combined consequence of quarrelling for the first time with Heathcliff and of seeing Linton and Heathcliff confronted and opposed. Their enmity makes a war within herself; her hatred (essentially of herself for creating her dilemma, knowing, as Ellen has told her, that she herself drove Heathcliff away) turns on to Linton, since it cannot turn to Heathcliff who 'is more myself than I am', and when Linton strikes Heathcliff he strikes, in effect, at his own wife. Her delirium and death follow.[3]

[1] Despite its homely and even trivial evidences, Catherine's fate feels almost tragic by the irony which surrounds it, in anticipation, at the time, and retrospectively. Being overheard by Heathcliff, she confesses her love when trying to conceal it, and by trying to aid him she drives him away; she suffers herself 'the fate of Milo' (an athlete who was trapped by the hands in the tree he was attempting to split, and was devoured by wolves) that she promises to anyone who tries to separate them, and hears only the following morning that Hindley was about to turn Heathcliff out, an act that would paradoxically have united him and Catherine for ever: 'if you do turn him out of doors, I'll go with him.' (Chapter 9)

[2] The years from her illness to six months after her marriage being bridged only by a return to Lockwood's narrative, a chapter division, and a few sentences from Ellen.

[3] But Emily Brontë takes care to persuade on the natural level as well as the spiritual: she has already hinted that Catherine is pregnant:

'She's her brother's heir, is she not?' he asked, after a brief silence.
'I should be sorry to think so,' returned his companion. 'Half-a-dozen nephews shall erase her title, please Heaven!' (Chapter 10)

and her pregnancy gives colour to her derangement, and the premature birth is the immediate cause of her dying.

Her delirium is as vital to our understanding as Lear's madness.[1] Catherine's delirium is even tragically moving; not least by contrast with the scene of violence before it, where she has actually repelled sympathy by exposing her weak husband to his powerful rival, and by apparently threatening to exploit her own frenzy to torment both her men:

> 'Well, if I cannot keep Heathcliff for my friend – if Edgar will be mean and jealous, I'll try to break their hearts by breaking my own.'
> (Chapter 11)

Her refuge in childhood, psychologically and naturalistically utterly convincing, is thematically and structurally vital. Her delirium evokes superstition, and seeing her own face in the mirror she sees her own 'fetch' and knows herself death-doomed:

> she *would* keep straining her gaze towards the glass.
> 'There's nobody here!' I insisted. 'It was *yourself*, Mrs Linton; you knew it a while since.'
> 'Myself!' she gasped, 'and the clock is striking twelve! It's true, then! that's dreadful!'
> (Chapter 12)

She returns in spirit to the moors and the Heights and the time when Heathcliff obeyed her, even in the trapping of lapwings, and then relives in images and in spirit the whole of her life between that and the present, thus rendering a spiritual history of the years the narrative omits. The unknown misery is explained by the intelligible one; Catherine imagines she is a child again

> 'and my misery arose from the separation that Hindley had ordered between me, and Heathcliff – I was laid alone, for the first time, and, rousing from a dismal doze after a night of weeping – I lifted my hand to push the panels aside, it struck the table-top! I swept it along the carpet, and then, memory burst in – my late anguish was swallowed in a paroxysm of despair – I cannot say why I felt so wildly wretched – it must have been temporary derangement for there is

[1] It is emphatically not weakness; there is no doubt of her power either 'to starve at once, or to recover, and leave the country' (Chapter 11); she has starved for two days when she says it, and the spirit that can control her body to its destruction is clearly a strong one.

scarcely cause – But, supposing at twelve years old, I had been
wrenched from the Heights, and every early association, and my all
in all, as Heathcliff was at that time, and been converted, at a stroke
into Mrs Linton, the lady of Thrushcross Grange, and the wife of a
stranger; an exile, and outcast, thenceforth, from what had been my
world – You may fancy a glimpse of the abyss where I grovelled!'

(Chapter 12)

The Heights become a symbol of her lost and unattainable whole-
ness and happiness, now to be reached only through the grave:

'Look!' she cried eagerly, 'that's my room, with the candle in it,
and the trees swaying before it ... and the other candle is in Joseph's
garret ... Joseph sits up late, doesn't he? He's waiting till I come
home that he may lock the gate. Well, he'll wait a while yet. It's a
rough journey, and a sad heart to travel it; and we must pass by
Gimmerton Kirk, to go that journey! We've braved its ghosts often
together, and dared each other to stand among the graves and ask
them to come ... But Heathcliff, if I dare you now, will you venture? If you do, I'll keep you. I'll not lie there by myself: they may
bury me twelve feet deep, and throw the church down over me;
but I won't rest till you are with me ... I never will!'

She paused, and resumed with a strange smile. 'He's considering
... he'd rather I'd come to him! Find a way, then! not through that
kirkyard ... You are slow! Be content, you always followed me!'

(ibid.)

The passage, epitomizing her relations with Heathcliff and Linton
(the one must follow her, the other may please himself), fore-
shadows the future of both herself and Heathcliff: she will die, and
so will he, unless he can find a way 'not through that kirkyard',
which for eighteen years after her death he tries to do; and her
spirit does indeed not 'rest' till he is with her. It reaffirms her as the
moving spirit of the partnership, conditioning us to feel her as the
power that will drive Heathcliff, invisibly, in a way not even Ellen
can perceive, for eighteen years to come. But something is still left
for her last great scene, since she will still not understand her fault:

'Why am I so changed? why does my blood rush into a hell of
tumult at a few words?'

(ibid.)

These are questions the reader can now answer, but not yet Catherine.

Her final scene and her greatest is in a way not so much hers as Heathcliff's, since her purpose here is mainly to force Heathcliff to reveal himself and to declare what neither has hitherto spoken to the other; consequently this is not so much the end of her earthly life as the establishment of the spiritual one she will assume until Heathcliff too dies in his turn. All the misunderstandings between them are cleared away. Heathcliff finally declares what the action has been persistently proving:

> 'Because misery, and degradation, and death, and nothing that God or satan could inflict would have parted us, *you*, of your own will, did it. I have not broken your heart – *you* have broken it – and in breaking it, you have broken mine. So much the worse for me, that I am strong. Do I want to live? What kind of living will it be when you – oh, God! would *you* like to live with your soul in the grave?'
>
> (Chapter 15)

She answer's Heathcliff's reproaches with confession: 'If I've done wrong, I'm dying for it,' and by so doing re-forges the bond between them so that though dead she will still hold him, he will still communicate with her (his soul) and she, the only one in the tale, will survive beyond the grave by the pull of the living. Her madness is a necessary condition of such knowledge, since it enables her to express contradictory truths without arousing disbelief:

> 'I shall not be at peace . . . should a word of mine distress you here-after, think I feel the same distress underground, and for my own sake, forgive me.'   (ibid.)

> 'I'm wearying to escape into that glorious world, and to be always there; not seeing it dimly through tears, and yearning for it through the walls of an aching heart; but really with it, and in it.'   (ibid.)

Both concepts of death are held henceforward, neither is a Christian one, and both are linked to the living Heathcliff. Even Ellen's valediction is not final but comparative:

> 'Far better that she should be dead, than lingering a burden, and a misery-maker to all about her.'   (ibid.)

21

Through Heathcliff she is to be both for another eighteen years.

Her spiritual existence invoked by Heathcliff the very night she dies is not suggested until seventeen years later (Chapter 29), where it is presented not as a fact but only as what Heathcliff believes. It is perversely what has kept him alive to perpetrate his revenge, since had he not imagined her presence – 'I appeared to feel the warm breath of it displacing the sleet-laden wind' (Chapter 29) – he would have died to be with her in the grave on the night she was buried. She is still intimate, perverse, and familiar like her living self, and therefore prepares for Emily Brontë's even more difficult achievement of making the reader believe in Heathcliff and herself as real ghosts, seen and believed by Joseph and the shepherd-boy.

If Catherine is the impetus of the story, Heathcliff is its structure. Lockwood asked Ellen for his history; he gets exactly and completely what he asked for. Every detail that Emily Brontë reveals is present because it is relevant to one or other of Heathcliff's two ruling forces – love, and the urge to revenge – whether it is recognized at the time or merely seen to be so in retrospect. Heathcliff is, paradoxically, frighteningly powerful and yet on analysis a passive character; whom one freely terms violent and cruel, yet whose actions on inspection are no more violent than those of other characters, and possibly less cruel. He presents a much harder problem than Catherine to his author, since he must be both hated and pitied, feared and understood, by the reader, when almost all the other characters feel only the hate and the fear, and even Ellen, the purveyor of understanding, does not herself comprehend him; he must be the instrument of suffering and death, yet his own suffering and his own death must be the main concern. He must be no monster, but a man accepted by those around him, whom the doctor Kenneth thinks of in the same terms as any other landowner, whom the lawyer will serve as readily as Linton, and who can employ two housekeepers besides Ellen who can take life with him at the Heights as a natural thing. His career is a spiritual one, and his power and passion are spiritual and moral, not physical, and find expression only at great crises, and often in terms other than action. Since most of Ellen's analyses of him, and all of Lockwood's, direct our understanding only by their obvious inadequacy, he is revealed mainly by what is done to him, and by his own self-revelations to Ellen.

As far as his part in the action is concerned, he is almost always a passive character, acted upon by others and arousing passions in them – hatred in Hindley, rivalry in Linton, love then hate in Isabella, terror in his son. Until Catherine rejects him, he is entirely passive: he cannot help old Earnshaw's affection, nor Hindley's hate, nor the love between himself and Catherine, and though he talks of vengeance he takes no steps to advance himself or alter his lot. It is her rejection that turns him into a destructive force and lets loose his impulse to revenge (always clearly a passion less powerful than his love); he leaves for two years and comes back having overcome his degradation, able to marry Catherine now, but, finding he is too late, yields to despair:

> 'I meditated this plan – just to have one glimpse of your face – a stare of surprise, perhaps, and pretended pleasure; afterwards settle my score with Hindley; and then prevent the law by doing execution on myself.'
> (Chapter 10)

Her manifest love prevents his plan, and he contents himself by way of revenge with driving Hindley bankrupt; while his mixed feelings towards Catherine for deserting and tormenting him make him marry Isabella, thus beginning his revenge on his other adversary, Edgar Linton. When Catherine is dead Heathcliff's influence actually restores the order which her actions and his own have torn apart. Hindley, the first wrongdoer, dies first, drunken and ruined, and his money and lands (rightfully Hareton's) go to Heathcliff. The younger Catherine, marrying Heathcliff's misbegotten and monstrous son by Isabella, becomes Heathcliff's heir, and Hareton, the Earnshaw heir, whom Heathcliff tries to degrade, is actually saved by him from a loveless unbringing by his dipsomaniac father, to become the husband of Catherine, the other surviving descendant of the Earnshaw house, the inheritor of the money as he is of the land. Clearly all this is part of the author's plan for Heathcliff, since once this is achieved, he begins to die, unaware that he has fulfilled his purpose, which he still thinks is to be the plague of both the houses:

'It is a poor conclusion, is it not?' he observed, having brooded a while on the scene he had just witnessed. 'An absurd termination to my violent exertions? I get levers, and mattocks to demolish the two houses, and train myself to be capable of working like Hercules, and when everything is ready, and in my power, I find the will to lift a slate off either roof has vanished! My old enemies have not beaten me – now would be the precise time to revenge myself on their representatives – I could do it; and none could hinder me – But where is the use? I don't care for striking, I can't take the trouble to raise my hand!' (Chapter 33)

In fact the climax of his revenge came at the time of greatest violence and agony, at the younger Catherine's marriage and Edgar Linton's death. That done, Heathcliff's work is done. The rest of his story is of the consummation of his union with Catherine.

Emily Brontë begins her novel with Heathcliff, a man in the prime of life, master of himself and his household, as Lockwood sees him a year before his death. She emphasizes his physical present reality, about forty, a 'dark-skinned gipsy in aspect, in dress and manners a gentleman' with 'an erect and handsome figure; and rather morose' (Chapter 1); she emphasizes his power, which responds to others' power with his first 'grin' to Lockwood's threatening to beat the dog that bit him; and she emphasizes the impossibility of dealing with him on normal social terms; Lockwood, with the dogs holding him down and his nose bleeding from rage, is a silly figure, but he need not have been so if Heathcliff had behaved as we expect a host to behave to a guest. He contrasts with the pseudo-misanthropist Lockwood, and with Lockwood's misreadings of him; he is clearly indeed 'a fierce, pitiless, wolfish man', and whatever his inner life, we are not being given the chance to be Byronic or sentimental about it. His first real emotion (apart from grim amusement at Lockwood's ineptitudes) is his greatest and ruling one in one of its most powerful manifestations:

He got on the bed, and wrenched open the lattice, bursting, as he pulled at it, into an uncontrollable passion of tears.
'Come in! come in!' he sobbed. 'Cathy, do come. Oh do – *once* more! Oh! my heart's darling, hear me *this* time – Catherine, at last!' (Chapter 3)

Heathcliff thus gains enormous power through being kept to his essentials, and through belonging to the 'present' of 1801 and Lockwood's account. When he re-enters this present again, after we know of his terrific past, when he calls on Lockwood in Chapter 10, and Lockwood calls on him in Chapter 31, it is like meeting the heroic dead.

In the earlier part of Ellen's story he is less important than in the later. As a child, he is less important in himself than Catherine. What is chiefly established is his personality and the feud between himself and Hindley: the familiar incident of the exchange of horses shows how Heathcliff, to gain his ends, can manipulate existing circumstances rather than creating them, and shows his absence of positive pleasure in the mere inflicting of pain, compared with Hindley – whom he could very easily have made to suffer as he himself suffers. His confidences to Ellen, natural in a child, establish his habit of confiding in her, so that we accept his much less natural but much more vital disclosures when he is a man. He is self-contained but by no means reserved, and is clearly habitually truthful. His first long dialogue shows him at his best, living the life offered to him to the full, telling Ellen of the escapade to Thrushcross; he shows himself perceptive in judging Edgar and Isabella, and selfless in his delight in seeing Catherine happy:

> 'I left her, as merry as she could be, dividing her food, between the little dog and Skulker whose nose she pinched as she ate; and kindling a spark of spirit in the vacant blue eyes of the young Lintons – a dim reflection from her own enchanting face – I saw they were full of stupid admiration; she is so immeasurably superior to them – to everybody on earth; is she not, Nelly?'   (Chapter 6)

Already all his feelings are centred exclusively in Catherine, and the sense of unity with her is evidently so strong that it requires no physical contact and prohibits any distress at being shut out where she, significantly and ominously, is welcomed in. Their union is already something far beyond that of the brother and sister Linton on the one hand, and the husband and wife Hindley and Frances on the other. It is emphasized further at this early stage by his sharing Catherine's manner of speech and thought; *he* rejects the Christian

God's right to vengeance – 'God won't have the satisfaction I shall' (Chapter 7) – in the same way as *she* rejects the Christian heaven, and they both thereby set themselves apart from everyone else and outside the conventional scheme of things. Catherine is indeed Heathcliff's only source of connection with life, which after this point of meeting with the Lintons we see being taken from him, in a way that necessarily arouses a sense of injustice and of sympathy for him, insulted as he is by Linton and beaten by Hindley (Chapter 7) and at last unfairly reproached by Catherine herself for 'knowing nothing and saying nothing' (Chapter 9). At the same time we are asked to feel him as something evil; 'from the very beginning, he bred bad feeling in the house', says Ellen (Chapter 8), a feeling which his own wild words intensify with his threats of 'flinging Joseph off the highest gable, and painting the housefront with Hindley's blood' (Chapter 6). Ellen's speculations (not necessarily true) play their part:

> (His countenance) expressed, plainer than words could do, the intensest anguish at having made himself the instrument of thwarting his own revenge. Had it been dark, I dare say, he would have tried to remedy the mistake by smashing Hareton's skull on the steps.
>
> (Chapter 9)[1]

We therefore give Heathcliff, even as a child, credit for the power both to experience and arouse excessive and exceptional emotions, while, since he has done nothing wicked, and his most powerful passion is a selfless one, we do not credit him with being criminal or, in any ordinary sense, evil. Emily Brontë is having her cake and eating it; having all the sensation value of an evil hero, without any of the moral opprobrium: she and her reader can respond, without feeling that by so doing they are partaking in wickedness.[2]

When Heathcliff returns to the story (Chapter 10) two years later, he is a 'tall, athletic, well-formed man', completely changed

---

[1] There is no doubt here of Heathcliff's violent nature, whose internal and invisible power is revealed by Ellen's powerful feelings about him; but that he would actually have murdered Hareton is only Ellen's guess.

[2] Thus far Emily Brontë shows a resemblance to Charlotte Brontë, who in *Jane Eyre* equally responds to passion which is yet not evil.

in all but his nature: 'a half-civilized ferocity', diagnosed by Ellen, 'lurked yet in the depressed brows and eyes full of black fire', his eyes, 'that couple of black fiends', being significantly the one feature that Ellen had wished the boy Heathcliff to change into 'confident, innocent angels' (Chapter 7). He is stronger now physically than both his enemies, Linton seeming beside him 'quite slender and youth-like' (Chapter 10), and stronger than Catherine; neither his body nor his reason breaks under his suffering as hers does, so that her power over him in general is the more striking.

The reader regains contact with him as quickly as Catherine does, through her reactions and through his own words. The two motives in his life are now confirmed and explicit, and Emily Brontë can refine on the nature of Heathcliff's love. The repulsive scene in which Catherine exposes Isabella's love before Heathcliff (Chapter 10) is an important one: Catherine openly names herself as Isabella's rival for Heathcliff's love, and yet Heathcliff goes on to consider Isabella seriously as a match:

> 'She's her brother's heir, is she not?' he asked, after a brief silence.
> 'I should be sorry to think so,' returned his companion. 'Half-a-dozen nephews shall erase her title, please Heaven! Abstract your mind from the subject at present – you are too prone to covet your neighbour's goods: remember *this* neighbour's goods are mine.'
> 'If they were *mine*, they would be none the less that,' said Heathcliff; 'but though Isabella Linton may be silly, she is scarcely mad.'
> (Chapter 10)

Marrying Isabella is clearly a way of revenge over Linton, but not felt to be at all a betrayal of his love for Catherine, whose goods even would still be hers, though they descended to him. All their most startling self-exposures are like this one, made in passing, even casually, when some other less remarkable matter (here Isabella's love) is supposedly the really startling thing. So we feel the relation of Catherine and Heathcliff as 'the unchanging rocks beneath' the thousand natural shocks of everyday life.

On this normal everyday level Heathcliff is still repulsive, talking of 'wrenching (nails) off fingers' (Chapter 10), accusing Catherine of 'torturing him to death' (Chapter 11) and spurning Linton as a 'milk-blooded coward' and a 'slavering, shivering thing' (ibid.).

By this time we are beginning to see, however, that such outbursts are not really a direct reaction to the situation, still less a sadistic one, but a breaking-out of the agony of frustration within him, usually entirely invisible, but appearing at crises. And the outbursts are more often verbal than active; though he talks of 'crushing those beneath him' (ibid.), or of 'painting on the white (of Isabella's face) all the colours of the rainbow, and turning the blue eyes black, every day or two' (Chapter 10), he does not actually do any bodily harm unless seriously provoked to it, as Hindley provokes him by shutting him out of the Heights, or as earlier the child Linton's ill-timed insult provoked him to hurl apple-sauce at him. Not always even then does Heathcliff retaliate, since he lays no hand on Linton when he is at his mercy, and even manages to endure 'full on the throat a blow that would have levelled a slighter man' (Chapter 11).[1]

Emily Brontë, only apparently wishing to arouse all the horror of violence and unrestraint, constantly drags us to a juster estimate of what we have seen. The whole of Isabella's story of what happens at the Heights on the night of Catherine's funeral is a masterpiece of conditioned response. Heathcliff in fight with Hindley disgusts us:

> The charge exploded, and the knife, in springing back, closed into its owner's wrist. Heathcliff pulled it away by main force, slitting up the flesh as it passed on, and thrust it dripping into his pocket.

[1] From the moment of the quarrel to the news of Catherine's death is in fact a continuous crisis for Heathcliff, extending over two months, in which, on inspection, Heathcliff is rather conspicuous for his physical (though not emotional) restraint than for violence. Married to Isabella and detesting her, he yet declares that Linton may 'set his fraternal and magisterial heart at ease':

> 'I keep strictly within the limits of the law. I have avoided, up to this period, giving her the slightest right to claim a separation.'
>
> (Chapter 14)

Isabella does not contradict, and we believe him. Ellen's report here does not demonstrate his cruelty, still less any joy in cruelty, but recreates the strain under which he is living, thinking Catherine cruel and heartless, knowing she is ill and dying, and holding Linton responsible (as we know in a way, on the evidence of Chapter 11, that he is right to do).

He then took a stone, struck down the division between two windows and sprung in. His adversary had fallen senseless with excessive pain, and the flow of blood that gushed from an artery, or a large vein.

The ruffian kicked and trampled on him, and dashed his head repeatedly against the flags; holding me with one hand, meantime, to prevent me summoning Joseph.

He exerted preterhuman self-denial in abstaining from finishing him, completely; but getting out of breath, he finally desisted, and dragged the apparently inanimate body on to the settle.

There he tore off the sleeve of Earnshaw's coat, and bound up the wound with brutal roughness, spitting and cursing, during the operation, as energetically as he had kicked before. (Chapter 17)

We see his violence, but we feel his reasons for it, since we know, as Isabella cannot, all that is implied by Heathcliff's being 'a stranger in the house from last Sunday (when Catherine died) until today (the night after her funeral)' (ibid.),[1] and know his sufferings to be greater than those driving the two who oppose him. Heathcliff, indeed, gains in grandeur by comparison of his own unpremeditated desperation, with, first, the calculated yet ineffectual crime of the drunken Hindley, and second, the unspeakably malicious tauntings of Isabella: she has guessed enough of how he loves Catherine to be judged as acting deliberately:

'If poor Catherine had trusted you, and assumed the ridiculous, contemptible, degrading title of Mrs Heathcliff, she would soon have presented a similar picture! *She* wouldn't have borne your abominable behaviour quietly; her detestation and disgust must have found voice.' (ibid.)

Catherine's death-scene is Heathcliff's confession of faith. The greatest moment in both their lives is really more vital to him than to her, since he understands better than she what has been done, and looks forward to what must be to come, for both of them:

---

[1] And later learn in retrospect what happened (Chapter 29): that he has come back to the Heights feeling Catherine's presence, and nearly certain of being reunited with her there.

'You teach me now how cruel you've been – cruel and false. *Why* did you despise me? *Why* did you betray your own heart, Cathy? I have not one word of comfort – you deserve this. You have killed yourself. Yes, you may kiss me, and cry; and wring out my kisses and tears. They'll blight you – they'll damn you. You loved me – then what *right* had you to leave me? What right – answer me – for the poor fancy you felt for Linton? Because misery, and degradation, and death, and nothing that God or satan could inflict would have parted us, *you*, of your own will, did it. I have not broken your heart – *you* have broken it; and in breaking it, you have broken mine. So much the worse for me, that I am strong. Do I want to live? What kind of living will it be when you – oh God! would *you* like to live with your soul in the grave?'   (Chapter 15)

Heathcliff is the same here as elsewhere, but more intensely so:

He gnashed at me, and foamed like a mad dog, and gathered her to him with greedy jealousy.   (ibid.)

Just as his scenes of horror are yet moving, so his most moving scene arouses horror, and rushes us emotionally headlong to the outburst to Ellen in which he refuses to acknowledge the barriers of mortality:

'I pray one prayer – I repeat it till my tongue stiffens – Catherine Earnshaw, may you not rest, as long as I am living! You said I killed you – haunt me then! The murdered *do* haunt their murderers. I believe – I know that ghosts *have* wandered on earth. Be with me always – take any form – drive me mad! only *do* not leave me in this abyss, where I cannot find you! Oh, God! it is unutterable! I *cannot* live without my life! I *cannot* live without my soul!'   (Chapter 16)

After Catherine's death, all the motives for Heathcliff's action are internal, of which his treatment of the next generation, and his occasional revelations to Ellen, are the only signs. He is still a mover of events only when compelled to be so, content with letting Hindley drink himself to death, content to let Isabella keep their son until the age when Heathcliff wants him, and content to let Linton's and Catherine's courtship take its own course, until his son's and Edgar Linton's imminent deaths compel him to speed up the marriage. During this period, between Catherine's death and

Linton Heathcliff's, in which Heathcliff achieves his revenge, Emily
Brontë stresses chiefly his power to inspire hate and fear. This is not
done primarily through his cruel acts, which are indeed few[1], but
through the spiritual effect he has on others. He dominates his feeble
son without touching him:

> 'I brought him down one evening, the day before yesterday, and
> just set him in a chair, and never touched him afterwards. I sent
> Hareton out, and we had the room to ourselves. In two hours, I
> called Joseph to carry him up again; and, since then, my presence
> has been as potent on his nerves, as a ghost.'   (Chapter 29)

while Ellen's terror of him, feeling more than once 'as if I had raised
a goblin', is all superstitious. He exerts his will always with a purpose,
gets no active pleasure from cruelty for its own sake, takes good care
of his feeble son for several years, and more than once actually warns
people to keep out of his way when he is violent:

> 'You must learn to avoid putting me in a passion, or I shall really
> murder you sometime.'   (Chapter 33)

His violence is always a clue to powers within himself breaking
momentarily out of his control. This suggests itself even at first
reading, and is absolutely clear in retrospect, when we know what
he tells Ellen of being 'beguiled with the spectre of a hope, through
eighteen years', of being killed by it 'not by inches, but by fractions
and hairbreadths' (Chapter 29). This retrospect makes us realize
startlingly that Heathcliff would have died to be with Catherine at
her death, but that Catherine's own spirit, by preserving his life,
has allowed him to complete his revenge, and made him an instrument and an almost impersonal force of purgation. Emily Brontë
thus again reveals, by manipulation of the action, the fascination
of the artistic and emotional full circle and completion.

Once Edgar is dead and can suffer no more, however Heathcliff
may deal with his daughter, Heathcliff's worldly task is done. He
begins to withdraw from life from the moment when, before
Edgar's funeral, he opens Catherine's grave and sees her uncorrupted

---

[1] Forcing the dying Linton out on to the sunny moors to meet Catherine, and
boxing Catherine's ears are practically all that he can be charged with.

body, and prepares to join her (Chapter 29). He has now only to work out his own happiness by joining Catherine. He has spent eighteen years on his revenge and on 'considering' – as Catherine in her delirium foretold:

> 'He'd rather I'd come to him! Find a way, then! not through that kirkyard ... You are slow! Be content, you always followed me!'
> (Chapter 12)

The end has to be told mainly by what Heathcliff, disburdening an overcharged spirit, tells Ellen. She, the only survivor of his generation and the only possible administrator after his death, is the natural recipient. Again Emily Brontë has covered a structural necessity with the air of naturalism, not least by making Ellen not fully understand what she hears.

From the opening of Catherine's grave begin the increasing allusions to 'disturbing the dead' (Chapter 29) and to the influence of the dead on the living, conditioning the reader to believe not only in Catherine, but in Heathcliff's power to fulfil his own threat that, if Ellen does not have him buried with Catherine, 'You shall prove, practically, that the dead are not annihilated!' (Chapter 34).

Although Emily Brontë is concerned to round off her tale and restore worldly order by restoring the two Earnshaw children to harmony and their rights, the end of the tale is Heathcliff's; the happiness of the young people, vivid though it is, being artistically an earthly parallel of the spiritual ecstasy he is struggling to attain. We spare not much more thought for Catherine and Hareton than Heathcliff himself does when they impinge on him as pale reincarnations of Cathy and himself. We are never actually told that Heathcliff sees Catherine's spirit, but the ambiguous allusions make it clear enough. We know, as Heathcliff does, the ambiguity of his saying:

> 'Today, I am within sight of my heaven – I have my eyes on it – hardly three feet to sever me!'
> (Chapter 34)

and take to heart his warning:

> 'You'll neither see nor hear anything to frighten you, if you refrain from prying.'
> (ibid.)

The judgement on a death like Heathcliff's, preceded by an ecstasy demonstrated in

> his frame shivering, not as one shivers with chill or weakness, but as a tight-stretched cord vibrates – a strong thrilling, rather than trembling. (ibid.)

cannot be done either literally of hyperbolically. Emily Brontë employs the utterly inadequate and the apparently contradictory. No one in the story comprehends, but together they make the reader comprehend. Ellen's accurate observation and Joseph's ramblings provide the material, and commonplace remarks and superstitious dread direct our attention as they have done before: we no more believe Heathcliff is a fiend than we believe that his nerves are disordered or that 'the divil's harried off his soul' (Chapter 34) – their various suggestions. But we do believe what Ellen does not wish to believe, that 'he *walks*', that 'that old man by the kitchen fire has seen two on 'em looking out of his chamber window, on every rainy night since his death' (Chapter 34), and that the little boy (and the sheep) know better than Ellen what they saw 'under t'nab' that made them refuse to go on.

Most of the imagery of the novel clusters round Heathcliff. His own speech is more figurative than anyone else's, he can hardly utter a sentence without a metaphor, and he is the greatest subject of figurative speech. Much of his power derives from the associations thus built up, and he partakes of the force of many even contradictory comparisons. To those who hate him he is the devil and excites hyperbole: old Earnshaw presents the child 'as dark almost as if it came from the devil' (Chapter 4); he is young Hindley's 'imp of Satan' (ibid.), and Joseph's 'flaysome divel of a Heathcliff' (Chapter 9); Isabella wonders if she has married 'a devil' (Chapter 13); Ellen sees his eyes and the spirit in them as 'that couple of black fiends' (Chapter 7), and can even call him 'Judas' for seeking to court Isabella (Chapter 11). She sees him often in folk-lore terms, running from him 'as scared as if she had raised a goblin' (Chapter 11). While to Catherine he is one with the great forces of nature and with herself:

'Whatever our souls are made of, his and mine are the same, and Linton's is as different as a moonbeam from lightning, or frost from fire.'   (Chapter 9)

and when speaking with deliberate truth to Isabella she keeps to such natural parallels:

'He's not a rough diamond, a pearl-containing oyster of a rustic; he's a fierce, pitiless, *wolfish* man ... He'd crush you, like a sparrow's egg.'   (Chapter 10, my italics)

His own speech reveals the violence that his actions cannot and is the cause of our common feeling that the action is violent and macabre in a way that cold summary denies. His torture-images reveal agony rather than desire:

'The tyrant grinds down his slaves and they don't turn against him, they crush those beneath them.'   (Chapter 11)

and his hatred and abuse find vent in the same terms as are used on himself: 'witch', 'the devil' (Chapter 29); and in natural images: 'I'll crush his ribs in like a rotten hazel-nut' (Chapter 11): 'He's such a cobweb, a pinch would annihilate him' (Chapter 12).

Heathcliff clearly owes a good deal to the romantic, solitary misanthropic heroes of the Byron of Emily Brontë's early reading. But *Wuthering Heights* must be one of the few instances where the result is greater than the original from which it derives. Emily Brontë has so re-created the noble sufferer and the effects of suffering long drawn out that Heathcliff has personally little in common with Manfred. Sin and guilt like Manfred's do not interest her, though his more than mortal passion does. The revelation and the consequences of a not conventionally moral way of responding to life, which defeat Byron, are Emily Brontë's triumph.

The rest of the characters are given just so much life as the absorbing preoccupation with Heathcliff and Catherine permits them. They are all as finely observed on their smaller scale as the two great ones, and repay study; but we are never allowed to become absorbed in them. The second generation are second in our attention too. They shrink because Ellen sees them all as children (even at the end, when Hareton is twenty-three and Catherine seventeen), as she never saw their parents, her coevals. The younger Catherine is attractive, but seen only when she is to impinge on Heathcliff, emphasized as she represents her parents, sympathetic in her love for her father and Linton Heathcliff, but so wilful that we feel little outrage when Heathcliff boxes her ears – a punishment she has deserved before this.

Linton Heathcliff is the most repulsive creation in the novel, the single instance of real enjoyment of suffering *per se*. He has just sufficient physical attraction to justify Catherine's childish, half-maternal fancy for him, but sympathy is kept to the minimum. He is dying at the age of thirteen when he enters the story, so we feel less pity for him, when Heathcliff forces him into unwilling action, than we do disgust at his senseless rages, petty tyranny over Catherine, and enjoyment at tormenting others. He is the means whereby Heathcliff gains his revenge on Edgar Linton, and whereby Emily Brontë secures our understanding of Heathcliff at a time when he is at his most inhuman.

Hareton gains by contrast. Uncouth in looks and mind, he has the power of vigour and health, and good impulses, reinforced by our consciousness of his inheritance (it is his name carved over the lintel of the Heights), by Ellen's love for him as a child, by Heathcliff's unwilling feeling for him, and most of all by his resemblance both to Catherine and to Heathcliff.[1]

Of the first generation, Hindley has enough passion to be an Earnshaw, a fit brother for Catherine, and a powerful though degraded father to Hareton. His drunkenness repels any sympathy Ellen may make us feel for him as Heathcliff's prey and a wasted life. Isabella Linton, essential to the plot though she is, barely exists, being rather a sharer in the prevailing atmosphere than a personality, yet her mere existence in her likeness to Edgar makes him something of a type and representative of society, to contrast with

[1] The few Gimmerton characters who appear pertain mainly to this second generation: Zillah and the earlier unnamed housekeeper, the lawyer Green, and the doctor Kenneth. They are chiefly important for noticing nothing much amiss at the Heights, demonstrating what the reader, absorbed, may miss, that the struggles are primarily spiritual ones.

the two great individuals. Linton himself (who might be called Emily Brontë's St John Rivers) is of considerable interest, as the man must be who can distract Catherine from Heathcliff, parallel-ing him in many ways. He is a mixture of attraction and repulsion from the first sight of him as the attractive fair-haired, blue-eyed child squabbling with his sister over 'who should hold a heap of warm hair' (Chapter 6). We are invited to scorn him for 'whining for trifles' (Chapter 10), and for the weakness which causes Cath-erine to call him 'not a lamb, but a sucking leveret' (Chapter 11), yet we are invited to admire his power and courage in striking the much stronger Heathcliff 'full on the throat a blow that would have levelled a slighter man' (Chapter 18). Like Heathcliff, he attracts curiously conflicting images, so that, in contrast with the gentle lamb-imagery, Joseph calls him 'yon cat o' Linton' (Chapter 9), and Ellen, seeing him charmed by love for Catherine, says aptly yet very strangely,

> He possessed the power to depart, as much as a cat possesses the power to leave a mouse half killed, or a bird half eaten.
>
> (Chapter 8)

His hold on life weakens steadily, making him a negative father to allow his daughter the freedom the story demands, and he desires death for rest and reunion with Catherine; so he diametrically opposes Heathcliff, for whom death is only to be won by desperate struggle, but who is in fact the one to be reunited.

Other than the two narrators, this leaves only Joseph, a magnifi-cent, rich and indispensable fellow, whose only difficulty is the look of his dialect on the page. Joseph, 'the wearisomest self-righteous Pharisee that ever ransacked the Bible to rake the promises to him-self and fling the curses to his neighbours' (Chapter 5), the single survivor of the original generation, who remains at the Heights when it is left 'for the use of such ghosts as choose to inhabit it' (Chapter 34), is full of such life and vigour as rouses us to reluctant joy at his awfulness. His views are always grotesque and always comic, making us aware of the very considerable comic powers of the other Heights characters, at the most startling times. Like Shakespeare's clowns he enriches and deepens great scenes by his very earthiness, incongruity, and misunderstandings, which often have a truth ironically not known to him:

> 'Have you found Heathcliff, you ass?' interrupted Catherine. 'Have you been looking for him, as I ordered?'
>
> 'Aw sud more likker look for th'horse,' he replied. 'It 'ud be tuh more sense.'
>
> (Chapter 9)

It would indeed. He promises damnation to all the wrong people in all the wrong places, yet is perversely right in his devotion to the Earnshaw blood even in young Hareton, and able to give a richly and comically illuminating summary of secondary narrative material, of characters, or of events, on occasions not otherwise visible:

> 'Does he niver say nowt of his fine living amang us, when he goas tuh t'Grange? This is t' way on't – up at sun-dahn; dice, brandy, cloised shutters, und can'le-lught till next day at nooin: then, t'fooil gangs banning un raving to his cham'er, makking dacent fowks dig thur fingers i' thur lugs fur varry shaume; un' th' knave, wha he carn cahnt his brass, un' ate, un' sleep, un' off tuh his neighbour's tuh gossip wi' t' wife. I'course, he tells Dame Catherine hah hor fathur's goold runs intuh his pocket, and her fathur's son gallops dahn t'Broad road, while he flees afore tuh oppen t'pikes?'
>
> (Chapter 10)

His fine last appearance – lamenting vigorously over the delinquent Ellen Dean for singing at her work, over Hareton for being 'witched' into happiness by Catherine, and then over Ellen again, welcoming Lockwood, for 'having followers at her time of life' (Chapter 32) – is a sign that all is well at the Heights, and is recognized as such with joy.

Even animals are treated seriously and responsibly by Emily Brontë and her characters. The Heights is a farm where sheep have to be brought in by Hareton and cows milked by Joseph by the light of a lantern. While people may at times partake of the nature of beasts, dogs and horses at least at times achieve a pleasant near-humanity. They have names and are called by them, and sexes which are recognized (no dog is ever merely 'it', though Heathcliff sometimes is). The bulldog Skulker who bites Catherine at Thrushcross suffers for a misreading of his duty, and is throttled off, but is humanely given some water to restore him (much as Heathcliff binds up Hindley's wound after beating him), and soon reappears in the drawing-room to partake of Catherine's food and have his nose pinched. His offspring Throttler recognizes Isabella, now not much better off than the animal, at the Heights (Chapter 13), and co-operates by clearing up her spilt porridge while she wipes the milk off the banister with her handkerchief.

Lockwood and Ellen Dean are set apart from the rest by being primarily structural characters, the bearers of the narrative rather than personalities who act or influence. Though Lockwood opens the story Ellen is far the more important, and the handling of her is both discreet and professional. Most of the features which form her are necessities of the story, and we even lose sight of her structural basis from the success with which it is concealed. On the whole she is the passive observer in whom others confide but whose advice they do not take. Though she has affections she has no personal commitments other than to the Earnshaw and Linton families. Even her ties with the children she brings up, Hareton and Catherine, are doomed to be broken, and known to be so before we know what the ties were. Her loyalties are quite clear: her earliest is to her foster-brother Hindley and the Earnshaw household generally, but the first we are told is that to the Lintons whom she thinks of as 'us' (Chapter 4). The difference between the reader's sympathies and hers is rich and complex, and gives an impression of subtlety to a narrative dealing only with simple and fundamental emotions. She is on the side of the younger generation, suggesting that they are more 'normal' than the first, and on the side of Hindley rather than Heathcliff or Catherine. She provides therefore a contrast of tone to that of Heathcliff and Catherine. She is the voice of hope for the future in her joy at Catherine's and Hareton's happiness. She is equally the voice of nostalgia for lost happiness, of sorrow for others' doom, and for one man's helplessness to help another:

'I smelt the rich scent of the heating spices; and admired the shining kitchen utensils, the polished clock, decked in holly, the silver mugs ranged on a tray ready to be filled with mulled ale for supper; and above all, the speckless purity of my particular care – the scoured and well-swept floor.

I gave due inward applause to every object, and, then, I remembered how old Earnshaw used to come in when all was tidied, and call me a cant lass, and slip a shilling into my hand, as a christmas-box; and, from that, I went on to think of his fondness for Heathcliff, and his dread lest he should suffer neglect after death had removed him; and that naturally led me to consider the poor lad's situation now, and from singing I changed my mind to crying.' (Chapter 7)

She gives a sense of the past quite as much as she gives a sense of immediacy:

'All at once, a gush of child's sensations flowed into my heart. Hindley and I held it a favourite spot twenty years before.

I gazed long at the weather-worn block; and, stooping down, perceived a hole near the bottom still full of snail-shells and pebbles which we were fond of storing there with more perishable things – and, as fresh as reality, it appeared that I beheld my early playmate seated on the withered turf; his dark, square head bent forward, and his little hand scooping out the earth with a piece of slate.

'Poor Hindley!' I exclaimed involuntarily. (Chapter 11)

We grow to wonder at her as a link between present life and a heroic past.

Being introduced to her as a woman of forty and Lockwood's housekeeper, we trust her to tell the truth, even though for the first part of the story she is only a child herself, and even though we soon come to feel differently from her, particularly about the elder Catherine, whom Ellen 'owns she did not like' (Chapter 8). Throughout the story up to Catherine's marriage she is both the young person reacting at the time of the events, and the mature woman looking back, giving a complexity like that Charlotte Brontë achieves in *Jane Eyre*. She feels life at the Heights with the intensity of a child, though a child sufficiently older than Catherine and Heathcliff (eight years) to judge them as well. She makes Catherine and Heathcliff seem unchildish: seem indeed as children seem to each other, not as they do to the adult observer. Thus she emphasizes the power of the first generation, for though her sympathies are with the second one, the younger Catherine and Hareton are never more than children seen by a superior and wiser adult.

Beginning when she is scarcely old enough to pass sound judgements – fourteen when the story begins and only twenty-two when Catherine confesses her engagement – she, childlike, accepts people's natures, and though she reacts and assesses, does not condemn. She leaves the way open for the reader, guided by her facts and warned by her inadequate responses, to pass judgement for himself, without feeling that he has been directed to a foregone conclusion. She comes to be the voice of normal human limitation, to represent the point at which the normal human standards of even a responsive and kindred being break down before Catherine and Heathcliff. Her responses are thus always the voicing of part of the reader's response, which is nullified by Ellen's too commonplace utterance:

> 'And now, let us hear what you are unhappy about. Your brother will be pleased ... The old lady and gentleman will not object, I think – you will escape from a disorderly, comfortless home into a wealthy respectable one; and you love Edgar, and Edgar loves you. All seems smooth and easy – where is the obstacle?' (Chapter 9)

This is plainly inadequate, though excellent sense, and it predisposes the reader in favour of the outburst it elicits from Catherine. Her comment on that outburst, that Catherine is 'a wicked, unprincipled girl' (ibid.), which again must be one of the things we have ourselves thought, is, when actually said, so far short of the mark that we respond even more powerfully to Catherine. And so Ellen commonly guides us; we do not agree because we know better; but her opinion is invaluable in teaching us how to know better. She is particularly valuable as the voice of religious orthodoxy, or of natural human reaction generally in the face of the spiritual world. Her remarks on death are all-important, since, entirely unsentimental (a notable feature in a nineteenth-century novel), and robust, and conventional though she is, her orthodoxy has a hard struggle; her appeal to Lockwood about the dead Catherine is startling, by its content as well as by the sudden jerk to the present:

'Do you believe such people *are* happy in the other world, sir? I'd
give a great deal to know.'   (Chapter 16)

The rest of the story is devoted to the answer Lockwood cannot
supply.[1]

In the second part of the story the plot demands that her structural
role of passive observer has to be distorted somewhat. Someone
must summon Linton to turn out Heathcliff in Chapter 11, for
instance; careful servant though she is always supposed to be, Ellen
must neglect Catherine and leave her alone with her delirium after
the quarrel; and though *in loco parentis*, she must be an ineffectual
guardian in order to give the younger Catherine freedom to seek
her own disaster. Much of the action takes place through other
narrators, an apparent failing which turns out to be an asset, since
Ellen remains the observer closest to the reader, and also the only
one in touch with Heathcliff, so keeping the focus on him when the
plot is actually growing away from him. The superstitious fear she
has exhibited from time to time reveals its function with respect to
him, investing him with a greater awe by the simple and inadequate
terms of Ellen's horror: to wonder whether Heathcliff dying in his
agony of desire is 'a ghoul or a vampire' (Chapter 34) is no more
than a groping in the right direction with grotesquely wrong terms.
Unlike most stories of the supernatural this one does not make the
reader care what the mortal observer Ellen feels at all, though she
undergoes fear and horror; a guide she has been and a guide she
remains, so that we concern ourselves, astonishingly and uniquely,
with the feelings and fates not of the living, but the dead.

[1] Ellen's personality occasionally shows signs of the strain put upon it. Many
have complained of her unrealistically literate style, but this, though obviously
true (and a danger felt by Emily Brontë, who makes a rather transparent attempt
to cover her tracks by having Ellen explain her self-education, Chapter 7) is not
very important, since one must accept a good deal of formality in the presentation of a first-person narrative. Ellen's is generally the speaking voice rather
than the written word, and not much more can be asked, or would be readable
or intelligible if offered. There are, however, occasional failures of verisimilitude.
When Heathcliff returns, for instance, Ellen leaves the room while he, Catherine
and Edgar Linton have tea, but the scene is still retailed; and when the younger
Catherine is twelve, Ellen declares herself 'too old to run up and down amusing
her' (Chapter 20) although she is barely forty – young enough to be her mother.

Lockwood is a character pared down to his function even more than Ellen.[1] He has just enough personality to get the action going, and deliberately not enough to occupy us for a moment once anyone at the Heights appears, or even the other narrator Ellen.[2] He has the interest in life to make him an accurate and keen observer, the romantic notions of a young man to respond to Catherine and make the reader respond even when she is at her worst, and a consciously affected cynicism and misanthropy to define by contrast the presence of the qualities in their genuine form at the Heights. He thus sets the tone without realizing it, and stifles before they are born not only sentimentality and platitudinous notions of what Catherine later terms 'rough diamonds' and 'pearl-containing oysters', but also the more insidious danger of the romantic, Byronic, exotic and alluring, undefined sin. He is shocked to discover in Heathcliff 'a genuine bad nature' of a kind that reveals itself very un-Byronically by speaking savagely to a pretty young woman. We believe very firmly in a ghost that must reveal itself to so unpromising a young man as Lockwood, heightened though his perceptions may be by a bad fright and a drenching with cold water. His consequent chill, neatly employed as the pretext for Ellen's story, is invaluable as a means of providing the sense of time at various levels that is so rich a part of the whole. Returns to the present of Lockwood's winter illness of 1801–2 are daringly and deliberately used, among the other methods of handling time, to be discussed with them later. Like Ellen, he provides facts which we trust and reactions and opinions from which, by differing, we see more truly. He conceives a very abstract fancy for the younger Catherine, seeing himself as her rescuer as Linton was her mother's; this usefully gets things into proportion, for though the younger

[1] This is why attempts to analyse his character always fail, and why the rumour that Branwell wrote the opening chapters doggedly persists. Lockwood refuses to seem 'foppish' (Introduction to *Wuthering Heights* in the Penguin English Library, 1965), still less to seem a 'dandy', as Mark Schorer describes him ('Fiction and the Matrix of Analogy,' *Kenyon Review*, XI, 1949.)
[2] For function and handling he recalls that other deliberately uninteresting introducer, Scott's Jedediah Cleishbotham who initiates the *Tales of My Landlord*. Emily Brontë read Scott, and owed a great deal to him, as has been so usefully demonstrated by Florence S. Dry. (*The Sources of Wuthering Heights*, Heffers, 1940).

Catherine has much less fire than her mother, we see clearly enough
that she has a great deal more than Lockwood, and ranges herself
thereby very much more readily with Hareton.

These two narrators – awkward though they have sometimes
been thought – are yet an essential part of Emily Brontë's narrative
method, which when examined shows itself to be necessarily
original from her original subject-matter, and very far from clumsy.
On reading one notices the detail within scenes rather than the
shape that scenes gathered into sections build up, as indeed Emily
Brontë intends, since successions of details are frequently successions
of conscious shocks, while the directing of attitudes over the larger
sections goes on unobtrusively.

Over the small stretch – the individual scene – she depends upon
speech and vivid detail. Speech varies between at one extreme the
literary monologue of Ellen and Lockwood, and the various
secondary narrators (Isabella and Zillah for instance) who supplement them, through the near-monologues of Catherine and
Heathcliff's various self-revelations, through passionate choric exchanges between them and others at moments when emotions
are much heightened, to short, truly dramatic dialogues occurring usually at moments of action, not reflection. It is only in
these last that speech is naturalistic and familiar; elsewhere
the weight of passion and sense combined turns to rhetoric and to
a kind of writing which, while being both powerful and completely convincing, is nearly unsayable except as a kind of poetic
declamation.

By contrast the details of scene, setting and action that accompany dialogue are wonderfully accurate, intensely vivid and relevant, and uncompromisingly realistic. They show just as much in
smaller scenes as great ones:

> Following her habit, my young lady descended early, and visited
> the kitchen: I watched her go to the door, on the arrival of a certain
> little boy; and, while the dairy-maid filled his can, she tucked
> something into his jacket pocket, and plucked something out.
>   I went round by the garden, and laid wait for the messenger; who
> fought valorously to defend his trust, and we spilt the milk between
> us.   (Chapter 21)

The billet-doux Catherine is sending to young Linton is the narrative concern here, but Emily Brontë realizes the whole scene for us, by concentrating on the other actual concern, the milk, and its fate. No scene is without its detail of this sort, which may well be taken up and used again later; Hindley's 'curiously-constructed pistol, having a double-edged spring knife attached to the barrel' (Chapter 13),. which so alarms Isabella, is later the weapon with which he is himself injured; or a single detail may reappear at intervals throughout the novel, making a complex series of connections, as does the catch on the window in the bedroom Lockwood occupies at the Heights, which, he noticed, had been 'soldered into the staple' (Chapter 3).

Emily Brontë works in terms of the individual, immediate, completely localized scene and moves from one scene to the next by a law of contrast, usually administering, while the reader is still shaken by one shock, another entirely different one. He is given no time to get back to his own conventional terms for assessment before the next scene resolves the former for him in some unusual way. There is no release from action except into a different kind of action. Hindley's drunken fit (Chapter 9) in which Hareton is almost killed, is only just over, and Ellen has only just sat down 'to lull my little lamb to sleep' when Cathy comes in to confess her engagement and, by doing so, to send Heathcliff into exile; this scene in turn is followed by the thunderstorm and Cathy's fever. Even on the morning after Catherine's burial we are hardly allowed to feel a break, since Isabella, escaped from the Heights, relives the last week for us in very different terms (Chapter 17). Clearly such effects are not done merely to shock the reader, but to increase understanding. Hindley's frenzy in which he drops Hareton over the banisters brings home to us what an urge Catherine must have to escape the Heights, while it and the thunderstorm serve in a very natural way to excite the characters above their ordinary level, and predispose them to act in an extraordinary way.

Breaks in time, whether long intervals or short, between these intense dramatic scenes are got over rapidly and unobtrusively in Ellen's narrative. Emily Brontë's time-scheme is exceptionally accurate, and dates and days are carefully expressed:

'Instead of leaping three years, I will be content to pass to the next summer – the summer of 1778, that is, nearly twenty-three years ago.'   (Chapter 7)

She is particularly good at covering gaps in a way that makes us actually feel the time that has passed. She does it usually by reference to circumstances or persons connected in Ellen's mind and in the narrative. Sometimes it is the brief effective phrase:

Cathy stayed at Thrushcross Grange five weeks, till Christmas.
                                                        (Chapter 7)

That Friday made the last of our fine days for a month.
                                                        (Chapter 17)

sometimes the general reflection, as when she gets over the first twelve years of the younger Catherine's life (Chapter 17), by describing Linton's resignation and Catherine's personality. Chapter endings frequently mark action endings, and are closed by some general utterance:

Her husband lies in the same spot, now; and they have each a simple headstone, above, and a plain grey block at their feet, to mark the graves.   (Chapter 16)

I felt that God had forsaken the stray sheep there to its own wicked wanderings, and an evil beast prowled between it and the fold, waiting his time to spring and destroy.   (Chapter 10)

Time in *Wuthering Heights* is retrospection and assessment as well as progression. The original narrator Lockwood obviously provides one level of retrospect and distancing, looking back at second-hand through Ellen. Ellen, looking back into the past, makes connections out of their chronological place, and by this means also covers the large gaps in time, even before they have, on the level of narrative, happened at all; for instance, Heathcliff, discussing the birth of his son with Ellen, says,

'But I'll have it, when I want it. They may reckon on that!'

and she goes on:

Fortunately, its mother died before that time arrived, some thirteen years after the decease of Catherine, when Linton was twelve, or a little more.   (Chapter 17)

But the next paragraph reverts to the present: 'On the day succeeding Isabella's unexpected visit', and goes on to tell of Hindley's death. Her turnings back are not assessments of time alone, but also, very movingly, of sensation:

> I kissed Hareton goodbye; and, since then, he has been a stranger, and it's very queer to think it, but I've no doubt, he has completely forgotten all about Ellen Dean and that he was ever more than all the world to her, and she to him! (Chapter 9)

We are constantly being called upon to feel the past in the present, whether it is the personal past summoned when the younger Catherine and Linton, wishing to play ball,

> found two, in a cupboard, among a heap of old toys; tops, and hoops, and battledores, and shuttlecocks. One was marked C., the other H. (Chapter 24)

or whether it is the historical past evoked by the name and date 'Hareton Earnshaw, 1500' among the 'wilderness of crumbling griffins and shameless little boys' (Chapter 1) over the door of the Heights, which it is the living Hareton's small triumph at last to learn to read.

Emily Brontë blending thus in a quite original and unique manner creates the feeling of eternity and grandeur surrounding the history of her two heroes.[1]

The ending to her history is magnificent, embodying all the reconciled contradictions of which the story has been so full, and we feel on reading the rightness of things: no contradiction between the ghosts in whose existence we believe, and Lockwood's faith in the 'quiet slumbers' of 'the sleepers in that quiet earth'. Hareton and Catherine fear nothing because they are the rightful inheritors among the living, Joseph's protests are silenced by the sweet ring of a sovereign at his feet, all is as it was, and the Joseph of the last chapter is again the Joseph of old Mr Earnshaw's prime. Lockwood

---

[1] She might well have learned the emotional effect of using historical time from Scott, who himself has heroes who work out their fates against a historical and foreordained past (which is their own future) and draws on its epic, tragic, and nostalgic powers, notably in *Waverley* and in *Old Mortality*. To create imaginary history, rather than using the real thing, is entirely her own.

leaves the living for the dead, where all is well. Mutability is perceived in the kirk which has been for so long an associate of Heathcliff's and Catherine's disunion:

> 'They may bury me twelve feet deep, and throw the church down over me; but I won't rest till you are with me.' (Chapter 12)

Heathcliff is with her and they are both at rest; the church may decay as it chooses. Lockwood's phrase 'unquiet slumbers' is, like many of his others, truer than he knows, and recalls Catherine's dream of being happy not in heaven but on the Heights, and Heathcliff's words on 'disturbing the dead' and on the nature of *his* heaven. They are very evidently at peace, in their own way, in their own heaven, a heaven inseparable from 'that quiet earth'.

Emily Brontë's greatness is in reaching her deeply impressive and most movingly ambiguous conclusion. Her central offering is the power of human feeling; the novel's great virtue is its courage in facing and bringing the reader to acknowledge what it sees as truth, and recognizing the power of forces whose existence has not hitherto been admitted. Emily Brontë has cast aside the duties of marriage (Catherine's to Linton), has claimed the invalidity of some kinds of love (Catherine's for Linton again, and Isabella's for Heathcliff), and has declared man's right to his own revenge, all without being either sensational or immoral. But her story ends in death. Hareton and Catherine, who inherit the earth that has now turned into a 'mighty stranger', are lesser figures than those who went before them. The novel is curiously sterile; it has no imitators of stature, and has had no influence on the novel after itself. One re-reads *Wuthering Heights* and responds and wonders, but one not only feels that Emily Brontë could not have written another novel, one does not even desire it – any more than one desires another *King Lear*.

2

THE PROFESSOR

The Professor, the first of Charlotte Brontë's prose works designed
for publication, is in many ways obviously the work of a beginner.[1]
Its interest is partly intrinsic and partly that of the promising early
work of a novelist who was soon to fulfil the promise. Even though
this beginner was nearer thirty than twenty, and even though her
remark in the preface that 'the pen which wrote it had been previously worn a good deal in the practice of some years' (which
alludes to her private fantasy epics) is an understatement as applied
to a larger quantity of writing in the past than she was to do in the
future, yet *The Professor* has deficiencies which are obvious. Its
writer is clearly not yet at ease with the balances required between
the various sections of a full-length work. She has not yet learned
to work in her characters evenly without disproportion between
what is minor in one part and major in another. She does not
always keep to what is artistically relevant, being led aside into
narrative cul-de-sacs – entertaining though some of these, like
Crimsworth's 'goûter' with the two pedagogic mothers Mesdames
Pelet and Reuter (Chapter 8), turn out to be. And she has not yet
realized the importance of the length of the whole: this is neither
novel nor short story, and feels inadequate in itself, apart from
being unlikely to gain publication in days when three volumes were
the norm.

The Professor is a minor work, but not necessarily a second-rate

[1] According to Charlotte Brontë's husband Arthur Nicholls, in his own preface
(1856) to the first edition (1857), it had been prepared for publication, and a
preface written to it, shortly after the appearance of *Shirley* (1849). However,
it must remain substantially as it was when written, in 1846, at about the same
time as Emily Brontë's *Wuthering Heights* and Anne Brontë's *Agnes Grey*.

one by comparison with others of its time. Had it been all Charlotte Brontë wrote, it might have gained paradoxically more favour than it now enjoys, since it has the same flavour as *Jane Eyre*, *Shirley* and *Villette*. We notice it less here, because these three main works are so much stronger meat.

Like them, *The Professor* is utterly original, in its material and its writer's view of life and of literary art. Her plot is entirely her own, and much of the matter is autobiographical. We see immediately her unfaltering belief that while it is proper to borrow *in extenso* and in ill-disguised form from life, it is out of the question to borrow in any fundamental way from literature, at any rate from the common stock of literary conventions. When the opportunity arises, even peripherally, she scorns it:

> I was no pope – I could not boast infallibility: in short, if I stayed, the probability was that, in three months' time, a practical modern French novel would be in full process of concoction under the roof of the unsuspecting Pelet. Now, modern French novels are not to my taste, either practically or theoretically. Limited as had yet been my experience of life, I had once had the opportunity of contemplating, near at hand, an example of the results produced by an example of interesting and romantic domestic treachery. No golden halo of fiction was about this example, I saw it bare and real, and it was very loathsome. (Chapter 20)

These are the hero Crimsworth's words, but, as will be examined later, he has a good many of his author's traits, and the literary terms in which he expresses his moral repudiation show very plainly his author's backing. While *he* will not accept life on a pattern laid down by fiction, *she* will not accept fiction either on these terms. She has no confidence that the conventions of fiction, even if seen by the light of common day, will lead her to the kind of literary truth she desires. In fact her aims are paradoxically high ones, while seeming very modest. This is one of the most important reasons why she leans so heavily on autobiographical material. She knows it is life not fiction, and believes that it cannot lead to the second-hand or debased. The plot of this novel therefore, even though it shows conscious and careful planning, betrays inexperience that a less candid and scrupulous writer could have avoided by depending on convention. Crimsworth morally and spiritually belongs in England, and the particular part of it in which the English scenes are set – the West Riding of Yorkshire as the author knew it, although she does not name it. The story rightly begins with six chapters of Crimsworth's experiences in his brother's employ at the counting-house of the mill in the busy and dirty industrial town of X——; and ends with a half-chapter in 'a sequestered and hilly region, thirty miles removed from X——' (Chapter 25) where Crimsworth returns with his wife and son to peace, prosperity and retirement. The shape is right, but a more experienced writer (as Charlotte Brontë soon became) would not have made such a broken-backed business of it. All that hold these English scenes to the Belgian ones are Crimsworth himself and Yorke Hunsden – Hunsden being, as I will show later, a dangerous tool. All the other characters and vividly created scenes and atmosphere of X—— are cast aside and forgotten, having no bearing on what happens in Belgium. Even in Belgium itself, there are too many events that lead nowhere, and too many that appear unprepared, perform one function only, and then drop into oblivion. The vigorous and near-rabelaisian mothers of Pelet and Mlle Reuter already mentioned are examples of the first, and the wealthy Dutch father Vandenhuten and his son whose life Crimsworth saved in a boating accident are an example of the second, appearing just in time to find Crimsworth a job when he has left Pelet's school. We see in *Jane Eyre* how rapidly Charlotte Brontë was to learn, not to change her methods, but to use them with real purpose; and when in *Villette* she seems to return to this casual introduction of material, the effect, as will be seen later, is very different in a work with very different intentions.

The Professor involves far fewer characters than Charlotte Brontë's other novels (another sign of a writer conscious of inexperience), and there is a very clear distinction between those of first and second rank. Crimsworth, his brother Edward, Pelet, Mlle Reuter, Yorke Hunsden and Frances Henri are quite unlike Edward's wife, his clerk Steighton, the two Bruxelloise mothers, the pupils of the pensionnat or Mr Vandenhuten. This distinction is one she preserves in *Jane Eyre*, and largely abandons in *Shirley* and *Villette*. But the distinction which is vital to structure and theme in *Jane Eyre* has much less use here, where the plot makes only minor use of characters felt to be major. There are no subordinate actions here, going on half-concealed from us, like all that concerns Bertha Mason, or the affairs of Jane Eyre's West Indian uncle, or Ginevra Fanshawe's ridiculous intrigue and Lucy's deliberate concealments from the reader in *Villette*. There are no parallel threads of experience like the Reed material in *Jane Eyre*, nor any separate sections to illuminate and finally combine with the main story, like the sections concerning the Rivers family. There are nevertheless some hints of this kind of structure, using offshoots from the main story of the kind which, particularly in *Villette*, she will make real use of later. There is for instance a tentative examination of the affairs of M. Pelet and Mlle Reuter, which feels for a time as though it may develop independently of the narrator's own *affaires du coeur* and counterbalance them, as the courtship of Graham Bretton and Paulina Bassompierre, or Ginevra and her toy Colonel, contrast with Lucy Snowe's and Paul Emmanuel's. There is also the suggestion of a source of incident in Sylvie, the one dutiful and intelligent child in Crimsworth's class, destined to be a nun 'early taught to make the dictates of her own reason and conscience quite subordinate to the will of her spiritual director' (Chapter 12). But she is never brought to bear on the protestant Frances Henri, as Helen Burns's true religion and Eliza Reed's arid one are brought to bear on Jane Eyre. These are tentative movements towards Charlotte Brontë's characteristic form, interesting, locally effective, and even artistically justified in a limited way.

Where the unity imposed on such disparate material is incomplete, as it is here, the writer's originality is all the more striking. *Jane Eyre* is so very much the achieved work of genius, and its originality so much obscured by later copies of it, that *The Professor*, less perfect, is a better witness. Writing it must have involved a choice as remarkable, on its own level, as Emily Brontë's when she conceived *Wuthering Heights*. Offered for publication in 1847, and written shortly before, *The Professor* is quite unlike anything available then as a model for a would-be writer. Like Emily Brontë's, the originality may be greater than the author realizes – despite the claims of the *Preface*.[1] It involves a new and idiosyncratic way of regarding the purpose of the novel: it also involves creating a unique area of experience which author and reader grow to share as the novel progresses. She feels clearly the purpose a novel has for her, and it is to be perceived most significantly when she seems to be following the novel's conventions most closely; that is, in allowing her novel to end with the married happiness of its leading character. This is not the mere convenient stopping-point it is generally for any of the novelists who could have influenced Charlotte Brontë – Fielding, Scott, Thackeray or Dickens notably – it is rather the artistic culmination of the whole, just as it is, even more clearly, in *Jane Eyre*. But Charlotte Brontë's materials here are not adequate to her purpose. The trivial round, the common task, do not furnish even Crimsworth, a clerk in a counting-house, with all he asks; nor does his flight to schoolteaching in Belgium furnish Charlotte Brontë with all she requires to reveal her hero's capacity for living, much less what she herself is capable of creating in a novel. Many of the ideas and states of mind revealed in Crimsworth reappear in the other three novels, where they seem completely and satisfyingly relevant, whereas here they do not. For example, after Crimsworth has proposed, successfully, to Frances Henri (Chapter 23) he suffers an intense and painful attack of hypochondria which lasts for a week, rendered briefly and vividly, and, in isolation, powerfully. He explains it rationally enough:

> I had been excited and in action all day, and had tasted no food since eight that morning; besides, for a fortnight past, I had known no rest either of body or mind. (Chapter 23)

But since his proposal to Frances has been so deliberately unimpassioned the reader cannot feel that the excitement has been great enough to produce so intense a reaction. When the same reaction into hypochondria recurs in Jane Eyre, suffering during Mr

[1] 'I had got over any such taste as I might once have had for ornamented and redundant composition, and come to prefer what was plain and homely. At the same time I had adopted a set of principles on the subject of incident, etc., such as would be generally approved in theory, but the result of which, when carried out into practice, often procures for an author more surprise than pleasure.'

Rochester's absence just before the wedding, the reader has already felt the force of Jane's passion through ten long chapters, and consequently acknowledges without question the rightness of the reaction into melancholia. Secondly, Charlotte Brontë makes structural use of the emotion to foreshadow disaster. The dreams which torment Jane foretell how she will be torn from Mr Rochester, and even how Thornfield will become a ruin. Other examples abound. Crimsworth's scorn and distaste for his young Belgian pupils are hardly natural in the competent and cool young man he is supposed to be; but are very right in *Villette* as the reaction of a nervous and not very competent young woman, of the same sex as her pupils and very little older. The violence and vigour of Yorke Hunsden are inappropriate to his concern over Crimsworth; they are fine and right when they reappear in *Shirley* as the concern of the radical, Hiram Yorke, over the troubles of mill-owners and workers in 1812.

As with emotional power, so also with moral forces. Crimsworth is placed in few moral dilemmas, for his situation does not admit of them. His only serious one occurs when he feels bound to resign his teaching post at the point when Frances, by finding one, prevents him from renewing his friendship with her. And even this is as much a matter for the emotions (his sensitiveness to impoverishment) as of moral testing. The actual decision to leave Pelet's (because it would be a dangerous folly to live in the same house as Zoraïde Reuter – now Mme Pelet) is presented as a social and aesthetic choice, quite as much as an ethical one, and causes Crimsworth no struggles. Yet we constantly feel the moral weight of Crimsworth's reflections, quite in excess of the circumstances provoking them. He feels it a duty to become his brother's clerk, and to remain so, however uncongenial the place may be:

> I am not of an impatient nature, and influenced by the double desire of getting my living and justifying to myself and others the resolution I had taken to become a tradesman, I should have endured in silence the rust and cramp of my best faculties. . . . I should have set up the image of Duty, the fetish of Perseverance, in my small bedroom at Mrs King's lodgings, and they two should have been my household gods, from which my darling, my cherished-in-secret,

Imagination, the tender and the mighty, should never, either by
softness or strength, have severed me.   (Chapter 4)

The heightened tone and utterance, mixing abstractions with the
comically concrete, is disproportionate here, but finds its place when
it recurs in Jane Eyre debating within herself about St John Rivers's
proposals, which, with all the weight of religious and social decorum
to recommend them to her, are a much more serious matter.

Yet despite these inadequacies, *The Professor* reveals quite clearly
and even powerfully an author working with topics and situations
which are original and her own, recognizing already where her
strength lies. When the feeling is in excess of the circumstances that
arouse it, the reader does not feel that the emotion is superfluous
or hysterical, but that the novelist's material is inadequate to her
purpose. The memorable and moving things in this novel are of
the same kind as those in her others. Crimsworth like Jane embodies
the urge to experience and learn from all that his personality is
capable of, to assert the claims of the individual over the pressures
of society and convention. He is an examination of the hero in
isolation, and, through him, of loneliness, of loss, of the experience
of great passions controlled by necessity and by a sense of duty and
decorum, and of the experiences of the whole personality when
anticipating, experiencing, and receding from crises.

For Charlotte Brontë the first person narrative is the natural
method of achieving her ends. For a writer who is just beginning
to work her own novel structure out of the nature of her material
it is also a practically useful one: it readily absorbs a good deal of
autobiographical matter, and it automatically imposes a kind of
unity and an elementary kind of emphasis on what is said and done.
Her first choice of hero is both interesting and significant. It is a
man, not a woman. This may well be partly because Charlotte
Brontë wished to be anonymous, and it would therefore be prudent
to conceal her sex – though not essential, as *Jane Eyre* proved.[1] But

[1] Writing as a man would not be at all strange or new to her after the extensive
practice she had had in the private family writings, for these involve even odder
feats than identifying herself with a self-created hero: she often chronicles in
the first person characters and events supplied by her brother, using the names
of actual persons, notably the Duke of Wellington and his sons.

the choice is more important in other ways. A reader is much less conscious of the sex of a male narrator than a female, particularly in a time when a woman's sphere was so much more restricted than a man's. One can never ignore for a moment that Jane Eyre or Lucy Snowe is female; Crimsworth is very often quite simply the neutral narrator, and the awareness of his sex can be put aside. Charlotte Brontë, as her letters and *Shirley* show, is conscious of the limitations society imposes on a woman, and therefore, by having a man as the central character, she avoids the limitations a heroine would impose on the novel, not yet realizing that to exploit such limitations is to be her great strength. Feminine though Charlotte Brontë is (and as Emily Brontë is not) she always seems to enjoy masquerading as a man – as in the long correspondence with her publishers as 'Currer Bell', and as in those parts of *Shirley* concerning 'Captain Keeldar' – and here she enjoys entering into the being of William Crimsworth. A male hero also solves neatly another of what could have been her problems, her heroine. She can now use aspects of what she clearly already feels her richest source of material – her own nature – to create the unusual heroine who is to be observed, understood and interpreted by the hero who has most convincingly much in common with her, since he also embodies some aspects of his author.[1]

William Crimsworth is remarkable not for being sometimes deficient as a portrayal of a man (so, if it comes to that, are David Copperfield and Pip, or that near-narrator Henry Esmond) but for being often impressive, and always answering his author's purposes. Crimsworth's personality is the result of a very proper reaction from the sensationalism of the private writings, and of a very proper feeling that it would be unsuitable for work for publication; a personality which in avoiding the sensational narrowly escapes

[1] Critics have objected that this implies emotional self-indulgence on Charlotte Brontë's part, since she creates herself twice over, and allows half herself to fall in love with the other half. When the result is a heroine who is both original and attractive, and when the novel itself offers the reader conspicuously less that can be used for his own emotional self-indulgence than her other, greater, ones, the charge seems the result (as so often with Charlotte Brontë) of letting what is known of biography and background intrude too far into a reading of the novel.

being bloodless. Yet Charlotte Brontë has managed a remarkably successful blending of the elements which make up Crimsworth: his delineations of himself and of others, his thought, action, conversation, and self-analysis. She describes his person very little – a sign of her confidence; like Emily Brontë she is always as assured about the physical as the mental and spiritual, so her characters achieve a physical presence which those of few other novelists attain. We are not asked to see Crimsworth except where his appearance is relevant to a full understanding of situation, or character other than his own; his first assessment of his brother is our first view of himself:

> I looked at him: I measured his robust frame and powerful proportions; I saw my own reflection in the mirror over the mantel-piece; I amused myself with comparing the two pictures. In face I resembled him, though I was not so handsome; my features were less regular; I had a darker eye, a broader brow – in form I was greatly inferior – thinner, slighter, not so tall. As an animal, Edward excelled me far.
> (Chapter 2)

The only other occasions on which his appearance recurs are when Hunsden scorns him for looking like an aristocrat, and when Mlle Reuter becomes infatuated. Her high-flown exclamation that he is 'beau comme Apollon quand il sourit de son air hautain' is promptly rejected by old Mme Reuter's remark that 'I had no point of a handsome man about me, except being straight and without deformity' (Chapter 20). It is a sign of Charlotte Brontë's originality and sureness of touch that we believe the old woman rather than the young one, and feel no sense of the inverted boast. The great opportunity for self-praise is completely passed over: Frances Henri never comments on his appearance at all. Like Jane Eyre's, Crimsworth's bodily presence is noted for its thematic relevance, even though its details cannot be so detailed or forceful.

Of his personality we hear more, for Crimsworth like Jane Eyre is self-conscious, though never self-absorbed. We hear what reveals the workings of his mind and the depths of feeling that the action cannot bring out; and also what explains his nature so that this in turn may interpret his behaviour. Although his personality does

not develop or change (in which respect he resembles the protagonists of *Shirley* rather than of *Jane Eyre* or *Villette*) the reader
grows to understand it gradually, since it reveals itself by degrees
through events and Crimsworth's responses to them.

> being a steady, reasonable man, I did not allow the resentment,
> disappointment, and grief, engendered in my mind by this evil
> chance, to grow there to any monstrous size; nor did I allow them
> to monopolize the whole space of my heart; I pent them, on the
> contrary, in one strait and secret nook. In the daytime, too, when I
> was about my duties, I put them on the silent system; and it was only
> after I had closed the door of my chamber at night that I somewhat
> relaxed my severity towards these morose nurslings, and allowed
> vent to their language of murmurs; then, in revenge, they sat on my
> pillow, haunted my bed, and kept me awake with their long, mid-
> night cry.   (Chapter 19)

Since Crimsworth's conduct must be all repression, it is only by
such a passage that the reader can find out that he feels distress, and
of what kind, at losing Frances Henri. The excellence is that this
repression is felt to be as much a part of his nature, self-imposed, as
a necessary exigency of the plot.

Analyses of other characters must necessarily be done through
the narrator, but they equally accord with and reveal the teller.
The skill which makes every character in *Jane Eyre* an extension
of Jane's apprehension and experience and so of herself is not yet
here, but there are many signs of it; and the handling of other
characters, often original, is never mechanical:

> I turned; at my elbow stood a tall man, young, though probably
> five or six years older than I – in other respects of an appearance the
> opposite to common-place; though just now, as I am not disposed
> to paint his portrait in detail, the reader must be content with the
> silhouette I have just thrown off; it was all I myself saw of him for
> the moment: I did not investigate the colour of his eyebrows, nor
> of his eyes either; I saw his stature, and the outline of his shape; I
> saw, too, his fastidious-looking *retroussé* nose; these observations,
> few in number, and general in character (the last excepted), sufficed,
> for they enabled me to recognize him.   (Chapter 3)

This does not in any way impede the flow of the narrative: it gives us the main points of Hunsden, particularly the faintly ludicrous and eccentric fastidiousness of his faintly ludicrous nose, and it has the half-mocking tone of familiarity and detachment that is to be the way the two young men regard each other. Similarly Zoraïde Reuter's appearance is retailed a little at a time, as Crimsworth notes it and its significance, and likewise Frances Henri's. The few set-pieces of personal description are deliberately done, and refer to personalities that have no emotional contact with the narrator. The formal sketches of those very remarkable pupils Aurelia Koslow, Adèle Dronsart, and Juanna Trista in Chapter 12 are a first attempt at those in *Villette*; Edward Crimsworth's wealthy empty-headed young wife anticipates Ginevra Fanshawe; and guests at his party return as the house-party in *Jane Eyre*.

Crimsworth's own thoughts do not take up as large a part as one might expect of a first-person narrative. Like Jane Eyre, and unlike Caroline Helstone, he is self-conscious, but not introspective or brooding. During most of the novel something, either conversation or incident, is taking place, the interest resting in the other characters as they affect Crimsworth or as he interprets them, rather than in his own thoughts. The set-pieces of thinking, in which Crimsworth reviews himself and his situation, are commonly put into dramatic or dialogue form. Charlotte Brontë would always rather reproduce thought and feeling than describe it. Crimsworth, when alone, like Jane Eyre and Lucy Snowe, thinks as though speaking, well aware of the reader's place in what is going on, exclamatory and consciously articulate. His nature and musings divide themselves, like Jane's and Lucy's, into dialogue, generally between an aspect of Reason or Conscience, and spontaneous feeling:

> I took several turns in my room, under the goading influence of most poignant remorse; I walked a quarter of an hour from the wall to the window; and at the window, self-reproach seemed to face me; at the wall, self-disdain: all at once out spoke Conscience:—
>
> 'Down stupid tormentors!' cried she; 'the man has done his duty; and you shall not bait him thus by thoughts of what might have been; he relinquished a temporary and contingent good to avoid a

permanent and certain evil; he did well. Let him reflect now, and when your blinding dust and deafening hum subside, he will discover a path.' (Chapter 21)

States of mind also present themselves as images, almost as visions, such as the reaction following his proposal to Frances Henri:

> At last I dozed, but not for long: it was yet quite dark when I awoke, and my waking was like that of Job when a spirit passed before his face, and like him, 'the hair of my flesh stood up'. I might continue the parallel, for in truth, though I saw nothing, yet 'a thing was secretly brought unto me, and mine ear received a little thereof; there was silence, and I heard a voice,' saying –
> 'In the midst of life we are in death'.
> That sound, and the sensation of chill anguish accompanying it, many would have regarded as supernatural; but I recognized it at once as the effect of reaction. (Chapter 23)

The style of such passages is rhetorical, here probably disproportionately so, yet it is far from trite in its use of biblical echoes; it is undeniably powerful, and is of course much more so in *Villette*, as the medium for the strained, heightened states of the hypersensitive Lucy Snowe. The artistic purpose even here is a most estimable one. Charlotte Brontë always intends her characters to be seen in relation to the world around them and to eternity. Her theme is man's relations with other men and with his moral duty to them, to himself, and to the eternal truths as he sees them. Hence introspection and analysis of personality is not her main concern, and she rarely indulges in it. We see in the above passage that man's feeling towards the supernatural must be taken into account as part of his feeling for life. Crimsworth interprets his vision as the image of his state of mind and it has no further use in the novel, but similar images in *Jane Eyre* prepare for the moment at which the supranormal cannot be thus explained away – when Jane, about to submit to St John Rivers, hears Mr Rochester's voice. The devices are most frequent of all in *Villette*, where they are so successful as a part of Lucy's nature that their further purpose, though felt, is less easily extracted.

·   ·   ·

When we come to the characters other than Crimsworth we find that Crimsworth is our guide. This is the method of *Jane Eyre*. While we are never asked to stand apart from the narrator and discount his judgement; while the other personalities actually are what he sees them to be, and his delineation of them is accurate and just; while their business is to elucidate him, not to have a life of their own apart from him; yet, while believing what the narrator says, the reader never forgets that narrator's presence as an intermediary; and so he feels that he can, in spite of it, judge for himself on the evidence supplied.

Probably the most achieved success in *The Professor* is Mlle Reuter, even above the heroine Frances Henri; while the most interesting creation is Yorke Hunsden – the one Belgian, and leading to *Villette*, the second Anglo–Swiss, containing seeds of Jane Eyre, the third English, and leading to *Shirley*. The rest of the characters also look forward in various ways to the later novels.

Mlle Zoraïde Reuter is plainly a working of the personality who appears as *Villette* as Mme Beck. Knowledge of Charlotte Brontë's own life makes it clear that both are to some degree portrayals of Mme Héger, principal of the school which Charlotte and Emily Brontë attended in Brussels. While speculation on the resemblance between art and life may be interesting to the biographer, it is not much relevant in assessing Charlotte Brontë's artistic achievement here. Mlle Reuter is generally agreed to be a quite considerable and successful creation. She shows most admirably her author's consistent fairness towards antipathetic persons. The reader dislikes Mlle Reuter, just as Crimsworth dislikes her, but is compelled to recognize and acknowledge her sense of decorum, her efficiency, her astuteness, and to feel the physical charm of the 'little and roundly formed woman' with her 'nut brown' curls and with a colour on her cheek 'like the bloom of a good apple, which is as sound at the core as it is red on the rind' (Chapter 9). The reader is forced to be fair to her just as (to compare with a greater) he is forced to be fair to George Eliot's Rosamond Vincy. He approves Mlle Reuter's management of her school, enjoys the dexterity with which she removes obstacles in her path (even when the obstacle is Frances Henri), and delights in her catlike deception and decorum:

'Mademoiselle,' I continued, 'you would greatly oblige me by directing me to that young person's abode.'

She seemed somewhat puzzled; and at last, looking up with an admirably counterfeited air of naïveté, she demanded, 'Does Monsieur think I am telling an untruth?'

Still avoiding to give her a direct answer, I said, 'It is not then your intention, mademoiselle, to oblige me in this particular?'

'But, monsieur, how can I tell you what I do not know?'

(Chapter 19)

Though she has, as Crimsworth observes, the makings of 'a fascinating little woman', we are not allowed to give her any sentimental credit for loving the hero, or to feel him aggrandized by being its object: his analysis comes early, exactly, and conclusively – 'blunt susceptibilities are very consistent with strong propensities' (Chapter 10).

The other woman who concerns Crimsworth deeply is Frances Henri, the Ango-Swiss teacher of lace-mending and embroidery who attends his classes. She occupies a large portion of the novel, she is its heroine, and ought therefore to be remarkable. In fact she is not. As I have indicated in talking of Crimsworth, she is a projection of aspects of her author that have not gone into the making of the hero. This need not make her a failure, but it must limit her. She is like both Jane Eyre and her author in appearance:

The shape of her head was different [from the Belgian girls], the superior part more developed, the base considerably less.

(Chapter 14)

She wears a 'well-fitting black stuff dress' with a 'spotless white collar', with no ornaments (Chapter 19) and is 'slight, straight, and elegant' (Chapter 23) – all of which agrees with what Mrs Gaskell tells us of her author. On the other hand Frances is idealized: even though she is no beauty, we hear of

the clearness of her brown eyes, the fairness of her fine skin, the purity of her well-set teeth, the proportion of her delicate form.

(Chapter 23)

The improvement on reality suggests, not narcissism, but a wish

61

to be acceptable to readers and publishers accustomed to heroines of charm and beauty. Indeed it is an original venture to have so modest and plain a heroine, 'not even a beautiful girl or a lady of rank' as the preface remarks, though the originality is now over-shadowed by that poorer, plainer, fiercer flouter of convention Jane Eyre. It is original also to emphasize the charm of personality above that of person: 'Frances' mental points had been the first to interest me, and they still retained the strongest hold on my pre-ference' (Chapter 23). The 'mental points' reveal themselves in her 'devoirs' in the same manner as Jane's personality reveals itself to Mr Rochester in her drawings: the difference in range between the two creations is that between the odd charm of Frances' little study of Alfred the Great, and the weird powerful imagination of Jane's visions of Latmos and the Evening Star.

Frances is restricted also, in comparison with Jane, by her few opportunities for speech. She has the chance to say very little, and that in inadequate English. Her idiom, necessarily stilted and formal, gives a flavour to dialogue, making Frances Henri the retiring pupil a more fully realized person than Frances Crimsworth the articu-late wife and head of her own school. The marriage of Crimsworth and Frances fails on another count: its essence is that it should seem unexciting and everyday, whereas Charlotte Brontë is by tempera-ment and experience (she had never seen in her own family the relations subsisting between husband, wife, and son which she describes in the closing chapters) better equipped to create the strange, the heightened and the abnormal. Imagination always serves her well, but in *The Professor* she has cut herself off from too many of the things that fire her.

Most of the Brussels characters are female. Charlotte Brontë clearly feels safer when depicting women, and rightly so: the only men she employs are M. Pelet, M. Vandenhuten, Mr Brown, and the ushers in Pelet's school. The ushers are mere background: 'bêtes de sommes' says Pelet, and Crimsworth makes no protest. Brown (to whom Crimsworth has letters of introduction from Hunsden for his first job) is a tool of the plot; so is Vandenhuten, who has the advantage over Brown of possessing a son and some sensibility, though it never rises above 'benignant content' (Chapter

23). After *The Professor*, Charlotte Brontë never again allows herself to use dull characters who make her work dull.

M. Pelet on the other hand, the remaining Bruxellois, appears at greater length than anyone but Hunsden. Being acute, corrupt, and a man of sentiment, he is automatically made 'a Frenchman by birth and parentage'. He is sophisticated and cynical, to contrast with Crimsworth and to demonstrate Mlle Reuter's calculation in marrying him; while as an older and more sophisticated man he is a useful implementation of Crimsworth. But after his one splendid bout of drunkenness he vanishes from view; his marriage and the interview at which Crimsworth resigns his post being merely reported. He does not fulfil the promise of his introduction and early appearances, another proof that *The Professor* cramps its author.

The remainder of the inhabitants of Brussels are women, of interest mainly for what they anticipate in the later novels. The two old women Pelet and Reuter, useful additions to the social setting, in their grotesquerie, their gusto in eating and drinking and the burlesque style Charlotte Brontë uses for them – 'a lace cap with *flourishing* red roses in the frill' (my italics, Chapter 8) – show an unexpected side of their author and look forward to the trio of curates in *Shirley*. Sylvie is the embodiment of Charlotte Brontë's anti-catholicism, which will find much more powerful expression in *Villette*. The trio of contrasted and unsatisfactory pupils and the trio of mistresses in Chapters 10 and 12 have an odd yet useful formality (as again in *Villette* where the same device recurs). A school always produces an illusion of stasis and permanence even though the pupils continually arrive and leave and change. Charlotte Brontë recognizes the illusion, and these portraits of the violent, and even corrupt and vicious, girls reveal the potentially dangerous forces under the calm. We are enabled therefore to sympathize with Mlle Henri who is unable to control them, and to look forward to *Jane Eyre*, with its much more extensive and confident handling of potential violence under seeming calm.

English characters are both shorter and simpler, partly because only seven of the novel's twenty-five chapters take place in England, and partly because Charlotte Brontë can assume that her reader is thoroughly familiar with English society. The one fully developed individual is Yorke Hunsden. He is the first use of the raw materials which later make up Mr Yorke in *Shirley*.[1] Both men combine brusque Yorkshire manners with cosmopolitan and cultivated taste and good French, both are blunt to the point of rudeness, both are eccentric in conduct and speech, both are liked by those very unlike them, and are, on the whole, intended for the reader to approve. But while Mr Yorke is one character among many in *Shirley*, Hunsden looms disproportionately large in *The Professor*. His power is in his language. His speech is racy and authentic and his exchanges startling and passionate as those of the foreign speakers cannot be. He is idiosyncratic and down-to-earth in a way characteristic not only of Charlotte Brontë, but also Emily and Anne. While his material anticipates Mr Yorke, his treatment suggests both Mr Rochester and Paul Emmanuel. The scenes he shares with Crimsworth have the excitement, and often the movement and phrasing, of those between Jane and Mr Rochester, notably that (too long to quote) in Chapter 6 where Hunsden, who has virtually lost Crimsworth his job, taunts him into exposing his hitherto suppressed ambition, and then encourages him to go to Brussels. Unfortunately the relationship between the two men (unlike Jane's and Rochester's) leads nowhere, so that the feeling seems in retrospect to be in excess of what the situation requires. A good deal is made of Hunsden's physical presence – his 'tall figure and long dark locks', and his significantly fastidious retroussé nose – and he is constantly presented in his relation to women, when the plot does not require it at all. Having seen Frances he remarks

> When I marry I must have straighter and more harmonious features, to say nothing of a nobler and better developed shape than that perverse, ill-thriven child can boast.　　　　　(Chapter 24)

The tone here is distasteful; Charlotte Brontë, in affecting the man of the world, has merely achieved the vulgar. In the final chapter he shows a miniature of the woman he wishes to marry, an actress. All this, irrelevant though interesting in a secondary character, be-

---

[1] Both were recognizable portraits of Mr Taylor, the father of Charlotte Brontë's close school-friend and lifelong correspondent Mary Taylor, who is herself the Rose Yorke of *Shirley*.

comes vital when it takes shape as the Bertha Mason and Céline Varens of the young Mr Rochester.

The only other significant English character is Crimsworth's brother Edward, who also has a force greater than the foreigners. He is Charlotte Brontë's first working of the dangerous minor character, who looks forward in violence to Mrs Reed in *Jane Eyre*, and, to a lesser degree, in his uncongenial authority, to Mr Helstone in *Shirley*. Like Mrs Reed he is a force that the hero must overcome as a stage in his own moral growth, though of course Crimsworth's victory as a grown man is slight compared with Jane's, rendering Edward Crimsworth's violent language and his brother's equally violent though briefer replies much less frightening than Jane's violence, and Mrs Reed's dangerous restraint or cowed silence.

The rest of the English characters are trivial but have occasional transitory but startling life, not so much for their functions here, but for what they foretell: Mrs Edward Crimsworth for instance

> spoke with a kind of lisp, not disagreeable but childish. I soon saw also that there was a more than girlish – a somewhat infantine expression. (Chapter 1)

or Mrs Lupton, the mother of a dashing and eligible young woman, who is 'a stout person in a turban' (ibid.). These seedlings take root in the soil of *Jane Eyre* and burgeon into Louisa Eshton and Baroness Ingram of Ingram Park, formidable mother of the formidable Blanche.

A novel using autobiographical material is likely to draw on parts of its narrator's experience which do not concern her relations with people. Charlotte Brontë like Emily is intensely aware of how the whole physical world affects the individual mind. Her sensitivity to place and atmosphere gives a great deal to *The Professor*. Though there is no question here of setting, landscape or weather being organic or symbolic, as they are in *Wuthering Heights*, and sometimes become in *Jane Eyre* and *Villette*, yet settings almost always illuminate the person with whom they are connected, characters' emotional states take account of their physical surroundings, and setting very often enriches the reader's understanding of events.

Place gives shape to the novel as a whole; England is the home from which Crimsworth departs to seek his fortune and to which he returns when he has succeeded and proved his worth in Brussels. Within this main framework place has its purpose, one of the most effective being Frances Henri's lodging (Chapter 19) where the economy, neatness, and charm, while plainly revealing Frances herself, reveal also the values of rationality and order which oppose those of impulse and passion in the novel as a whole. Such details occur only where they might naturally be observed, and when they intensify the mood. They are generally, as in her best work, both unobtrusive and memorable: one remembers Frances' 'painted floor and square of green carpet in the middle', and her 'black cat roused by the light [of the fire] from its sleep on a little cushioned footstool' who is 'fed with provisions brought forth on a plate for its special use'; just as much as one remembers the 'tea-equipage [that symbol of England] whose pattern, shape and size denoted a remote antiquity' (Chapter 19). Similarly other characters and events are pinned down by the odd precise detail; Edward Crimsworth and his private, complacent, thick-skinned prosperity are indicated in one over-stuffed easy chair, covered with red morocco, in his library; while his brutal business success receives substance in the following:

> we passed through two massive gates into a great paved yard, and we were in Bigben Close, and the mill was before us, vomiting soot from its long chimney, and quivering through its thick brick walls with the commotion of its iron bowels. Work people were passing to and fro; a waggon was being laden with pieces. (Chapter 2)

Crimsworth's emotions never make him unconscious of his surroundings; they rather make him unusually sensitive to them, and make them a part of his experience. Frustrated and lonely as his brother's clerk, with 'thoughts not varied but strong', he seeks relief in walking, noting that

> there was a crescent curve of moonlight to be seen by the parish church tower, and hundreds of stars shone keenly bright in all quarters of the sky. (Chapter 4)

66

After he is dismissed he again walks to calm himself. His state of mind is revealed in what he sees when he finally rests and looks about him:

> A chill frost-mist was rising from the river on which X — stands and along whose banks the road I had taken lay; it dimmed the earth, but did not obscure the clear, icy blue of the January sky. There was a great stillness near and far; the time of the day favoured tranquillity, as the people were all employed within doors, the hour of evening release from the factories not being yet arrived; a sound of full-flowing water alone pervaded the air, for the river was deep and abundant, swelled by the melting of a late snow. I stood awhile, leaning over a wall; and looking down at the current, I watched the rapid rush of its waves ... Grovetown church clock struck four; looking up, I beheld the last of that day's sun, glinting red through the boughs of some very old oak trees surrounding the church – its light coloured and characterized the picture I wished. I paused yet a moment, till the sweet, slow sound of the bell had quite died out of the air; then ear, eye and feeling satisfied, I quitted the wall and once more turned my face towards X —.   (Chapter 5)

The cold accords with his loneliness and lack of prospects, and the 'full-flowing' river, full with the effects of bad weather, reveals the nature of the calm in Crimsworth's own mind. Yet the term 'pathetic fallacy' cannot be used of such writing. It is not that scenery or weather are rigged to implement sensations, but that the sensation itself finds its own release through its surroundings. The Belgian scenery which delights Crimsworth on his drive to Brussels is neither beautiful nor in harmony with his mood:

> Green, reedy swamps; fields fertile but flat, cultivated in patches that made them look like magnified kitchen-gardens; belts of cut trees, formal as pollard willows, skirting the horizon; narrow canals, gliding slow by the roadside; painted Flemish farm-houses; some very dirty hovels; a grey, dead sky; wet road, wet fields, wet house-tops.   (Chapter 7)

What harmony this comes to have is not intrinsic, but what Charlotte Brontë creates by lively, felicitous, and precise writing. She is as aware here of the harmony and contrast between man and his surroundings as she is in *Jane Eyre*, where the same brilliant summer weather shines on Jane's love in the orchard, and on her agonized despair on the heather-covered moors.

Just as Charlotte Brontë shows none of the usual awkwardnesses of a beginner in handling her material, so she is already individual in her expression. Her highly original style, seen in the passages above, is already formed: with the precise choice of words, the formal idiom, and the always rather elevated tone which permits her to use poetic or uncommon words without jarring. It and the ways in which she uses it are completely assured. The way she narrates, presents her characters, and conducts her dialogue have already the unmistakable flavour which invite Mr Rochester's exclamation: 'It is rich to see and hear her! Is she rich? Is she piquant?' Here, as in her other novels, her dialogues are rarely entirely natural in idiom or movement. Perhaps she could not produce 'polite conversation'. There is no evidence that she ever did. It is quite clear even in *The Professor*, though, that polite conversation would hardly ever serve her purpose. The kind of communication involved when Jane addresses Rochester or, here, Crimsworth faces his brother or Yorke Hunsden, is that of crisis, of the moments when the ordinary standards of behaviour and speech break down. Charlotte Brontë is caught up in situations and feelings that might well be thought more the business of poetry or drama than the novel. It is not surprising then that she uses the vocabulary of poetry and the oratorical elevated manner of the drama. A formal style has the second advantage that it avoids the danger on the one hand of losing the personality of the speaker in the business of narration and on the other of over-insisting on the speaker's personality when it is least relevant.

One other of Charlotte Brontë's personal idiosyncrasies deserves mention: her habit of addressing the reader. She has good precedent for the device, in Fielding and Scott, and in her own much-admired contemporary Thackeray. But these writers do not use the auto-biographical method at the same time, a combination which can disconcert and even repel the modern reader, and which will demand closer consideration in the other novels. Even here its use is always justified, occurring where a break must come in pace, or in feeling between episodes, where aphorism or general reflection allow a review of things before moving forward again. The transition between Chapter 6 where Crimsworth takes summary leave of Hunsden, and Chapter 7 where he travels to Brussels, is done with the opening sentence:

Reader, perhaps you were never in Belgium?

economical, precise, and making perfectly both the break in time and scene and the join in mood and interest required. The apostrophe can also be, as so often in *Jane Eyre*, a retreat from threatening sentimentality, an excellent intention, though somewhat brutally carried out here after Crimsworth's successful proposal of marriage:

> Now, reader, during the last two pages I have been giving you honey fresh from flowers, but you must not live entirely on food so luscious; taste then a little gall – just a drop, by way of change.
> (Chapter 23)

There follows his attack of hypochondria.

> 'Something real, cool, and solid, lies before you; something unromantic as Monday morning. . . . Cold lentils and vinegar without oil, and no roast lamb.'

These words from the opening of *Shirley* are equally apt to what Charlotte Brontë proposed to do in *The Professor*, and are about equally true. As with many authors, what she consciously intends is not always what she performs, and while it was a valuable aim for her to avoid the romantic and melodramatic fancies she had indulged in private writings for her family (the Angrian epics in which she collaborated with her brother) her successes here, just as in her major works *Jane Eyre* and *Villette*, are not the result of being commonplace; they are rather the result of the tensions, and the resulting balance, between her natural impulse towards the thrilling and the supranormal, and her firm belief in the importance of the rational and the everyday.

3

JANE EYRE

Jane Eyre still bursts upon the reader as it burst upon its first readers in 1847. Even though most people are now conscious of works by two sisters accompanying it, and now know that it is one of four novels by its author, and that it was preceded by *The Professor* and a huge quantity of writing never intended for publication, it still seems to spring into the world as an achieved masterpiece: an Athena from the head of Jove, or a Venus from the sea. There are very few signs of the writer still learning his trade, a rare state for any first book to enjoy. *Jane Eyre* has many idiosyncrasies, and its structure and method are highly unconventional, so inevitably praise has been accompanied and qualified by condemnation of a whole range of 'faults', which vary according to the climate of criticism when they are discovered. But these faults are never those of an apprentice, and are never attributed to immaturity; as indeed they should not be, since the same qualities are to be seen again in both *Shirley* and *Villette*. One must examine *Jane Eyre* with a candid judgement, as free as possible from preconceived notions both of what a novel should contain and how it should achieve its ends. This is generally agreed to be the case with *Wuthering Heights*, but not so much with *Jane Eyre*, mainly because Charlotte Brontë seems to be working with the common stuff of the novel, the adventures of a central character which end with a marriage. Consequently *Jane Eyre* has suffered with time, since the two main kinds of novel which give the modern reader these preconceived notions are the great Victorian and nineteenth-century novels which are almost all written later than *Jane Eyre*, and the large number of second-rate Brontë-imitations, which take over some of the situations and character types from Charlotte and Emily

Brontë's works, without any real understanding of their model.[1] This recognizable novel form – adventure ending in marriage – was one of the qualities which made *Jane Eyre* acceptable to the novel-reader of the 1840s when *Wuthering Heights* was not; it is also the quality which has swung critical opinion over the last forty years the other way, so that while *Wuthering Heights* is an accepted master-piece *Jane Eyre* has sunk in esteem. *Wuthering Heights* compels us to examine its purpose, that of its characters, its structure, and the style and expression used. *Jane Eyre* does not. Yet those features are equally the demonstration of its kind, and the proof of its excellence, are equally original and independent, and in fact have more in common with *Wuthering Heights* than with any other writer or work.

Any study of a work begins with the essential and the obvious, since these are by definition likely to be more enlightening than the abstruse. The most obvious things in *Jane Eyre* are the simple single story and the personality of its narrator Jane herself, with Mr Rochester coming a very close third. Everything that is done bears directly on these three. This is partly the result of having a narrator who is also the hero, but the concentration shows it is more than a natural consequence. There are no sections of this novel like the story of Steerforth in *David Copperfield* (another 'autobiography') which has a life and artistic significance beyond what the career and character of the narrator require. This perfectly proper and legiti-mate use of a narrator, which Charlotte Brontë employs in *Villette*, is not present in *Jane Eyre*. Like *Wuthering Heights*, *Jane Eyre* might be called a love story. This would be true in one way, since it shows that the marriage at the end is the moral and artistic culmination of the whole – not merely a convenient rounding-off of a whole collection of different kinds of material, like Amelia Sedley's marrying Dobbin at the end of *Vanity Fair*, or even Dorothea Brooke's marrying Ladislaw in *Middlemarch*. In another way it is

[1] Most of these latter books are not literature at all, and so, while they are part of most readers' consciousness, they are not recognized as having any bearing on their habits of criticism. Examples one might mention are the novels of Ethel M. Dell, of Daphne du Maurier, and of countless contributors to women's magazines.

considerably less than the truth, since by the time this marriage is reached it has come to represent the resolution of moral and emotional conflicts, and the growth of moral and emotional grasp of life as a whole; for all of which the word 'love-story' is a very inadequate counter. The story really examines that period of life in which its heroine (and in secondary place its hero also) makes the most influential decisions of her life; the period which arouses the most extreme emotions of which her nature is capable, and brings out and tests the strength of the moral principles which rule her.

Such complete concentration on the moral and emotional growth of an individual, done wholly by self-revelation, had not been attempted before.[1] Charlotte Brontë, therefore, doing something new, had to work out her own way of doing it. Her way is the fictional autobiography. It is her great claim to genius, proved by the claims to greatness of *Villette* and *Jane Eyre*, and demonstrated conversely by *Shirley*, which, trying the more customary author's narrative, is far less successful. The autobiography not only allows Charlotte Brontë to reveal the main character, it imposes a form on the material available – we can perceive only what it is possible for the narrator to perceive – and it forces the reader to share in that character's growth and self-knowledge. The reader's emotional and moral sympathy with Jane Eyre is vital, and no one questions Charlotte Brontë's power of obtaining and keeping it. But complete emotional sympathy generally suggests complete identification, the reader feeling that he actually becomes the character throughout, or for long portions of the action. *Jane Eyre*

[1] Earlier novelists who spring to mind are Defoe, Richardson and Jane Austen. Defoe, while using the first-person narrative, does not concern himself primarily, if at all, with either moral or emotional development; Richardson's heroines (even Clarissa) do not grow, change, and learn from what they suffer to anything like the extent Jane Eyre does (they do not begin as children), and a good deal of the revealing of them is done by others – to achieve what Charlotte Brontë achieves Richardson would have to write letters from his heroine exclusively. Jane Austen does not use the first-person narrative, and when in *Emma* she comes close to seeing life through the perceptions of a single personality, she is still concerned with a whole society and the heroine's moral obligations towards it.

obviously approaches this state at points, but this is not really the whole truth, and Charlotte Brontë never meant the story to produce so total an immersion. It would come much too near the emotional state Jane Eyre herself rejects during Mr Rochester's courtship:

> 'I'll not sink into a bathos of sentiment: and with this needle of repartee I'll keep you from the edge of the gulph too; and, moreover, maintain by its pungent aid that distance between you and myself most conducive to our real mutual advantage.'
>
> (Chapter 24)

Jane, who cares passionately for Mr Rochester, preserves her detachment from him; and Charlotte Brontë takes care that the reader, who comes rapidly to care passionately about Jane, shall preserve his degree of detachment as well. The reader is quite often addressed, and so forced to think of himself and his own personality as very much a thing apart from the narrator's, and the demands that he shall do so grow more frequent as the story goes on. They increase in direct proportion to the emotional and moral complexity of the material. The first exhortation is unobtrusive:

> Have I not described a pleasant site for a dwelling, when I speak of [Lowood] as bosomed in hill and wood, and rising from the verge of a stream? Assuredly, pleasant enough: but whether healthy or not is another question. (Chapter 9)

and it is followed soon by a short discourse to the reader on Helen Burns. It is an indication of two things: first, that we are to watch, as well as feel, at Helen's death, since the incident's artistic purpose is to increase Jane's emotional and moral understanding; and second, that we are now drawing away from Lowood, for the next chapter (10) is the one in which Jane resigns her post as teacher and prepares to move to Thornfield. Apostrophes to the reader continue to be used in the same way: to mark the opening of a new scene (Chapter 11) or to mark a stage in the emotional development (Chapter 18), and also, originally and remarkably, at moments of extreme emotional tension, when it would seem like artistic sacrilege to destroy the willing suspension of disbelief. This is the most remarkable and original use of the device, and the one that jars the reader's

73

sensibility the most if he is reading in a spirit of mere emotional indulgence. They occur equally at joyful and painful moments:

'Jane, you look blooming, and smiling, and pretty,' said he: 'truly pretty this morning. Is this my pale, little elf? Is this my mustard-seed? This little sunny-faced girl with the dimpled cheek and rosy lips; the satin-smooth hazel hair, and the radiant hazel eyes?' (I had green eyes, reader; but you must excuse the mistake: for him they were new-dyed, I suppose.)   (Chapter 24)

Gentle reader, may you never feel what I then felt! May your eyes never shed such stormy, scalding, heart-wrung tears as poured from mine. May you never appeal to Heaven in prayers so hopeless and so agonized as in that hour left my lips: for never may you, like me, dread to be the instrument of evil to what you wholly love.

(Chapter 27)

The caged eagle, whose gold-ringed eyes cruelty has extinguished, might look as looked that sightless Samson.
    And, reader, do you think I feared him in his blind ferocity? – if you do, you little know me.   (Chapter 37)

These apostrophes occur so consistently that they must be there for a purpose. They are clearly a call to attention from author to reader,[1] but not to draw closer, to share in the experience, but to detach oneself momentarily from something that may lull one's rational or moral awareness.[2]

This detachment in varying degrees is consistently maintained, and the tension between it and emotional involvement is one of the work's great achievements. Detachment of the usual kind – that

[1] As Robert Martin observes (*The Accents of Persuasion*).
[2] In the first example, the remark about green eyes, it would be easy to fall into a number of false attitudes here; one might not notice the false note, might accept it as an example of the power of 'the loving eye' which has already given Mr Rochester himself 'a power beyond beauty' (Chapter 22), or might think Charlotte Brontë is romantically indulging her heroine at last with a small share of good looks. But the word 'reader' jolts us, we are forced to notice that Mr Rochester is being ridiculous, because his attitude to Jane is a wrong one – contrast his proposal, where he frankly calls her 'small and plain' (Chapter 23); and, though Jane's humorous comment keeps the tone light, this incident combines with others to make us see that Mr Rochester is morally wrong, in the way he treats Jane, in small details just as much as in attempting bigamy.

JANE EYRE

resulting from an observing author and a reader who observes the author in his turn – is largely done away with. Autobiography involves an apparently simplified narrative viewpoint: that solely of the teller of the story; and Charlotte Brontë preserves the impression of simplicity. She never disagrees with Jane, and neither does the reader. Even so, there are many fine distinctions in the degrees of detachment of writer from material. They are not immediately obvious or obtrusive on reading, but the effects they have on how the reader perceives what is happening are very considerable, and are a vital part of the intellectual and emotional control which, despite the more obvious passions, one feels throughout the story. There are two obvious narrative stances available: the story can either be seen and revealed by Jane at the age at which she experiences it, or it can be interpreted by the Jane who is supposedly looking back at her youth from the age of about thirty – the age she claims to be in the last chapter, where she says she has been married ten years. Charlotte Brontë uses both stances frequently. But as the action develops, other points of view are taken up within this main framework. The eighteen-year-old Jane at Thornfield has the opportunity to revisit the scene of her first sufferings and her first defiance, Gateshead, and to reassess both herself and those who hurt her; and there are many other equally vital but even smaller time-lapses and retrospects: Jane at Lowood looks back and tells her sufferings at Gateshead to Miss Temple; at Morton, she contrasts herself as schoolteacher with what she would have been as Mr Rochester's mistress; and the whole of the section at Thornfield is punctuated by pauses for Jane to review, analyse or assess what has gone before. These degrees of involvement make it easy to suppose that when we have reached the most detached narrator, we have reached the author. It is easy to feel that Jane Eyre at her wisest and most omniscient is Charlotte Brontë herself, and probably the majority of readers do so, consciously or not, at some time during their acquaintance with the work. It is the measure of Charlotte Brontë's triumph. It is natural to like Jane, and when we know that many of the things that happen to her, and many of the places she goes to, belong equally to Charlotte Brontë, it is both natural and inviting to think that Jane and Charlotte may be equated. It is a

75

temptation that must be resisted if one intends to get the most
possible out of the novel.[1]

These degrees of detachment are never automatic or system-
atized; they are always determined by the emotion and the attitude
to it that is necessary both in Jane and in the reader. At the beginning of the story the method is created and established. It would be
all too easy here to assume complete identification with the ten-
year-old Jane, see all through her eyes, and make her sufferings
quite unnaturally painful, and her adult tormentors monstrous or
merely ridiculous. Charlotte Brontë never permits it. From the
magnificently simple and dramatic opening paragraphs, describing
John, Georgiana and Eliza Reed in the comfort of the drawing-
room, and Jane in disgrace reading Bewick in the window of the
cold breakfast-room, she moves to Jane's opinions on her book –
a book which sets the sinister tone for Jane's future superstitious
agonies in the red room:

> Of these death-white realms I formed an idea of my own: shadowy,
> like all the half-comprehended notions that float dim through
> children's brains, but strangely impressive. The words in these
> introductory pages connected themselves with the succeeding
> vignettes, and gave significance to the rock standing up alone in a
> sea of billow and spray; to the broken boat stranded on a desolate
> coast; to the cold and ghastly moon glancing through bars of cloud
> at a wreck just sinking.
>
> I cannot tell what sentiment haunted the quite solitary churchyard,

[1] The obvious case against this identification theory – that the novelist's mind
contains his whole work whereas the mind of any one character within it
manifestly does not – is not easy to maintain here, since the mind of Jane Eyre
comes very near to containing the whole work. However, it is pretty clear that
if Jane Eyre were Charlotte Brontë, there would have been no *Shirley* and no
Villette. And the case for identification of author and character can, if one
wishes, be made out equally effectively with Lucy Snowe, and Lucy is patently
not like Jane in many fundamental ways. Likewise the evidence of biography
and letters will corroborate one's critical opinion that Charlotte Brontë's
personality – irrespective of her experiences – is not Jane Eyre's. There are, in
particular, occasional remarks which suggest that the 'I' speaking is further
from the events than even a thirty-year-old Jane can be, and that we are very
close to hearing the voice of Charlotte Brontë herself, and this suspicion receives
support from *Shirley*, where the same astringent note occurs very frequently.

with its inscribed headstone; its gate, its two trees, its low horizon, girdled by a broken wall, and its newly-risen crescent, attesting the hour of even-tide.

The two ships becalmed on a torpid sea, I believed to be marine phantoms.

The fiend pinning down the thief's pack behind him, I passed over quickly: it was an object of terror.

So was the black, horned thing seated aloof on a rock, surveying a distant crowd surrounding a gallows.

Each picture told a story; mysterious often to my undeveloped understanding and imperfect feelings, yet ever profoundly interesting.
(Chapter 1)

Here we see clearly that what Jane thinks is not fact, but an imaginative heightening and distortion – 'half-comprehended notions that float dim through children's brains', 'mysterious often to my undeveloped understanding and imperfect feelings' – and this prepares the way for her dealings with people to show equally 'undeveloped understanding and imperfect feelings'. There is no emotional indulgence in Jane's childish sufferings and the reader is not allowed to indulge either: in the red room Jane wonders pitifully whether she is indeed as wicked as everyone declares:

I grew by degrees cold as a stone, and then my courage sank. My habitual mood of humiliation, self-doubt, forlorn depression, fell damp on the embers of my decaying ire. All said I was wicked, and perhaps I might be so: what thought had I been but just conceiving of starving myself to death? That certainly was a crime: and was I fit to die? Or was the vault under the chancel of Gateshead Church an inviting bourne? In such vault I had been told did Mr Reed lie buried; and led by this thought to recall his idea, I dwelt on it with gathering dread.

(Chapter 2)

and from this grows her 'singular notion':

I doubted not – never doubted – that if Mr Reed had been alive he would have treated me kindly; and now, as I sat looking at the white bed and overshadowed walls – occasionally also turning a fascinated eye towards the dimly gleaming mirror – I began to recall what I had heard of dead men, troubled in their graves by the violation of their last wishes, revisiting the earth to punish the perjured and avenge the oppressed; and I thought Mr Reed's spirit, harassed by the wrongs of his sister's child, might quit its abode – whether in the church vault or in the unknown world of the departed – and rise before me in this chamber. I wiped my tears and hushed my sobs; fearful lest any sign of violent grief might waken a preternatural voice to comfort me, or elicit from the gloom some haloed face, bending over me with strange pity. This idea, consolatory in theory, I felt would be terrible if realized: with all my might I endeavoured to stifle it – I endeavoured to be firm.   (ibid.)

But in between these two passages which brilliantly reproduce Jane's feelings is an interpolation:

I could not remember him; but I knew that he was my own uncle – my mother's brother – that he had taken me when a parentless infant of his house; and that in his last moments he had required a promise to Mrs Reed that she would rear and maintain me as one of her own children. Mrs Reed probably considered she had kept this promise; and so she had, I dare say, as well as her nature would permit her; but how could she really like an interloper not of her race, and unconnected with her, after her husband's death, by any tie? It must have been most irksome to find herself bound by a hard-wrung pledge to stand in the stead of a parent to a strange child she could not love, and to see an uncongenial alien permanently intruded on her own family group.   (ibid.)

This is clearly a mature mind looking back, and, while it breaks the emotional continuity, serves in the long run to make Jane's sufferings even more dreadful (since we are not allowed the emotional relief of thoroughly loathing her tormentors), and they are even more potent for having a recognizable relation with common life. This scene establishes a moral attitude, and a sense of claims other than merely those of the child's sufferings, a state which is continued throughout the novel. This moral poise is unusual in any writer concerned with children, as a comparison with any other would show. In Charlotte Brontë's closest contemporary, Dickens, the Murdstones are as terrible to the young David Copperfield as the Reeds to Jane, while the pathos is probably even more painful to the reader, since David cannot rise against them as Jane does, and since he has to watch them torture his mother too; yet to the reader the

Murdstones are mere grotesques, on whom he is never asked to spend a serious thought. The superiority of Charlotte Brontë's method is proved in the novel as a whole, since the Reeds return eight years later, and while they impress Jane the independent young woman very differently, they are still – especially Mrs Reed – very recognizably themselves. Later in *David Copperfield* Miss Murdstone appears as Dora's chaperone, and David meets Mr Murdstone buying his marriage licence to another unfortunate victim. But there is no life in them now their place in the child David's mind is no more: they have no function and no personality.

When the Gateshead experience appears again, and Jane tells her story to Miss Temple, we can measure Jane's emotional and moral development by the combined effects of the two levels of narrative comment in the first chapter:

Exhausted by emotion, my language was more subdued than it generally was when it developed that sad theme; and mindful of Helen's warnings against the indulgence of resentment, I infused into the narrative far less of gall and wormwood than ordinary. Thus restrained and simplified, it sounded more credible: I felt as I went on that Miss Temple fully believed me.

In the course of the tale I had mentioned Mr Lloyd as having come to see me after the fit: for I never forgot the, to me, frightful episode of the red room; in detailing which, my excitement was sure, in some degree, to break bounds; for nothing could soften in my recollection the spasm of agony which clutched my heart when Mrs Reed spurned my wild supplication for pardon, and locked me a second time in the dark and haunted chamber. (Chapter 8)

Again there are two narrative levels: the first paragraph is all ten-year-old (though already a wiser one than she was at Gateshead); the latter half of the second one suggests the eye of an ever maturer self, looking back on both Lowood and Gateshead.

When Jane again meets Mrs Reed, she has been proved to be still structurally and emotionally important, and we recognize her by the insight the earlier detached comments have given us:

The well-known face was there: stern, relentless as ever – there was that peculiar eye which nothing could melt; and the somewhat raised, imperious, despotic eyebrow. How often had it lowered on me menace and hate! and how the recollection of childhood's terrors and sorrows revived as I traced its harsh line now! And yet I stooped down and kissed her: she looked at me.   (Chapter 21)

This is the largest and longest single retrospect in time, and involves us in two levels: Jane at eighteen seeing Jane at ten and measuring her development, and Jane at thirty seeing both.

When Jane is grown up – at Thornfield and at Morton – there are of course the obvious retrospects, like this, at Morton:

... to have been now living in France, Mr Rochester's mistress; delirious with his love half my time – for he would – oh, yes, he would have loved me well for a while. He *did* love me – no one will ever love me so again. I shall never more know the sweet homage given to beauty, youth, and grace – for never to any one else shall I seem to possess these charms. He was fond and proud of me – it is what no man besides will ever be. – But where am I wandering, and what am I saying; and, above all, feeling? Whether is it better, I ask, to be a slave in a fool's paradise at Marseilles – fevered with delusive bliss one hour – suffocating with the bitterest tears of remorse and shame the next – or to be a village-schoolmistress, free and honest, in a breezy mountain nook in the healthy heart of England?   (Chapter 31)

Passages such as this show Jane's attempts to subdue and control her own grief, as she has subdued and controlled her sense of anger and injustice at Mrs Reed, to see life steadily and see it whole; at the same time it reminds the reader of the passion and suffering that the action at this point cannot disclose. Yet it would seem natural on the whole for the narrative detachment to decrease and simplify, as it does in *David Copperfield*. In fact the tendency is the opposite, and the more the emotional pressure increases, the more Jane's understanding of herself and ours of her is clarified by the way the narrator reveals them. The closest-knit section of the book in all ways is that at Thornfield, from Mr Rochester's first appearance on the icy causeway to his last in despair when Jane leaves him. This section consists of a series of emotional surges forward, with pauses or even withdrawals between them, like the waves of a rising tide. At every pause the reader is made to stand away from the emotional experience, and assess it in relation to others, to moral standards, or simply to ordinary common life. This is achieved by a shift in the narrator's view, and Jane herself stands away from events. After she has rescued Mr Rochester from the fire, Jane thinks of Grace Poole, and rejects the idea that she may have some romantic hold over Mr Rochester:

> . . . Mrs Poole's square, flat figure, and uncomely, dry, even coarse face, recurred so distinctly to my mind's eye, that I thought, 'No; impossible! my supposition cannot be correct. Yet,' suggested the secret voice which talks to us in our own hearts, '*you* are not beautiful either, and perhaps Mr Rochester approves you: at any rate you have often felt as if he did; and last night – remember his words; remember his look; remember his voice!'
>
> I well remembered all: language, glance, and tone seemed at the moment vividly renewed. I was now in the school-room; Adèle was drawing; I bent over her and directed her pencil. She looked up with a sort of start.
>
> 'Qu'avez-vous, mademoiselle?' said she; 'Vos doigts tremblent comme la feuille, et vos joues sont rouges: mais, rouges comme des cerises!'
>
> 'I am hot, Adèle, with stooping!' She went on sketching, I went on thinking.
>
> I hastened to drive from my mind the hateful notion I had been conceiving respecting Grace Poole: it disgusted me. I compared myself with her, and found we were different. Bessie Leaven had said I was quite a lady; and she spoke truth: I was a lady. And now I looked much better than I did when Bessie saw me: I had more colour and more flesh; more life, more vivacity; because I had brighter hopes and keener enjoyments. (Chapter 16)

Though love is not yet mentioned, we now see the force of the feeling Jane is refusing to admit to herself, we see the sound sense on which she bases her belief in Mr Rochester's favour, and the feeling that it is not preposterous or improper, as his association with the commonplace Grace undoubtedly would be. Jane's assessments are usually – when Blanche Ingram has appeared – repressions, but they show the same uncompromising and rational fairness, and the following extract is an example of the use of the multiple narrative stance revealing the number of levels at which we are asked to view a single situation: Jane has now admitted to herself that she loves Mr Rochester, that there is no longer any question of, as she says 'extirpating from her soul the germs of love there detected' (Chapter 17), but she now tries to come to terms with the situation when it seems very plain that he is going to marry Blanche Ingram. Though the reader is certain he will not (even on a first reading), this must not seem a preposterous situation, nor Jane a fool for being deluded.

> I have not yet said anything condemnatory of Mr Rochester's project of marrying for interest and connexions. It surprised me when I first discovered that such was his intention: I had thought him a man unlikely to be influenced by motives so common-place in his choice of a wife; but the longer I considered the position, education, etc., of the parties, the less I felt justified in judging and blaming either him or Miss Ingram, for acting in conformity to ideas and principles instilled into them, doubtless, from their childhood. All their class held these principles: I supposed, then, they had reasons for holding them such as I could not fathom. It seemed to me that, were I a gentleman like him, I would take to my bosom only such a wife as I could love; but the very obviousness of the advantages to the husband's own happiness, offered by this plan, convinced me that there must be arguments against its general adoption of which I was quite ignorant: otherwise I felt sure all the world would act as I wished to act.
>
> But in other points, as well as this, I was growing very lenient to my master: I was forgetting all his faults, for which I had once kept a sharp look-out. It had formerly been my endeavour to study all sides of his character: to take the bad with the good; and from the just weighing of both, to form an equitable judgment. Now I saw no bad. (Chapter 18)

This is an important review, taking place just after the charade in which Mr Rochester has 'married' Blanche Ingram, an incident which leads naturally to such a train of thought. Charlotte Brontë guides us wonderfully through Jane's situation. The first paragraph reveals a very young Jane, who does not know enough of the world to be sure of her own opinion that it is best to marry for affection ('there must be arguments against its general adoption of which I was quite ignorant'), and who accepts, without understanding, the 'ideas and principles instilled into them, doubtless, from their child-hood'. Such a view shows us the difficulties which beset Jane, and which she triumphantly surmounts. However, the second para-graph involves a shift, for the Jane who objects to sliding over Mr Rochester's faults is at a further remove, both wiser and older, and the reader is being led towards the belief that the first attempt at marriage is morally wrong for more subtle reasons than that it is bigamous, a belief that is expressed most fully much later: 'I could not, in those days, see God for his creature: of whom I had made an idol' (Chapter 24). The comments are not restricted to the ends of scenes, nor do they all reduce the emotion: the effect of distance can produce nostalgia and turn simple statements into pathos:

> What charade Colonel Dent and his party played, what word they chose, how they acquitted themselves, I no longer remember; but I still see the consultation which followed each scene: I see Mr Rochester turn to Miss Ingram, and Miss Ingram to him; I see her incline her head towards him, till the jetty curls almost touch his shoulder and wave against his cheek; I hear their mutual whisperings; I recall their interchanged glances; and something even of the feeling roused by the spectacle returns in memory at this moment.
>
> (Chapter 18)

Finally, there are the comments which seem to come from some personality even further from the protagonist then her mature self is, and to speak with a more general authority. An example is the outburst on modern poetry occasioned when St John brings *Marmion*,

> one of those genuine productions so often vouchsafed to the for-tunate public of those days – the golden age of modern literature. Alas! the readers of our era are less favoured. But, courage! I will not pause either to accuse or repine. I know poetry is not dead, nor genius lost; nor has Mammon gained power over either, to bind or slay: they will both assert their existence, their presence, their liberty, and strength again one day.   (Chapter 32)

And another example, a less obtrusive one, is the comment:

Miss Ingram was a mark beneath jealousy: she was too inferior to excite the feeling. *Pardon the seeming paradox: I mean what I say.* She was very showy, but she was not genuine: she had a fine person, many brilliant attainments; but her mind was poor, her heart barren by nature: nothing bloomed spontaneously on that soil; no un-forced natural fruit delighted by its freshness. She was not good; she was not original: she used to repeat sounding phrases from books: she never offered, nor had, an opinion of her own.

(Chapter 18, my italics)

The rarity of such comments shows how thoroughly Charlotte Brontë has subdued herself to her purpose, as we can see by recalling *Shirley*, where, there being no artistic impropriety, they appear very much more often.

It is clear that on the question of attitude to material alone, the first-person narrator is being used with great subtlety and with a sure hand. Jane is a great advance on Crimsworth in this respect. Even though *Wuthering Heights* and *Agnes Grey* both precede *Jane Eyre*, Charlotte Brontë has not borrowed from them, since neither uses its narrator in this way. But the use does show that Charlotte Brontë shared with Emily this desire to make her novel a complete vision of life, where one event does more than merely follow another, and events are constantly seen in the light of the significant events which precede and come after them, even though Charlotte's methods are on the surface less revolutionary than Emily's. This constant reference of past to present action may account for another resemblance between *Jane Eyre* and *Wuthering Heights*: there is no real attempt at anything approaching a sub-plot. Charlotte Brontë's publishers protested to her about the 'want of *varied* interest' (my italics) in *The Professor*, but it does not apparently occur to her to remedy the deficiency by adding variety, but by adding, as she says, 'a more *vivid* interest', that is, intensity.[1] It is not until she has succeeded – and indeed attained something like perfection – that, in *Shirley*, she tries her hand at the multiple plot. The resolve to chronicle the moral and spiritual growth of a single character deter-mines her choice of material and her shaping of it.

[1] Letter to Messrs Smith and Elder, 6 August 1847.

As a mere love story, the Thornfield and Ferndean sections seem to be the only vital ones, and the others – the two Gateshead ones, Lowood and Moor House – become extraneous padding or biographical self-indulgence. This very elementary carping is easily done away with. No reader denies the power of Jane's story of her childhood, and few would fail to see that the qualities of the adult Jane are present or developed or foreshadowed in the ten-year-old cousin at Gateshead, and the passionate friend of Helen Burns. But Charlotte Brontë has undoubtedly taken great risks with her plot; no writer could use it as a model and expect coherence in his own work; the Gateshead section is a complete plot in itself, the story of an oppressed child who rises against her tyrants and succeeds in escaping them; so is the Lowood story, that of a lonely girl, who, through Helen Burns, experiences suffering and death and the value of friendship; even more striking is the apparently completely separate Moor House story, where Jane begins a new life as a village schoolmistress, acquires three new cousins, comes into a fortune, and is sought in marriage by St John Rivers. What is more, all these plots are more realistic, more obviously likely, than the central one – of a man of property, with an insane wife concealed in the house he actually uses, who courts the governess of his illegitimate daughter, attempts to commit bigamy, and when that has failed, loses his sight and his hand in attempting to save the life of his wife, before being reunited (through a supranormal event) with the woman he has injured. But their common purpose unifies them: and great care is taken on the practical level to make sure that no detail is inaccurate. A sound structural basis is provided, and while the effect is frequently an emotional one, there are no practical inconsistencies. The amount of knowledge various characters have about Bertha Mason provides a useful demonstration of apparent anomalies and shows the author's complete control. Jane knows nothing, and, as Mr Rochester says,

'I charged them to conceal from you, before I ever saw you, all knowledge of the curse of the place; merely because I feared Adèle never would have a governess to stay if she knew with what inmate she was housed'
(Chapter 27)

but from time to time she hears hints from servants and from Mrs Fairfax: when we first hear the sinister laugh we have Mrs Fairfax's cryptic remark, 'Too much noise, Grace. Remember directions' (Chapter 11), and later Jane overhears Leah and the charwoman discussing Grace Poole:

> 'Ah! – she understands what she has to do, – nobody better,' rejoined Leah, significantly; 'and it is not every one could fill her shoes; not for all the money she gets.'
> 'That it is not!' was the reply. 'I wonder whether master —'
> The charwoman was going on; but here Leah turned and perceived me, and she instantly gave her companion a nudge.
> 'Doesn't she know?' I heard the woman whisper.
>
> (Chapter 17)

We wonder what they know, and how much, and Charlotte Brontë satisfies our curiosity, when all is known:

> 'At last I hired Grace Poole, from the Grimsby Retreat. She and the surgeon, Carter (who dressed Mason's wounds that night he was stabbed and worried), are the only two I have ever admitted to my confidence. Mrs Fairfax may indeed have suspected something; but she could have gained no precise knowledge as to facts.'
>
> (Chapter 27)

I doubt whether it occurs to one reader in a thousand to wonder why Grace or Carter did not tell what they knew; and Grace at least has been employed to be secret and it will pay her to continue. The rest of the intrigue also concerns the West Indies, and it is much more artistically fitting for the revelation to come from the same place. Mason stops the wedding because he has heard from Jane's uncle, whom Jane herself informed (Chapter 24). This same information is the reason why he leaves his fortune to Jane instead of to his other nieces and nephew the Riverses, so the plot is entirely and economically coherent, and entirely centred on Jane. Although Charlotte Brontë does not shirk the coincidence involved in Jane's meeting her cousins –

> The two girls, on whom, kneeling down on the wet ground, and looking through the low, latticed window of Moor House kitchen,

I had gazed with so bitter a mixture of interest and despair, were my near kinswomen; and the young and stately gentleman who had found me almost dying at his threshold, was my blood relation.

(Chapter 33)

– yet she has used coincidence as little as her given plot permits, and really very little by comparison with other novelists – Dickens and Hardy for instance – who make it a prerequisite.

The characters other than Jane and Rochester are of widely different types, and are presented in very different styles. While there have been many to disparage the presentation of the gentry, at the house-party, there have been few to praise the many successes who are necessarily less obtrusive: Mrs Fairfax, or Bessie, or St John Rivers. Again the problem is one of recognizing the novel's purpose. None of these characters can exist and stand alone as characters can when the narrator is the author. They exist as Jane sees them, not as Charlotte Brontë might have done. Again *Shirley* provides a useful comparison. Nothing so elementary as the house-party appears in *Shirley*, and there are many full-length portraits of forceful and original characters for which there is no parallel in *Jane Eyre*. It was not incapacity which prevented their appearing in *Jane Eyre* (as *The Professor* proved); it is a difference in function: in *Jane Eyre* Charlotte Brontë allows characters to reveal themselves only when what they do and are reveals Jane, or creates or illuminates her predicament. The range from which characters are drawn corresponds to the society in which Jane moves. The degree to which they are congenial indicates their worth, and by implication the moral worth of their kind and class. This moral worth is always an element in their presentation, a matter on which the reader is never left in any doubt, the only possible exceptions to the generalization being Mr Rochester and St John Rivers, who will be dealt with in due course. At the highest end of the social scale are the titled personages of the house-party, country gentry who descend in rank from young Lord Ingram[1] by way of Sir George and Lady

[1] What kind of Lord is not made clear – he has inherited the title from his father, since his mother is the Dowager, which is itself odd since he is not married.

Lynn, Colonel and Mrs Dent, to the magistrate Mr Eshton; and at
the lowest are the family servants Bessie and Robert Leaven at
Gateshead, Hannah at Moor House, Leah and Grace Poole at
Thornfield, John and Mary at Ferndean. At intervals between these
range the Reed family, the Rivers family, Mrs Fairfax, Adèle,
Bertha Mason and her brother, the Lowood characters Miss Temple,
Helen Burns and Mr Brocklehurst, and a few vividly-realized
incidental persons such as the few people Jane meets at Morton, and
the proprietor of the inn, who tells her where to find Mr Rochester.
The characters group themselves obviously according to the place
and episode in which they appear, but there are resemblances and
parallels between them and their relation to Jane, which appear as
the story progresses. Generally speaking, characters are simple in
the opening sections, and grow more subtle the further the story
progresses, as Jane's capacity for subtle appreciation increases, and
as the moral growth requires elaborate personalities to reveal it.

The first people we meet besides Jane herself are representatives
of Gateshead life: her cousins Eliza, John and Georgiana, her aunt
Mrs Reed, the nurse Bessie and the apothecary Mr Lloyd. The
Reed family are a demonstration of Jane's power to overcome her
circumstances, and link with and balance the Riverses – another
family of two sisters and a brother, whose relations with Jane are
another, more searching, test of her powers of resistance. Eliza and
Georgiana Reed have only the personality necessary to show in
contrasting forms the absence of human sympathy Jane suffers:
Eliza 'would have sold the hair off her head if she could have made
a handsome profit thereby' (Chapter 4), while Georgiana's curls
are essential to her; they are her virtues, and claims to affection.[1]
The simplicity of the representations make them forceful, and
emphasize the pain they cause the child Jane, yet the simple attributes can be taken and made to work morally when they reappear
as grown-up young women. Both are credible recreations, since
the basis of character is the same. We believe easily in the plump
and fashionable Georgiana and in the less predictable evolution of

[1] 'Yes, I doat on Miss Georgiana!' cried the fervent Abbot. 'Little darling! –
with her long curls and her blue eyes, and such a sweet colour as she has; just
as if she were painted!'   (Chapter 3)

Eliza into the rigorous recluse. Their soullessness contributes to the grimness of their mother's death, and the fact that they can no longer hurt Jane and that she can be useful to both is a measure of her development. They are deliberately balanced and opposed:

> True, generous feeling is made small account of by some: but here were two natures rendered, the one intolerably acrid, the other despicably savourless for the want of it.   (Chapter 21)

John Reed is a spoilt brute: his sisters' physique represents their mentality; he is wholly physical and lives, tortures Jane, and dies in physical terms: we never find out what kind of despair led to suicide, or even how he died. 'I dream sometime that I see him laid out with a great wound in his throat, or with a swollen and blackened face,' says his mother (Chapter 21); and so artistically he dies by two ways, both brutal; an end in keeping with the boy with 'a dim and bleared eye and flabby cheeks', who, in the one incident when we see him, is 'thrusting out his tongue at me as far as he could without damaging its roots' (Chapter 1). He has a borrowed power from being the physical expression of his mother's repressed impulses. Mrs Reed is a more developed person, adult and dangerous. She is no mere childhood monster, and Jane is painfully fair in speaking of her:

> I know that had I been a sanguine, brilliant, careless, exacting, handsome, romping child – though equally dependent and friendless – Mrs Reed would have endured my presence more complacently; ...
> Mrs Reed probably considered she had kept the promise [to rear and maintain Jane as one of her own children]; and so she had, I dare say, as well as her own nature would permit her.   (Chapter 2)

> She was an exact, clever manager, her household and tenantry were thoroughly under her control; ... she dressed well, and had a presence and port calculated to set off handsome attire.
>
>   (Chapter 4)

These comments feel absolutely just, having no tinge of Jane's hatred in them; they render Mrs Reed both more interesting and more terrible, and they prove that the child Jane is not at all sentimentalized, a fact which is proved again when Jane sees recognizably the same Mrs Reed through adult eyes and perceptions. We can see Mrs Reed has feelings of her own that can be troubled – she is distressed by Jane's passionate defiance in Chapter 4 – and so we are prepared for her deathbed to be troubled by remorse (though not repentance), while her desire to put herself in the right does not, ironically, prevent her from still hating Jane: 'My last hour is racked by the recollection of a deed, which, but for you, I should never have been tempted to commit' (Chapter 21). Her death is a conscious and structural partner to Helen Burns's, a measurement of Jane's spiritual independence and understanding:

> nothing soft, nothing sweet, nothing pitying, or hopeful, or sub-dued, did it inspire; only a grating anguish for *her* woes – not *my* loss – and a sombre tearless dismay at the fearfulness cf death in such a form. (Chapter 21)

Bessie has as much structural importance as the Reeds, though less thematic relevance, and is in many ways more interesting. She attracts our attention by being the only person to show any affection for Jane, though again there is no concession to sentimentality:

> I remember her as a slim young woman, with black hair, dark eyes, very nice features, and good clear complexion; but she had a capricious and hasty temper, and indifferent ideas of principle or justice. (Chapter 4)

By visiting Jane just before she leaves Lowood, and by being the subject of odd allusions and recollections when quite other matters are the first concern, she keeps Gateshead in the reader's mind when it would otherwise be forgotten. She connects with all that large part of Jane's perception which expresses itself by means of folk-lore: her stories of the Gytrash introduce Mr Rochester to us; her belief that 'to dream of children was a sure sign of trouble, either to one's self or one's kin' (Chapter 21) prepares us, when Jane dreams too, first for Jane's return to Gateshead and Mrs Reed's death, and second for Jane's dreams of a child just before her wedding (Chapter 24) to be seen as a serious omen of disaster.

Mr Brocklehurst is one of the links between Gateshead and Lowood. He is unlike the Reeds in the attitude we adopt towards him, and an example of one of the attributes Charlotte Brontë is often denied – humour. He is a comic grotesque.[1] The Rev. Carus Wilson may or may not be the original of the portrait, but we have no doubt of its truth to the type.

> I looked up at – a black pillar! – such, at least, appeared to me, at first sight, the straight, narrow, sable-clad shape standing erect on the rug: the grim face at the top was like a carved mask, placed above the shaft by way of capital. (Chapter 4)

He reveals himself ironically and unconsciously (to us) in his own words and behaviour, and Jane, the over-literal child, registers, though not consciously analysing, his absurdity:

> 'I buried a little child of five years old only a day or two since, – a good little child, whose soul is now in heaven. It is to be feared the same could not be said of you, were you *to be called hence*.'
> Not being in a condition to remove his doubt, I only cast my eyes down at the two large feet planted on the rug, and sighed; wishing myself *far enough away*. (Chapter 4, my italics)

Jane is capable of seeing him in a ridiculous light, and so he is a measure of her resilience – he contrasts with Mrs Reed who is not seen until her power and presence are proven – and he continues to be so at Lowood: in spite of being terrified of public disgrace, Jane can still observe him as 'longer, narrower and more rigid than ever', and the irony of the portrait of his wife and children 'splendidly attired in velvet, silk, and furs' (Chapter 8) needs no demonstration. His idiom is excellent:

> 'This girl, this child, the native of a Christian land, worse than many a little heathen who says its prayers to Brahma and kneels before Juggernaut – this girl is – a liar!'
>
> (Chapter 8)

The conclusion is both an anticlimax (not so dreadful a failing, after all) and a surprise: this is almost the last sin to apply to Jane, whose

---

[1] And one of the few figures to suggest that Charlotte Brontë learned anything from the writer she so much admired – Thackeray. He has much of the gusto and the comic horror of old Sir Pitt Crawley.

frankness is perhaps the only genuine virtue we have seen in her so far.

The teachers Miss Miller, Miss Scatcherd, and Mlle Pierrot are of the stock types that she used in *The Professor*, and uses again in *Villette*; they serve their purpose and are unobtrusive, allowing us to concentrate on the more vital Miss Temple and Helen Burns. These two both have the literary virtue of being interesting though noble characters. There is tact in stressing Helen's slovenliness before revealing her fortitude, and in deliberately underplaying her learning: she is first seen reading *Rasselas*, which daunts Jane, and probably the reader as well; and tact also in keeping Miss Temple at a distance: we never see her relations with Jane as she grows older and more intimate with her. If Jane learns 'patience under apparent injustice, and the wholesome distrust of too much reliance on human affections' from Helen (as Robert Martin thinks),[1] we also learn a great deal about Jane. Both Helen and Miss Temple demonstrate Jane's need simply for human affection, and her power to inspire it, before she meets Mr Rochester and the force of love is added. They prove also that Jane chooses the highest when she sees it.[2] From Miss Temple we learn also Jane's characteristic willingness to acknowledge her superior, which in its turn prepares her and us for the way she submits happily to her cousins Diana and Mary, both for the energy of their characters and for their learning.

At Thornfield there is another change in the type and the presentation of characters. As governess, Jane now has a social as well as a personal position, and the people she meets are consequently seen in their place in society as well as in their individual selves. Social position is to be at odds with personal worth and personal relationships at Thornfield: it is the essence of these society characters that their rank is wholly disproportionate to their personal

---

[1] *The Accents of Persuasion.*

[2] This is the only reason for the appearance of Mary Ann Wilson, who enhances Helen Burns by the contrast she provides, which also has an important relevance to Mr Rochester. Having seen Jane's choice of friends here, we accept without hesitation Mr Rochester's worth too, which might otherwise be a matter for serious doubt. We have, after all, only his care for Adèle as proof of any kind of virtue.

worth; and the culmination is Mr Rochester's social contract to his mad wife. Startling and sensational as the burlesques of the house-party and the final revelation are, the way is prepared for them from even before Jane arrives at Thornfield, when she receives Mrs Fairfax's answer to her advertisement:

> Mrs Fairfax! I saw her in a black gown and widow's cap; frigid, perhaps, but not uncivil: a model of elderly English respectability.
>
> (Chapter 10)

It is position, not personality, which is being suggested by 'widow' and 'respectability', and it is significant of the way things are to go that Jane is mistaken: Mrs Fairfax is not the mother of Adèle, nor the lady of the house, but only the housekeeper.

Mrs Fairfax, 'a placid-tempered, kind-natured woman, of competent education and average intelligence' (Chapter 12), 'kindly as usual – and, as usual, rather trite' (Chapter 13) – the perfect foil for Jane and Mr Rochester in their first interviews – is something new, and creates, assisted by Sophie and Adèle, the atmosphere of positive, if placid, goodwill that is a necessary feature of Thornfield, and a strong contrast to what has gone before. Charlotte Brontë will abandon verisimilitude if occasion demands,[1] yet Mrs Fairfax's personality and idiom are as accurate as Bessie's, and recognizably of a generation or more before Jane's:

> 'I'm sure last winter (it was a very severe one, if you recollect, and when it did not snow, it rained and blew), not a creature but the butcher and postman came to the house, from November till February; and I really got quite melancholy with sitting night after night alone; I had Leah in to read to me sometimes; but I don't think the poor girl liked the task much: she felt it confining.'
>
> (Chapter 11)

The only other adult resident of the house of any significance is Grace Poole, faintly comic with her unexpectedly commonplace appearance, homely speech, and her prosaic 'pint of porter and bit of pudding on a tray' (Chapter 16). She is in her way a modest

---

[1] Mrs Fairfax is unable to analyse Mr Rochester in Chapter 11 (where mystery is requisite), but can do very well with Blanche Ingram in Chapter 16 when there is need of someone to be explicit.

triumph, since she is the antithesis of the sinister servant of Gothic romance, whose sinister machinations come to naught in the light of common day. When the light is let in on Grace's function, it is in fact something much worse than Jane or the reader could suspect, and knowing that she is commonplace makes us more ready to accept anything so sensational as a secretly kept insane wife. At the same time she helps us to see Jane as a person of sound sense, who, while preceiving a mystery, never lets her imagination get the better of her:

> 'What if a former caprice (a freak very possible to a nature so sudden and headstrong as his) has delivered him into her power, and she now exercises over his actions a secret influence, the result of his own indiscretion, which he cannot shake off and dare not disregard?' But, having reached this point of conjecture, Mrs Poole's square, flat figure, and uncomely, dry, even coarse face, recurred so distinctly to my mind's eye, that I thought, 'No; impossible! my supposition cannot be correct.' (Chapter 16)

She is right when she thinks Grace has some power over Mr Rochester, equally right in rejecting a romantic connection: and the incident is structural in that it ironically directs and prepares us for Bertha: it is indeed 'a former caprice' that has delivered him into her power.

The house-party displays a different type of minor character, with less relevance outside the incidents where they actually appear and a great deal less realism – or, as Charlotte Brontë might have said, 'more real than true'. They resemble Mr Brocklehurst in distressing Jane and being comic and grotesque at the same time. Once one recognizes the comedy, the obvious improbabilities become much less offensive, and one reads Blanche and her corsair-song, and the resplendent dowagers Lady Lynn and Lady Ingram, not so much as one reads Thackeray's satiric portraits, but Fielding's.[1]

---

[1] The mixture of tones is like Fielding – unemotional approval of the two Eshton girls, who demonstrate a degree of worth by playing with Adèle, sudden gentleness for Mrs Colonel Dent and her liking for flowers, 'especially wild ones', flat disregard of the 'apathetic and listless' Lord Ingram and his sister Mary, limited and humorous approval of Colonel Dent (a 'père noble de théâtre'), and the hyberbolical ridicule of the Dowagers; all these range round Blanche.

There is a gusto in Charlotte Brontë's language which prevents any suspicion that Jane is envious of these people, and suggests that she may know very well that she is exaggerating details of dress and modes of speech.[1] We are prepared for distortion when they first appear:

> There were but eight; yet somehow as they flocked in, they gave the appearance of a much larger number. Some of them were very tall; many were dressed in white; all had a sweeping amplitude of array that seemed to magnify their persons as the mist magnifies the moon.

> (Chapter 17)

The elevated diction here is a symptom of coming burlesque, which is promptly developed in the case of the dowagers:

> Her dark hair shone glossily under the shade of an azure plume, and within the circlet of a band of gems.

> She had Roman features and a double chin, disappearing into a throat like a pillar: these features appeared to me not only inflated and darkened, but even furrowed with pride; and the chin was sustained by the same principle, in a position of almost preternatural erectness. She had, likewise, a fierce and a hard eye: it reminded me of Mrs Reed's; she mouthed her words in speaking; her voice was deep, its inflections very pompous, very dogmatical, – very intolerable, in short. A crimson velvet robe, and a shawl turban of some gold-wrought Indian fabric, invested her (I suppose she thought) with a truly imperial dignity. (ibid.)

It is a brave writer and a superbly confident one who can use the same means for comic inflation as for serious writing: this passage recalls in turn Mr Brocklehurst (the pillar) and Mrs Reed (a direct allusion), anticipates Bertha Mason ('inflated and darkened'), and, best of all, epitomizes the whole supranormal intensity of the story in the very characteristic word 'preternatural'. The chief functions

[1] Robert Martin claims that the unreality of the portraits may deliberately suggest how young and inexperienced Jane is. It may well be that Charlotte Brontë is not capable of a psychologically realized full-length portrait of a frivolous character – Ginevra Fanshawe at least suggests it – but the failure to do one here rises from a different intention, and not from incompetence.

of this house-party group are to provide a setting for Blanche Ingram, to be the instruments performing the highly significant charade, to show us Jane's passive fortitude (since the earlier episodes have all shown her ability to act), and to force Jane and the reader to assess and acknowledge the relationship between Jane and Mr Rochester. It is not until the society of his social equals separates him, apparently, from Jane, that she admits what she feels, and names it – 'I had not intended to *love* him' (Chapter 17) is the first use of the word – and goes on,

> 'He is not of their kind. I believe he is of mine; – I am sure he is, – I feel akin to him, – I understand the language of his countenance and movements: though rank and wealth sever us widely, I have something in my brain and heart, in my blood and nerves, that assimilates me mentally to him.' (ibid.)

The presence of Blanche has forced into utterance something never before expressed in the novel, something which is essentially the same as Edgar Linton's proposal precipitates in Catherine's declaration of her feelings for Heathcliff:

> 'Nelly, I *am* Heathcliff! He's always, always, in my mind: not as a pleasure, any more than I am always a pleasure to myself, but as my own being.' (*Wuthering Heights*, Chapter 9)

Charlotte's expression is less poetic than Emily's, but her achievement is to make so revolutionary a relationship a part of something much closer to recognizable everyday existence than *Wuthering Heights* can ever be. Blanche herself may be unrealistic – even if at this late date we must take Miss Rigby's word that ladies did not dress as Charlotte Brontë describes Blanche,[1] there can be little doubt that no young lady talked like her – but she is superbly and comically convincing in her way, with her elementary Italian and French, and her outdated sentimental romantic enthusiasm for bandit heroes and highwaymen, contrasting with the painfully genuine and repressed feelings of Jane and Mr Rochester. Jane does not waste much narrative on her, and we do not care twopence for her feelings at being jilted by Mr Rochester, and this again shows

[1] Review of *Vanity Fair* and *Jane Eyre*, *The Quarterly Review*, December 1848.

the sound tact of Charlotte Brontë's portrait, which completely precludes pity for her, and consequent disapproval of Mr Rochester for deceiving her. However, she has taken up time in the courtship of Mr Rochester and Jane; we know and feel that Mr Rochester has had plenty of time in which to decide his course of action: he has committed bigamy out of calculation as well as passion, and so merits the moral judgement which he suffers.

Bertha Mason (whom it is offensive even to think of as Bertha Rochester) is the incubus of Thornfield, who has no 'character' until Mr Rochester reveals her history in Chapter 27, and whose character when it is finally exposed is no real surprise, though her existence is a shock. She is the embodiment of ungoverned passion, contrasting with Blanche, who has none (but who yet looks like her: 'I found her a fine woman in the style of Blanche Ingram; tall, dark and majestic,' Chapter 27), and demonstrates both the power and the failing of Mr Rochester, who will not send her to Ferndean because it is unhealthy, but insists on his right to act as if she does not exist. She develops from the vague to the explicit, from the unseen possessor of the laugh, who starts a mysterious fire in the night, to the violent attacker of Mason which seems the climax to her activities but is not so, since her worst offence is simply to exist as Mr Rochester's wife. She is the purveyor of horror, but is not herself revolting until it is most necessary for her to be so, when her full story is heard, and we must be made to pity Mr Rochester.

A character more important to the novel as a whole than her part in the action would suggest is Adèle Varens. Seemingly only the pretext for Jane's presence at Thornfield, Adèle is structurally invaluable. She is clearly a touchstone of character: Amy and Louisa Eshton call her 'a love of a child' (Chapter 17) and convict themselves of sentimentality; Blanche calls her a 'puppet' (ibid.) and demonstrates her own deficiency. Adèle herself is fond of her 'chère Mlle Jeannot' and so proves that Jane can attract more than merely her superiors, while Jane is cool but just about Adèle:

> She had no great talents, no marked traits of character, no peculiar development of feeling or taste which raised her one inch above the ordinary level of childhood; but neither had she any deficiency or vice which sunk her below it. (Chapter 12)

And this very coolness helps her to be useful. Mr Rochester is no monster for not loving her, and he is clearly philanthropic in bringing her up, when she may not even be his daughter. The way he treats her, providing a governess and keeping her at Thornfield (when he might have got her out of the way at a boarding school) predisposes us to accept his keeping a mad wife at home instead of having her shut up. Adèle is living evidence of Mr Rochester's past, which, literary and conventional as his expression of it is, gains solidity by her recollections of life 'chez maman'.[1] She has numerous incidental structural uses: commentary on the house-party, the pretext for Jane to appear in the drawing-room with the guests (not normally a governess's privilege); the recipient of Mr Rochester's whimsical badinage about Jane; another temptation not to leave Thornfield and Mr Rochester; and one of the few things to survive the fire.

In sharp contrast to anyone at Thornfield are the characters at Morton: St John, Diana and Mary Rivers, Hannah, Rosamond Oliver and the few villagers and farmers. Charlotte Brontë's touch with the rustics is sure: when Jane is starving, their equally unsentimental and unmalevolent treatment gives vivid conviction to her sufferings:

> At the door of a cottage I saw a little girl about to throw a mess of cold porridge into a pig trough. 'Will you give me that?' I asked.
>   She stared at me. 'Mother!' she exclaimed; 'there is a woman wants me to give her these porridge.'
>   'Well, lass,' replied a voice within, 'give it her if she's a beggar. T' pig doesn't want it.'   (Chapter 28)

The servant Hannah is another 'Bessie' character, helping Jane to return to contact with society, and re-establish her own place in it, clearly not as a beggar nor even a servant, and Hannah's verdict, 'You look a raight down dacent little crater' (Chapter 29), is entertaining in its inadequacy.

---

[1] That Adèle can say her La Fontaine fable with 'a flexibility of voice and appropriateness of gesture unusual at her age' (Chapter 11) suggests that Céline could act, a fact not indicated by her performance of outraged virtue as retailed by Mr Rochester in Chapter 15.

Mary never appears without Diana, and is really a shadow of her, and both are overshadowed by their brother. They are the first women friends Jane has had since she left Lowood and Miss Temple, and represent the pleasures of the intellect, which Jane has not had, or missed. Despite their beauty, they are not at all young-lady-like and nor are their conversations with Jane. St John is a finely-observed study of a man who turns egotism and ambition to the service of religion. He is the most important single character in the book after Mr Rochester, and is obviously his antithesis, religious, idealistic, handsome, cold-blooded, seeing in Jane 'nothing attractive ... not even youth – only a few useful mental points' (Chapter 37). He is indeed not attractive himself, and all his speeches are about, or soon turn to, himself. The following exchange, a discussion of Jane's post as schoolmistress, is characteristic:

> 'You will not stay at Morton long: no, no!'
> 'Why! What is your reason for saying so?'
> 'I read it in your eye; it is not of that description which promises the maintenance of an even tenor in life.'
> 'I am not ambitious.'
> He started at the word 'ambitious'. He repeated, 'No. What made you think of ambition? Who is ambitious? I know I am: but how did you find it out?' (Chapter 30)

He implicitly condemns himself and his aspirations: his sermon is symptomatic:

> Throughout there was a strange bitterness; an absence of consolatory gentleness: stern allusions to Calvinistic doctrines – election, pre-destination, reprobation – were frequent; and each reference to these points sounded like a sentence pronounced for doom. When he had done, instead of feeling better, calmer, more enlightened by his discourse, I experienced an inexpressible sadness. (ibid.)

His decision to become a missionary saddens his sisters, and is against his dead father's wishes. Even his passion for the elementary Miss Oliver indicates his deficiency, in caring in such a way for a woman so clearly inferior to what he has been accustomed to in his sisters, apart from Jane herself. His treatment, solemn, using Biblical allusion, and constantly described in terms of marble, and even as a pillar, all recalls that other columnar clergyman, Mr Brocklehurst. It is surprising that he can generate enough power to become the danger he is to Jane at the end of the episode, and that the reader shares her unwilling admiration for one who tempts her to do violence to her own nature, in antithesis to Mr Rochester, who tempted her to violate her moral standards. The impression of his influence builds up gradually: Rosamond links them:

> She said I was like Mr Rivers (only, certainly, she allowed, 'not one-tenth so handsome; though I was a nice neat little soul enough, but he was an angel'). I was, however, good, clever, composed, and firm, like him. (Chapter 32)

He understands Jane up to a point:

> 'Well, if you are not ambitious, you are —' He paused.
> 'What?'
> 'I was going to say, impassioned; but perhaps you would have misunderstood the word, and been displeased. I mean, that human affections and sympathies have a most powerful hold on you.'
> (Chapter 30)

And Jane herself increases their intimacy and consequently his power over her by invading his feelings for Rosamond. Impersonal though he may be, Charlotte Brontë yet makes us and Jane very conscious of him physically: his handsomeness makes him interesting at the same time as it separates him from Jane:

> The thing was as impossible as to mould my irregular features to his correct and classic pattern, to give to my changeable green eyes the sea-blue tint and solemn lustre of his own. (Chapter 34)

It can even make him moving:

> I waited, expecting he would say something I could at least comprehend; but his hand was now at his chin, his finger on his lip: he was thinking. It struck me that his hand looked wasted like his face. A perhaps uncalled-for gush of pity came over my heart.
> (Chapter 33)

There remain only the two people at the heart of the book – Mr Rochester and Jane. Mr Rochester has been seen by many as the idealized, even the impossible, hero: 'No flesh and blood man could be so exclusively composed of violence and virility and masculine vanity as Mr Rochester,' says David Cecil.[1] But he does not completely fill the romantic bill, and we are pulled up smartly if we try to make him; he is no nineteenth-century Sir Charles Grandison, nor even a Victorian re-working of the Byronic outcast. As usual, the attempt to identify the character with an actual person does not get us very far. M. Héger lurks at the back of every critic's mind, as with every hero in Charlotte Brontë's work, as though it were impossible for her either to depend on her imagination, or to adapt the material of life to her purpose. The other more respectable impulse, to explain historically, and analyse Mr Rochester's undoubted debt to Byronism, does not go far either, since the great interest of Mr Rochester is in what Charlotte Brontë creates out of her materials, rather than the nature of the materials themselves. Proof of this is that although in his place in the novel he convinces us completely, he cannot be taken out of his context: he exists as part of Jane's consciousness, and for his relation to her. But within this context we have no reservations about him other than those Charlotte Brontë specifically intends, and the impulse to think of him as isolable, as if 'real', is a measure of the success she has achieved by her autobiographical method. To describe a hero only by what the heroine sees, when the former must reveal more of himself to the reader than the other can observe, and when that other must be hampered by youth, inexperience, and passion, is a great achievement.

Mr Rochester is both the remote hero and the man whom Jane understands because she is 'akin' to him; he is a man whose moral nature is like Jane's, who is yet the one who tempts her to evil; he is a good man who suffers a dreadful punishment for his sin. Here for the first (and perhaps the only) time we have the romantic hero who becomes not less but more exciting as he becomes familiar, for whom marriage is the triumph, not merely the convenient and correct end to the adventures of courtship, who does not

[1] *Early Victorian Novelists.*

'dwindle into a husband' as Millamant deplored dwindling into a wife.

The essence of Mr Rochester is to be unpredictable, to shock with the unconventional and the unexpected; but it is essential that the reasons for his behaviour shall be clearly and unambiguously discernible, in retrospect if not at the time. A useful example is the conversation after Jane has rescued him from the fire (Chapter 15), and the events which immediately follow.[1] This is all sensational enough, but the receptive reader is able to understand Mr Rochester's behaviour in the light of what follows. Like Jane we believe Mr Rochester:

> 'I knew,' he continued, 'you would do me good in some way, at some time; – I saw it in your eyes when I first beheld you: their expression and smile did not – (again he stopped) – did not (he proceeded hastily) strike delight to my very inmost heart so for nothing.'
> (Chapter 15)

But unlike her, we understand his precipitate departure and return with Blanche Ingram. One reason he gives himself:

> 'I wished to render you as madly in love with me as I was with you; and I knew jealousy would be the best ally I could call in for the furtherance of that end.'
> (Chapter 24)

This is obvious and elementary. Another is suggested in another scene, when in his gipsy disguise Mr Rochester muses to himself with Jane kneeling before him in the firelight:

> 'I should wish to protract this moment *ad infinitum*; but I dare not. So far I have governed myself thoroughly. I have acted as I inwardly swore I would act; but farther might try me beyond my strength.'
> (Chapter 19)

After the fire the emotional situation has clearly got very nearly

---

[1] It comes immediately after he has recounted his affair with Céline Varens, and is his first profession of affection, and the first time he uses Jane's Christian name. The next morning he leaves for the Leas for an indefinite period, leaving Jane with feelings stirred by his words and actions, which she attempts to crush with the idea of Blanche Ingram.

out of hand, as Mr Rochester's hesitant words indicate.[1] We realize also that Mr Rochester must make up his mind about his moral position; he does so between the fire and the house-party, and returns having resolved on his right to commit legal bigamy. This is the reason why we hear of his mistress Céline Varens so very early in his acquaintance; it is indeed almost the first thing we find out about him other than what the immediate present reveals. Mr Rochester must be attractive (as Céline Varens's attachment proves indeed), but all the associations of illicit union must be kept in mind as repellent, since we must never for a moment think that Jane is wrong in refusing to live unmarried with Mr Rochester; we must see and feel, as well as know, that Mr Rochester himself abhors the idea, and that by his own lights he is no mere self-indulgent seducer of yet another mistress.

While he does a good deal of the explaining himself (being a man of vigour in words as well as actions, and being 'self-conscious' in the same way as Jane is self-conscious), we are constantly being called upon as the action progresses to try to judge Mr Rochester at the same time as we come with Jane under his spell, by standards which he himself is not aware of and will not admit. In almost every one of his conversations with Jane we are prepared for the moral impasse of Chapter 27: in their second conversation Mr Rochester declares 'unheard-of combinations of circumstances demand unheard-of rules' (Chapter 14); by his own admission later,

'If I bid you do what you thought wrong, there would be no light-footed running, no neat-handed alacrity, no lively glance and animated complexion.' (Chapter 20)

while he recognizes the danger that Jane will refuse him, he does not yet realize as we do the violence he is doing to her personality in deceiving her, and that Jane's moral sense just as much as her

[1] It is far too soon to make love to Jane, when he has no reason to believe she is fond of him; and it is in any case a considerable risk for a man near middle age, with a fortune, to put himself in the power of a penniless girl of eighteen with no background or family. And these are the objections we see as soon as the house-party arrives.

passion is what distinguishes her: it is not until Ferndean that he realizes the part of her that declared:

> '*I* care for myself. The more solitary, the more friendless, the more unsustained I am, the more I will respect myself. I will keep the law given by God; sanctioned by man. I will hold to the principles received by me when I was sane, and not mad – as I am now.'
>
> (Chapter 27)

We have learned to respond to Mr Rochester's moral predicament, and sympathize, while not condoning his behaviour.

The whole of his association with Jane is a series of surprises, of shocks to which Jane responds and draws back for periods of assessment, before the next shock impinges. By this means, he, like St John Rivers, develops a kind and degree of power we should not suspect from his beginnings, natural though it seems when we reach the end. These delays Mr Rochester introduces into the courtship have many uses, besides the obvious ones of producing suspense and excitement. They allow Jane to classify and come to terms with her experience; they show Mr Rochester's self-control and consciousness of his feelings and so make him worthy of Jane, since he is not acting merely on passion and impulse; at the same time there can be no doubt that he is morally at fault in committing a calculated legal crime, and violating Jane's known nature. He clearly enjoys the invidious relationships of this long courtship (as in a way Jane clearly does also), deliberately building up the excitement: almost all his speeches to Jane after Blanche arrives are ambiguous declarations or invitations.[1] He is rightly the mover of the romance and these many half-declarations are emotional attacks, and make Jane's position an artistically and emotionally satisfying one: she has had ample opportunity to see that he loves her when in Chapter 23 she does not receive the conventional proposal and conventionally submit, but attacks in her turn and so asserts her equality – as Mr Rochester says, 'it was you who made me the offer'.

Information about him is given as Jane acquires it, where it is

[1] Note for instance how he says good-bye when Jane leaves for Gateshead, Chapter 21; both of them know that a kiss is the form of farewell in both their minds.

most appropriate. The various ways in which we are invited to perceive him blend into a whole, and gain richer meaning as others accumulate. At first he is a figure of folklore; his dog is perhaps the Gytrash, and he himself is described in terms which are both physical and violent, and remote from the commonplace:

> Still, he looked preciously grim, cushioning his massive head against the swelling back of his chair, and receiving the light of the fire on his granite-hewn features, and in his great, dark eyes – for he had great, dark eyes, and very fine eyes, too: not without a certain change in their depths sometimes, which, if it was not softness, reminded you, at least, of that feeling. (Chapter 14)

There is physical vigour even in 'the *swelling* back of the chair', the 'massive head' recalls Pilot's 'lion-like' one (Chapter 18), and the passage is reinforced by the mention earlier of 'purple curtains', the imperial colour. The suggestion of something superhuman remains and the amoral and physical is taken up and shifted, by way of the oriental charade, so that during the month's engagement Mr Rochester as the imperial sultan is deliberately rejected and even ridiculed (Chapter 24): it stands for that side of him which distresses Jane and causes his downfall, since if he had not patronized Jane so that she feels like 'a second Danaë with the golden shower falling daily round [her]' (Chapter 24) she would not have written to her uncle, and *he* would not have told Mason of the wedding. Similarly the feeling of his violence is taken up and used. Mrs Fairfax says, 'the Rochesters have been rather a violent than a quiet race in their time' (Chapter 11), yet by Chapter 27 the physically violent, like that in *Wuthering Heights*, is merely a reflection of much greater spiritual turmoil.[1]

Mr Rochester at Thornfield is coherent enough, but many readers have wondered whether he is the same man whom Jane meets and

---

[1] We never fear that Jane is in danger of physical rape and Jane's reaction to the threat is a most robust one: 'I still possessed my soul, and with it the certainty of ultimate safety' (Chapter 27); indeed we feel as she says that 'the crisis was perilous, but not without its charm: such as the Indian, perhaps, feels when he slips over the rapid in his canoe' (ibid). This is the *Clarissa* situation utterly transmuted, and rendered both more realistic and more wholesome, leading now to life instead of death.

marries at Ferndean. Charlotte Brontë is careful to provide many links, perhaps the most notable of them being the Samson image; this was first expressed in Chapter 24 ('I was thinking of Hercules and Samson with their charmers'), reappears when Mr Rochester exclaims 'I long to exert a fraction of Samson's strength' (Chapter 27), and finds its true application at Ferndean where he is indeed 'a sightless Samson' (Chapter 37). He is certainly changed, just as Mrs Reed changed between Chapters 1 and 21; but Charlotte Brontë has no doubts about him: what is emphasized is that he is still essentially the man he was, vigorous and in the prime of life. He is reintroduced by his full name, his relationship with Jane is instantly re-established, he speaks with the same voice in the same terms, using the pet-name Janet, and seeing her as 'a fairy', making the same brisk leaps from the impassioned to the practical:

> 'And you do not lie dead in some ditch under some stream? And you are not a pining outcast amongst strangers?'
> 'No, sir; I am an independent woman now.'
> 'Independent! What do you mean, Jane?'
> 'My uncle in Madeira is dead, and he left me five thousand pounds.'
> 'Ah, this is practical – this is real!' he cried: 'I should never dream that.'
> (Chapter 37)

The main differences are that he is blind and maimed, and that he hesitates to ask her to marry him. Again it is over-sentimental to over-estimate the disaster, and Charlotte Brontë never does so. Mr Rochester blind is still a romantic figure, to be seen as a falcon or as Vulcan (as he could not be with one leg for instance). Jane's attitude is the robust one she showed in happiness: she discounts his injuries:

> 'I thought you would be revolted, Jane, when you saw my arm, and my cicatrized visage.'
> 'Did you? Don't tell me so – lest I should say something disparaging to your judgment.'
> (ibid.)

and rejects emphatically any suggestion of 'sacrifice' in marrying him.[1] He is realistically allowed to recover a good deal of his sight.

---

[1] We believe her the more because St John has offered her sacrifice already, to a religious ideal, and been rejected as repulsive.

Mr Rochester and Jane are now felt to be more equal and better suited than they were at Thornfield; we feel that Jane is right when she says:

> 'I love you better now, when I can really be useful to you, than I did in your state of proud independence, when you disdained every part but that of the giver and protector.' (ibid.)

At last it is impossible for Jane to seem 'an English Céline Varens' (Chapter 23) to be showered with favours, even though a marriage ceremony has taken place. The danger has always been lurking, all the more because Céline has managed to bear Mr Rochester's child, and so assume one of the chief functions of a wife. These considerations annihilate the other question that besets most readers: whether there is not an emotional indulgence, whether Charlotte Brontë is making Mr Rochester more of a Samson and Jane more a Delilah than she consciously intends, in letting Mr Rochester be so dreadfully maimed. It is right, too, that Mr Rochester's injuries are not his moral punishment for the suffering he caused Jane (his mental tortures are that). He is injured as a paradoxical reward for virtue: if he had not tried to save Bertha he would not have been hurt. This is not at all poetic justice, but there is a real psychological rightness about it, just as there was when he would not shut Bertha away at Ferndean because it was too unhealthy (Chapter 27) and she might die.

There remains very little to be said about Jane Eyre herself, because more than most eponymous heroines she is the whole of the novel in which she appears. Sympathy with her is essential, and there can be few characters in fiction to whom it has been so readily given. She calls up emotions every reader must recognize and probably have experienced, and at the times and ages that most people felt them, though in the novel they are intensified: Jane in terror of a bullying boy cousin, hating a powerful aunt, cringing from public exposure at school, giving her heart to a school-friend and a kind teacher, all readily find echoes in the reader's past; and when Jane's circumstances become stranger, we continue to respond as she does, and feel the truth of the response. With her passions Jane combines qualities more rational, equally sympathetic, which every reader's

vanity flatters him he possesses too: sound common sense, the power
to see herself as others see her, a robust sense of humour, the power
to act right under the most powerful of temptations, and survive
the most testing physical conditions. Charlotte Brontë is quite safe,
with such a basis, in making her heroine small and plain and
'Quakerish' in matters of dress, and in making her not incidentally
but genuinely so, as the occasional pointed comments of others
prove:

> 'You are genteel enough; you look like a lady, and it is as much as
> ever I expected of you.'   (Chapter 10)
> 'Il m'a demandé le nom de ma gouvernante, et si elle n'était pas
> une petite personne, assez mince et un peu pâle.'   (Chapter 13)

Bessie's faint praise and Adèle's candid summary are utterly convincing.[1] We even accept the excessive independence which makes
her declare that when married

> 'I shall continue to act as Adèle's governess: by that I shall earn my
> board and lodging, and thirty pounds a year besides. I'll furnish my
> own wardrobe out of that money, and you shall give me nothing
> but [your regard].'   (Chapter 24)

When Mr Rochester calls this 'cool native impudence, and pure
innate pride' we feel he is understating the case; but we are still on
Jane's side. This is the obvious strength of the book, this power to
involve the reader so intensely in Jane's fortunes.[2] Although a nar-

[1] We must bear in mind what beauty was in 1847, not what it is today: 'I
sometimes wished to have rosy cheeks, a straight nose, and small cherry mouth;
I desired to be tall, stately, and finely developed in figure.'   (Chapter 11)
[2] It is worth while by way of contrast to consider *David Copperfield* again,
which, though based on its author's own experiences, does not exact the same
emotional commitment of its reader: David the narrator regards the young
David's love of Dora, and the whole of their marriage, with a detachment and
a sense of 'knowing better' quite different from the way the mature Jane ever
regards her young self. Jane is much more like Ann Elliot in *Persuasion* (who is
incidentally the same age):

> 'I have been thinking over the past, and trying to judge impartially of the
> right and wrong, I mean with regard to myself; and I must believe that I was
> right, much as I suffered from it.' (*Persuasion*, Chapter XI of *Northanger Abbey
> and Persuasion*, Vol. IV, ed. R. W. Chapman, Oxford 1923.)

rating heroine in one sense reveals herself, in another Charlotte
Brontë avoids doing so as much as possible. There is proportion-
ately very little retail of thought and states of mind in *Jane Eyre*.
Wherever possible Charlotte Brontë uses action and dialogue.
Thought or state of mind, when it must be done, is done by various
objectifying devices: the interior dialogue, the address to the reader,
the use of imagery to reveal by parallels, or a simple flat statement
using almost eighteenth-century abstract concepts. The result is
that we never approach the sentimental or the mawkish.

The shape of the novel is very much represented by the places
where the action occurs, which Charlotte Brontë makes an essential
part of the structure, as well as the atmosphere, of her stories. Places
have indeed as much character as people, and serve many of the same
purposes, a use which *Jane Eyre* shares with *Wuthering Heights*, or,
to name a later novelist, Hardy. They operate by accurately and
vividly selected detail, and often on more than one level. Just as a
single person is felt and judged in different ways at the same time,
so places may arouse a variety of conflicting feelings, and the tensions, beginning fairly simply with the child's view of Gateshead,
increase in complexity through Lowood, Thornfield, Morton, and
Ferndean. Gateshead is plainly a place of torment, the house of the
Reeds, where all the rooms are places of cold and dread, whether in
company or isolation; even in the nursery Jane cannot touch the
dolls' house furniture 'for the tiny chairs and mirrors, the fairy
plates and cups were [Georgiana's] property' (Chapter 4), and the
windows are fretted with 'frost-flowers'. Jane's only pleasures there
are melancholy, uncertain, fleeting, and solitary: the vignettes in
Bewick,

> The rock standing up alone in a sea of billow and spray; the broken
> boat stranded on a desolate coast; the cold and ghastly moon glancing
> through bars of cloud at a wreck just sinking.   (Chapter 1)

are a brilliant choice: Bewick's vignettes do arouse such feelings,
so Jane's reactions seem authentic. Bessie's kindness, represented by
'a tart on a certain brightly painted china plate, whose bird of paradise, nestling in a wreath of convolvuli and rosebuds, had been wont

to stir in me a most enthusiastic sense of admiration' (Chapter 3), is, when she obtains it, 'like most other favours long deferred and often wished for, too late! I could not eat the tart: and the plumage of the bird, the tints of the flowers, seemed strangely faded' (ibid.). Yet these pleasures remain with Jane: Bewick can be clearly seen as an influence on the visionary paintings Jane does at Lowood and shows Mr Rochester at Thornfield: the pleasure in brilliant artefacts inspires her admiration for

> a very pretty drawing-room, and within it a boudoir, both spread with white carpets, on which seemed laid brilliant garlands of flowers; both ceiled with snowy mouldings of white grapes and vine-leaves, beneath which glowed in rich contrast crimson couches and ottomans; while the ornaments on the pale Parian mantel-piece were of sparkling Bohemian glass, ruby red; and between the windows large mirrors repeated the general blending of snow and fire. (Chapter 11)

– which Mr Rochester later dismisses (with reason):

> 'The glamour of inexperience is over your eyes,' he answered; 'and you see (Thornfield) through a charmed medium: you cannot discern that the gilding is slime and the silk draperies cobwebs; that the marble is sordid slate, and the polished woods mere refuse chips and scaly bark.' (Chapter 20)

reproducing thus the movement of the earlier passage about the plate.

Lowood is physically hard and aesthetically repulsive. A reader's immediate recollections of it are of burnt porridge, 'a strong steam redolent of rancid fat', 'a keen north-east wind, whistling through crevices of our bedroom windows all night long, [that] had made us shiver in our beds, and turned the contents of the ewers to ice' (Chapter 6), girls 'in brown stuff frocks of quaint fashion, and long holland pinafores' (Chapter 5), whose hair is not allowed to curl, even naturally. But the pleasures are more mature and more extensive. Sensuous pleasure remains; in food for the famished such as Miss Temple's supper ('How fragrant was the steam of the beverage, and the scent of the toast', and that ever memorable 'good-sized seed-cake' (Chapter 8)); and in the scenery ('prospects of noble summits girdling a great hill-hollow, rich in verdure and shadow; a bright beck, full of dark stones and sparkling eddies' (Chapter 9)). It is also the place of congenial companionship – Miss Temple, Helen Burns, and even Mary Ann Wilson; and intellectual pleasures are added – of drawing, learning French and conversing with Miss Temple.

Such simple combinations of good and bad prepare for the much more subtle use of Thornfield. The place has several aspects: freedom and happiness are embodied in some parts of the house, in its gardens, and in the surrounding landscape; while the sinister and evil are embodied in the upper storeys (especially at night); the grand world of society, heartless and tasteless, belongs in the drawing-room. These are all directly related to Jane's association with Mr Rochester, and help us to feel the moral weight of what happens. Jane first meets Mr Rochester outside, in Hay Lane; he tells her about Céline in the cold wintry garden, standing outside the house as he is standing, mentally, outside his own experiences and coldly assessing them; after Mason has been attacked and departed, Mr Rochester sits in the garden in summer sunrise with Jane, reviewing in the dawn of his new emotions the painful and violent ones of his youth, which link so closely with what has just happened inside the house; he proposes to Jane in the garden, in the orchard on Midsummer-eve, where all is 'Eden-like' and as he said before 'all is real, sweet and pure' (Chapter 20). The proposal is unlawful, but its spirit is not, and the setting of it cannot fail to make us feel so. By contrast what happens indoors is ambiguous or evil. When she has just met Mr Rochester, Jane, returning from Hay in the evening and loitering outside, sees the house as a 'grey hollow filled with rayless cells' (Chapter 12); the suggestion of prison and place of the dead continues: Bertha Mason is shut up on the third floor, and when she escapes, setting fire to Mr Rochester's bed, visiting Jane and tearing her veil, and setting fire finally to Jane's room, all she does is done indoors and upstairs. Downstairs the Gothic terror is replaced by vapid society and the pressure it exerts on Jane and Mr Rochester: he can only half-communicate with her, 'in mortal dread of some prating prig of a servant passing' (Chapter 17), or disguised as a gipsy, and as soon as they enter the hall after the proposal, Mrs

Fairfax, 'pale, grave, and amazed' (Chapter 23), recalls us to the standards of society, Thornfield is precious because Jane has 'lived in it a full and delightful life' (ibid.); but it is insubstantial and doomed to perish, representing the falsity that must be burned away by suffering before Jane and Mr Rochester can come together, and that Jane's dreams of it as a crumbling ruin fore-shadow (Chapter 25).

Moor House is in many ways its antithesis: the building is a symbol of security and family unity, a place Jane can 'care for' in the most practical sense, as the 'cleaning down' process with Hannah proves (Chapter 34). It provides Jane with a family and a function, but subjects her to more anxiety than Thornfield ever did, when St John's calls her to submit to a soulless and self-destroying marriage of duty. To read about Moor House reproduces Jane's experiences there: it is both less absorbing than Thornfield, and a great deal more trying. On the other hand, Moor House and Jane's life there gain dignity, power and health from the surrounding hill-country. Moorland comforts her in her flight:

> Beside the crag, the heath was very deep: when I lay down my feet were buried in it; rising high on each side, it left only a narrow space for the night-air to invade. I folded my shawl double, and spread it over me for a coverlet; a low, mossy swell was my pillow.
>
> (Chapter 28)

It is also a fitting background for St John, a stern setting for his stern proposals, which are made high in the hills where

> 'the mountain shook off turf and flower, had only heath for raiment, and crag for gem – where it exaggerated the wild to the savage, and exchanged the fresh for the frowning – where it guarded the forlorn hope of solitude, and a last refuge for silence'[1] (Chapter 34)

Jane's schoolteacher's cottage – one-up, one-down – offers a con-trast to Thornfield (the bare necessities of life, physical, mental and

---

[1] The reader's mind recalls the hills round Lowood, the 'noble summits' which also provided a setting both for suffering, when 'mists chill as death wandered to the impulse of east winds along those purple peaks' (Chapter 9), and for a new companionship and intellectual growth.

emotional), just as the moorland landscape offers a noble but barren contrast to the fertile country round Thornfield:

> A little room with white-washed walls, and a sanded floor; containing four painted chairs and a table, a clock, a cupboard, with two or three plates and dishes, and a set of tea-things in delf.
>
> (Chapter 31)

Here are merely the essentials for physical life, to correspond with the meagre mental life offered by teaching ignorant farmgirls; the setting makes one understand how Jane can say, 'I felt desolate to a degree. I felt . . . degraded', and then, in the next paragraph, be thankful to be 'a village schoolmistress, free and honest, in a breezy mountain nook in the healthy heart of England' (Chapter 31).

The story ends at Ferndean Manor, about thirty miles from Thornfield, 'quite a desolate spot', 'deep buried in a wood' in an 'ineligible and unsalubrious site', with 'dank and green decaying walls' (Chapters 36 and 37). Though the house and its milieu obviously provide a new setting for what is to be a new relationship, a setting in harmony with a meeting where 'rapture is kept well in check by pain' (Chapter 37), they are not relevant in the same way as the others have been, since they contrast with the present action, rather than reveal it. Although Jane does not tell us, we can safely assume that once married, she and Mr Rochester leave so unhealthy and gloomy a place, where it is difficult to accommodate even one guest. The house and its setting as seen at the beginning of Chapter 37 present the epitome of what Mr Rochester has suffered and become in the last year; and as soon as possible, on the morning after her arrival, Jane leads Mr Rochester 'out of the wet and wild wood into some cheerful fields' (ibid.) where 'the flowers and hedges looked refreshed' by the 'sad sky, cold gale, and small penetrating rain' of the night before, just as his sufferings have at last brought new life to Mr Rochester.

Thus the various sections of the story have a moral and artistic relevance to the main action and to each other which helps to prevent any feeling that the book has a broken back. The story is unified also in ways more obviously structural. Innumerable threads of association and construction link section to section and incident to incident; and Charlotte Brontë creates proportioned emphasis, subtle parallels, and a sense of layers of simultaneous action to her basically linear story. The mere proportion of space occupied plays a large part in suggesting relative importance to the reader: four chapters for Gateshead, six for Lowood, fifteen for Thornfield (interrupted by a single very long chapter when Jane returns to Gateshead); one long chapter for her suffering and starvation, seven for Morton, and three for Ferndean. Within the Thornfield period there is only one chapter before Mr Rochester appears, twelve chapters for the courtship (more than is spent on anything else in the novel), but also two very long ones which cover the span between the wedding and Jane's flight. It can clearly be seen that the narrative movement runs against the natural passage of time, but nevertheless time and the hour run through the roughest day. References to season and weather, and even dates and days of the week, are frequent and exact as well as atmospheric: the intervals of time between Jane's arrival at Thornfield in October and Mr Rochester's proposal on Midsummer Eve are carefully noted, and equally accurate are those between her midsummer agony on the moors, St John's news of her fortune brought on a snowy November the fifth, and her return to Ferndean on a wet Thursday summer evening (the third of June). Jane does not live wholly in the present (as fictional characters so often do) but is always aware of her own past and possible future – she imagines with frightening truth what marriage to St John would entail – and she recognizes death as an accepted fact for others and herself:

> I laughed at him as he said this. 'I am not an angel,' I asserted; 'and I will not be one till I die: I will be myself.' (Chapter 24)

The single long chapter in the middle of the Thornfield episode, when Jane revisits Gateshead and Mrs Reed dies, is probably the finest example of Charlotte Brontë's sure sense of shape. This chapter (21) covers the space of a month (May), the month immediately after the dreadful night when Mason is attacked, and the summer dawn when Mr Rochester almost tells Jane about his marriage and almost proposes to her. The next main event, two weeks after her return, is his real proposal. No one can fail to feel that the emotional effect of the interruption and return is right, but the reasons why Charlotte Brontë takes such a risk as to break off here, when things between Jane and Mr Rochester are clearly reaching a culmination, are not immediately clear.

The most obvious and mechanical reason why Jane returns is to hear Mrs Reed's deathbed confession telling her of the uncle to whom she will owe both the breaking off of her wedding and also her fortune. It is much more organically a culmination of what has gone before, and an anticipation of what is to come. The culmination is necessary because Jane is to return to Thornfield to face the two greatest emotional experiences of her life: Mr Rochester's and her own mutual declarations, and her renunciation of him. For these to have their full power we must see Jane as a whole being, a part of all that she has met, moulded to this experience by all that has happened to her hitherto. The return to Gateshead recreates her childhood and its sufferings, and charts her moral and emotional growth. Georgiana and Eliza can no longer oppress her, and of Mrs Reed she can say, and we can believe:

> I had left this woman in bitterness and hate, and I came back to her now with no other emotion than a sort of ruth for her great sufferings, and a strong yearning to forget and forgive all injuries.
>
> (Chapter 21)

The episode is equally vital as anticipation and preparation in perhaps more separate ways. It separates Mr Rochester's proposal from the scenes which have led up to it, and sets it apart from them. Jane, away from Mr Rochester and Thornfield for the first time, shows no weakly conventional or self-indulgent pain at the temporary separation; we are therefore the more ready to credit her extreme agony when she is forced to leave for good. So utterly unsentimental a handling of death prepares for the equally unsentimental love and agony to come:

> A strange and solemn object was that corpse to me. I gazed on it with gloom and pain: nothing soft, nothing sweet, nothing pitying, or hopeful, or subduing, did it inspire; only a grating anguish for *her* woes – not *my* loss – and a sombre tearless dismay at the fearfulness of death in such a form.
>
> (ibid.)

Gateshead and its affairs have reached a climax, which prepares for the even greater climax to come. As a climax, it is the antithesis of Mr Rochester's proposal; dreadful and unfeeling, it moves us and Jane, so that we are moved even more by the intense happiness which follows. Jane's power to hate intensely and to express it, recalled here, presupposes that her love and its expression will be equally intense. The episode puts before us distinctions we shall have to make at Morton, where 'judgement untempered by feeling' (ibid.) will again be offered, but in a more subtle guise, as religious renunciation. A view of life is created in which death takes a realistic place, so that when Bertha Mason dies, this convenient event seems not improbable, since four (Helen Burns, John Reed, his mother, and the West Indian uncle) have died before her.

Within the larger individual sections of the action, the movement varies, but Charlotte Brontë tends always to work in terms of the big scene, completely realized and dramatically presented. She likes to use the effect of shock on her reader, but she never loses her emotional continuity; she therefore moves from one big scene to the next, by a variety of methods: the smaller (but significant) intermediate scene, the pause for Jane's reflection and analysis of what has passed, and, very rarely, the juxtaposition of sharply contrasting important scenes. She is also careful to provide proper preparation where shock is unsuitable; and the prefatory material, though of various kinds, is always concerned with building up the right associations, or recalling the necessary personalities. The result is a wave-like movement, with a drawing-back between each surge of an incoming tide. Attention to continuity descends even to the nice placing of chapter divisions. The most interesting place to examine her structural methods is where they are at their finest and most sustained, that is, during the fifteen chapters chronicling the events at Thornfield. These move by a series of exciting, even sensational, events, seen in entirety. The sense of shock is as much in the material as the presentation, and Charlotte Brontë never cheats by cutting a scene off short to get her excitement. The first of these big scenes is the one where Mr Rochester falls off his horse in Hay Lane (Chapter 12), but this is unmistakably being underplayed, partly to gain power in retrospect, and partly so as to keep plenty of power in reserve. Mr Rochester is at this point, as Jane says, 'only a traveller taking the short cut to Millcote'. There must, after all, be no suggestion of falling in love at first sight – though this is what Mr Rochester almost does: 'It was well that I had learnt that this elf must return to me – that it belonged to my house down below – or I could not have felt it pass away from under my hand, and seen it vanish behind the dim hedge, without singular regret' (Chapter 12). Thereafter Charlotte Brontë has a good deal to do in the way of establishing relationships, and filling in past history, which all prevents action. But immediately this is done, the movement begins in Chapter 15, with the fire, the very night after Mr Rochester has told Jane about Céline Varens. The next is the first evening Jane and Adèle meet the house-party (Chapter 18), where Jane suffers her social inferiority, Mr Rochester's flirtation with Blanche, and finally Mr Rochester's all too perceptive questions; the charade comes next (18), then the fortune-telling gipsy (19), then the dreadful night when Mason is attacked, and the tête-à-tête in the orchard at dawn which follows (20); then at last (after Mrs Reed's death) and the very brief scene where Jane meets Mr Rochester in Hay Lane again, the proposal at midsummer (23). These chapters form an entity. The scenes are splendidly varied: there is the passionate tête-à-tête after the fire, and the disguised one of the fortune-telling; there are scenes when Mr Rochester makes the advances (the fire, his few words in the hall, his confession in the orchard when Mason has left), and scenes where Jane does (the proposal itself, and the little scene in Hay Lane preceding it); there are scenes where others are the real actors, and the relevance is in the emotions Jane feels (the 'polite' conversations about governesses, and the charade), scenes where the action is shared (Mason's terrible night). They take place at night, and by day, indoors and out (and not arbitrarily, for the setting is always significant); but however they occur, whoever is concerned, and wherever and whenever they happen, they each sweep things a little nearer to that Midsummer Eve in the orchard. After them comes another movement, whose motive is foreboding, which works in terms of fantasy and illusion, where dreams seem more real than life, where an ecstatic daylight reality runs alongside frightening omens at night, which coalesce after the abortive wedding, and culminate when Jane tears herself away from Thornfield. Similarly the chapters at Morton move by way of various excitements and pressures until Jane hears Mr Rochester's voice and breaks free from St John.

The transitions between these scenes are as varied as the scenes themselves, and equally superb. We never feel that Charlotte Brontë is having to summon her resources, or rest between engagements. The action has all the continuity of real life, and the interest never slackens. What goes on in between the events absorbs us just as much as the events themselves, since our eye never leaves what absorbs us most – Jane herself – though *her* eye of course may wander very considerably. Hence the variety in the interludes. These are generally a pause for breath, and for reassessment. The day after the fire is a fine example of Charlotte Brontë's method, involving in a short space a number of the devices she employs. After the fire Jane cannot sleep, and admits to us and herself for the first time how she feels about Mr Rochester – not yet explicitly but in images:

> Till morning dawned I was tossed on a buoyant but unquiet sea, where billows of trouble rolled under surges of joy ... [but] a counteracting breeze blew off land, and continually drove me back. Sense would resist delirium: judgment would warn passion.
>
> (Chapter 15)

The following day (Chapter 16) bears out what she says. The first incident is the servants Leah and Grace Poole putting the bedroom to rights, sense and the light of common day taking over the scene of delirium. Grace in person de-romances herself, with her 'pint of porter and bit of pudding' (Chapter 16). Having left her, Jane tries to explain Mrs Poole's position to herself: Mr Rochester may once have put himself in her power; they are the same age: 'she may possess originality and strength of character to compensate for the want of personal advantages. Mr Rochester is an amateur of the decided and eccentric.' Jane's reasoning is quite sensible, and even more sensible is the way she rejects the hypothesis when she considers Mrs Poole in person. The passage has an extra layer of significance, since all the points which make her reasoning sound here point to herself, not Mrs Poole, as the partner for Mr Rochester, as Jane herself recognizes. At this point Jane's thoughts again im-pinge upon action:

> I was now in the schoolroom; Adèle was drawing; I bent over her and directed her pencil. She looked up with a sort of start.
> 'Qu'avez-vous donc, mademoiselle?' said she; 'Vos doigts trem-blent comme la feuille, et vos joues sont rouges: mais, rouges comme des cerises!'
> 'I am hot, Adèle, with stooping!' She went on sketching, I went on thinking. (ibid.)

The day ends with conversation between Jane and Mrs Fairfax at tea, with the same kind of external manifestation of feeling:

> 'You must want your tea,' said the good lady, as I joined her; 'you ate so little at dinner. I am afraid,' she continued, 'you are not well today: you look flushed and feverish. (ibid.)

and the conversation reveals that Mr Rochester has left, and that the events are about to take a new course, with the arrival of the house-party and Blanche. Jane accepts this check to her feelings, and supplements it by contrasting herself with Blanche and drawing the two portraits. The whole interlude is 'sense' resisting 'delirium':

> When once more alone, I reviewed the information I had got; looked into my heart, examined its thoughts and feelings, and endeavoured to bring back with a strict hand such as had been straying through imagination's boundless and trackless waste, into the safe fold of common sense. (ibid.)

The use of incident as well as thought demonstrates at the same time that her conduct is always ruled by this sense, and that her feelings are so powerful as to break through the restraint she imposes on herself; the conclusion to the chapter drives home its point and directs us forward to what is to happen next:

> Ere long, I had reason to congratulate myself on the course of wholesome discipline to which I had thus forced my feelings to submit: thanks to it, I was able to meet subsequent occurrences with a decent calm; which, had they found me unprepared, I should probably have been unequal to maintain, even externally. (ibid.)

As the action at Thornfield sweeps itself forward speed gathers, the intervals between scenes get shorter and less obtrusive. After Jane's dreadful night with Mason, her talk with Mr Rochester in the orchard immediately follows. The events of the month of courtship rush on upon another without pause, and make their own comment on themselves, so Jane need interpose no more than

> My future husband was becoming to me my whole world; and more than the world: almost my hope of heaven. He stood between me and every thought of religion, as an eclipse intervenes between man and the broad sun. I could not, in those days, see God for his creature: of whom I had made an idol. (Chapter 24)

We are swept forward to the disaster at the altar, on past Mr Rochester's public admission, into his confession and persuasion of Jane; their agonizing battle of wills, from one startling revelation to the next, and have no pause to breathe until Jane gets into the coach which leaves her at Whitcross;

> Gentle reader, may you never feel what I then felt! May your eyes never shed such stormy, scalding, heart-wrung tears as poured from mine. May you never appeal to Heaven in prayers so hopeless and so agonized as in that hour left my lips: for never may you, like me, dread to be the instrument of evil to what you wholly love. (Chapter 27)

Since Charlotte Brontë's method is in many ways a dramatic one, she uses a good deal of dialogue. *Jane Eyre* has the advantage over *Villette* and *The Professor* that its characters (all except Adèle and Sophie) are English-speaking. Charlotte Brontë has a fine ear for characteristic idioms of class and age, which the deliberate and obvious artificiality of the house-party dialogues tends to obscure. She moves in a narrow compass, making little use of dialect, having no character to compare with Emily Brontë's Joseph; Hannah, the only really broad speaker, is generally reported, and her direct speech gets its flavour from idiom rather than pronunciation:

> 'Are you book-learned?' she inquired presently.
> 'Yes, very.'
> 'But you've never been to a boarding-school.'

'I was at a boarding-school eight years.'

She opened her eyes wide. 'Whatever cannot ye keep yourself for, then?'   (Chapter 29)

The idiom of the respectable servant is precisely caught, whether in Leah, Grace Poole, Bessie or Robert Leaven here:

'And how is Bessie? You are married to Bessie?'

'Yes, Miss: my wife is very hearty, thank you; she brought me another little one about two months since – we have three now – and both mother and child are thriving.'

'And are the family well at the House, Robert?'

'I am sorry I can't give you better news of them, Miss: they are very badly at present – in great trouble . . . Mr John died yesterday was a week, at his chambers in London.'   (Chapter 21)

Mrs Fairfax (whatever the actual or ostensible date of the book) goes back a generation or more, and her idiom recalls Jane Austen. Dialogue between Jane and others, expecially Mr Rochester, performs many functions besides verisimilitude: it is often not naturalistic, yet it almost always convinces, and always has a flavour of its own. Like the speech in *Wuthering Heights* it is often quite literally unspeakable, and is, despite its dramatic method, quite unlike that of a play or of life.

Charlotte Brontë's style is like no one else's. This is generally agreed and immediately obvious. Being odd, it has often been called bad, by those who have preconceived notions of what a novelist's style should be, and in particular a Victorian lady novelist's. But as Mr Rochester says in another context, 'unheard-of combinations of circumstances demand unheard-of rules' (Chapter 14). Both Charlotte Brontë and Emily found this to be so in their writing; both solved their own problem in their own way, and while Charlotte occasionally allows herself to copy other novelists (the voice heard most frequently besides her own is that of Thackeray, whom she greatly admired), her best effects are always her most individual ones. Again the distinction must be made between Charlotte Brontë and her creation Jane Eyre. While Jane has many of Charlotte Brontë's characteristics, it is clear that what she says is almost always 'in character', and Charlotte Brontë's success is so complete that it is only noticeable in her occasional failures, where an idiom is heard that we recognize from *Shirley* or *Villette*:

> Women are supposed to be very calm generally: but women feel just as men feel; they need exercise for their faculties, and a field for their efforts as much as their brothers do; they suffer from too rigid a restraint, too absolute a stagnation, precisely as men would suffer; and it is narrow-minded in their more privileged fellow-creatures to say that they ought to confine themselves to making puddings and knitting stockings, to playing on the piano and embroidering bags. It is thoughtless to condemn them, or laugh at them, if they seek to do more or learn more than custom has pronounced necessary for their sex.
> (Chapter 12)

> I know poetry is not dead, nor genius lost; nor has Mammon gained power over either, to bind or slay: they will both assert their existence, their presence, their liberty and strength again one day. Powerful angels, safe in heaven! They smile when sordid souls triumph, and feeble ones weep over their destruction. Poetry destroyed? Genius banished? No! Mediocrity, no; do not let envy prompt you to the thought. No; they not only live, but reign, and redeem: and without their divine influence spread everywhere, you would be in hell – the hell of your own meanness.
> (Chapter 32)

Both these jar by being generalizations, and being divorced from the topic, though the one is meditative and the other rhetorical. Generally, however, Charlotte Brontë's expression is determined by the speaker, by the occasion, by the emotional content of what is being said, or by the atmosphere of the episode, always bearing in mind that everything that is not spoken by one of the other characters is, whatever else it is doing, being used to express Jane.

With *Jane Eyre* Charlotte Brontë establishes what the novel is to be and do in her hands, and has found her course between what she herself summarized as the 'real' and the 'true', between which she was confused in *The Professor*.

4

SHIRLEY

Charlotte Brontë plainly intended *Shirley* to be different from *Jane Eyre*. She contrived it by conscious professional methods: by writing on a historical and social topic, by having no single all-absorbing central heroine, by having an original (then) and striking provincial setting, and by having an author-narrator instead of a character-narrator. She succeeded; *Shirley* contains many delights for which the material and method of *Jane Eyre* gave no opportunity. But she succeeded at a price, since it also inhibits her from much of what she does best.

'L'état, c'est moi.' Charlotte Brontë herself is the strongest personality in *Shirley*, and colours all the rest. In her first and only published attempt at the third-person narrator she produces a completely original work, while clearly feeling that she is using a well-known and orthodox mode. Though she is scrupulously fair in creating authentic events and investing her characters with sound motives, distorting neither action nor personality to suit her views, these views continually break through, and curiously colour the action. An account of the story and the people of *Shirley* would never suggest the mixture of rebellious suffering, impassioned stoicism, and personal loneliness that pervades it. They are produced by the attitude of the teller. These qualities, strong in *Jane Eyre*, have become much stronger, and now constitute a view of life that seems at times even bitter, since they speak to the reader directly, not as part of a fictional personality. They are part of Charlotte Brontë's development, governing equally the tone of her next novel *Villette*, where, however, they again acquire the artistic authenticity they had in *Jane Eyre* by being the essence of another first-person narrator Lucy Snowe, and become again an organizing power of the kind that suits Charlotte Brontë best. In *Shirley* they control the tone, but they cannot control the material.

Charlotte Brontë is still very much drawn to the self-revelatory method, though now the teller is not an actor in the story, and is, as far as any narrator is, the individual writer's own self.[1] She had the precedent of her well-read and much-loved Scott for her man-to-man tone to the reader in the conveying of unfamiliar material and solid general reflection; and the precedent of her much-admired contemporary Thackeray for an even more familiar tone and a sardonic and disillusioned view of the 'comédie humaine'. She must have felt that, in the main current now of the English novel, and protected by anonymity and her apparently masculine pseudonym, she was in safe waters – much safer than she was in the very original and very feminine *Jane Eyre*.

Such a method imposes, of itself, much less discipline on the author than the autobiographical, which automatically selects and proportions material and determines an attitude to it. The attitude of the narrator as used by Thackeray (and Fielding before him) can be much more flexible, and is largely at the discretion of the writer. When the narrator is handling a wide range of social topics and types, as such narrators commonly do, he needs to be, generally speaking, a person of some sophistication, urbane, balanced, and reasonably free from bias, not deeply and personally involved with any of his characters. Charlotte Brontë as narrator in *Shirley* has many engaging qualities, but these are not the epithets one would apply to her. She invariably succeeds where she can temporarily merit them – notably in comic scenes like those with the curates, or with characters like Mr Helstone whose idiosyncrasies are so pronounced as to make her own invisible, or where, as in the return of the wagons with the smashed machinery (Chapter 2), action

---

[1] The identification of the teller and Charlotte Brontë need not be complete: the tone of the reflections here is often not that of Charlotte Brontë's letters to her friends on similar topics, even allowing for the difference between private confidences and public dicta. And she had had practice as the narrator who is also a personality in the juvenile Angrian tales, many of which are told by 'Charles Wellesley', who is the passive, sardonic, and detached commentator brother of the actual hero.

predominates over analysis. All these talents not able to be revealed in *Jane Eyre* show a new development in Charlotte Brontë's art as a novelist, and capacities unguessable hitherto – though by hindsight we may see clues to them in *The Professor*.

On the other hand, by maintaining the stance, Charlotte Brontë would deprive herself of what was her greatest power: to engage rational and emotional commitment in the reader by employing her own. The detached narrator is really alien to her. She is both passionate and eccentric – 'original' is the word she herself used in *Jane Eyre* – and so, often, is the narrator in *Shirley*, notably in her own apostrophes to the reader, and in her analyses of Caroline Helstone. She is never ineffectual, and never fails of response; yet the result is to make the reader uneasy, and the book, in the last analysis, incoherent, when two such disparate tones are alternated.

Charlotte Brontë nevertheless selected the type of narrator most suited to her, that involving the closest contact with the reader. She was fond of apostrophizing her reader in *Jane Eyre*, and continues to do so here at moments both serious and comic, both of involvement and detachment, with equal success. She is flexible and assured; effectively burlesquing her curates on the opening page:

> The present successors of the apostles, disciples of Dr Pusey and tools of the Propaganda, were [in 1811–19] being hatched under cradle-blankets, or undergoing regeneration by nursery-baptism in wash-hand-basins. You could not have guessed by looking at any one of them that the Italian-ironed double frills of its net cap surrounded the brows of a pre-ordained, specially-sanctified successor of St Paul, St Peter, or St John; nor could you have foreseen in the folds of its long night-gown the white surplice in which it was hereafter cruelly to exercise the souls of its parishioners, and strangely to nonplus its old-fashioned vicar by flourishing aloft in a pulpit the shirt-like raiment which had never before waved higher than the reading-desk.
>
> (Chapter 1)

and effectively suggesting a personality:

> It is time, reader, that you should have some idea of the appearance of this same host: I must endeavour to sketch him as he sits at table.
> He is what you would probably call, at first view, rather a strange-

looking man; for he is thin, dark, sallow; very foreign of aspect, with shadowy hair carelessly streaking his forehead: it appears that he spends but little time at his toilette, or he would arrange it with more taste. He seems unconscious that his features are fine, that they have a southern symmetry, clearness, regularity in their chiseling; nor does a spectator become aware of this advantage till he has examined him well, for an anxious countenance, and a hollow, somewhat haggard, outline of face disturb the idea of beauty with one of care. (Chapter 2)

She continues the method, and continues to hold her reader until the last delightful dismissal of Malone:

Perhaps I ought to remark, that on the premature and sudden vanishing of Mr Malone from the stage of Briarfield parish (you cannot know how it happened, reader; your curiosity must be robbed to pay your elegant love of the pretty and pleasing), there came as his successor another Irish curate, Mr Macarthey. I am happy to be able to inform you, *with truth*, that this gentleman did as much credit to his country as Malone had done it discredit: he proved himself as decent, decorous, and conscientious, as Peter was rampant, boisterous, and – (this last epithet I choose to suppress, because it would let the cat out of the bag). (Chapter 37)

In such dealings with the reader she never fails, and the high spirits and gusto continue to effervesce from time to time throughout the novel.

Yet the view of life offered in *Shirley* is a grim one. The fate of Caroline Helstone, who concerns Charlotte Brontë more than anyone else, calls forth most of the utterances on life and the human predicament with which the novel abounds. These are not the settled convictions provoked by the action with which any reader may agree, as are Thackeray's, but passionately felt outbursts that seem to be as much the result of the author's own sufferings as of the character's. These impassioned judgements are most memorable, and have the robust ring of truth:

A lover masculine so disappointed can speak and urge explanation; a lover feminine can say nothing; if she did, the result would be shame and anguish, inward remorse for self-treachery. Nature would

brand such demonstration as a rebellion against her instincts, and
would vindictively repay it afterwards by the thunderbolt of self-
contempt smiting suddenly in secret. Take the matter as you find it:
ask no questions; utter no remonstrances: it is your best wisdom.
You expected bread, and you have got a stone; break your teeth on
it, and don't shriek because the nerves are martyrized: do not doubt
that your mental stomach – if you have such a thing – is strong as an
ostrich's – the stone will digest. You held out your hand for an egg,
and fate put into it a scorpion. Show no consternation: close your
fingers firmly upon the gift; let it sting through your palm. Never
mind: in time, after your hand and arm have swelled and quivered
long with torture, the squeezed scorpion will die, and you will have
learned the great lesson how to endure without a sob. For the whole
remnant of your life, if you survive the test – some, it is said, die
under it – you will be stronger, wiser, less sensitive. This you are
not aware of, perhaps, at the time, and so cannot borrow courage of
that hope. Nature, however, as has been intimated, is an excellent
friend in such cases; sealing the lips, interdicting utterance, com-
manding a placid dissimulation: a dissimulation often wearing an
easy and gay mien at first, settling down to sorrow and paleness in
time, then passing away, and leaving a convenient stoicism, not the
less fortifying because it is half-bitter.   (Chapter 7)

The difficulty is that such passages frequently seem in excess of
what the situation demands, or the character can bear. When the
above passage confronts us, we have seen only the charming inexperienced Caroline yielding to affection for her relative Robert
Moore, its quite suitable object. There is as yet nothing in her dis-
appointment to suggest that she should suffer so hopelessly and
intolerably as to merit this advice, or that she has a nature powerful
enough to do so. The form that selected and channelled from Charlotte Brontë's nature only that which belonged properly to Jane
Eyre now no longer operates; and even the passionate Jane Eyre's
advice to herself to suppress her love for Mr Rochester was not so
vicious as this. One must admit there are passages in *Shirley* where
Charlotte Brontë makes her reader wince. They are those in which
she is consciously 'writing up' her material, in the visionary pseudo-
religious mode she herself reproduces for Shirley's extraordinary
essay on 'La Première Femme Savante' (Chapter 27).

Yet such passages are rare, and in her natural and unself-conscious dealings with her reader Charlotte Brontë never fails; as in *Jane Eyre*, in narrative she rarely offers too much or the wrong kind of information (she is quite clear what is unusual in Yorkshire life and what she can safely presume familiar), events are splendidly handled, and emotions powerfully revealed. As a story-teller she is still superb, and while events are taking place or emotions are being analysed her hold never slips.

By allying herself more closely with the reader than with any of her characters except Caroline, Charlotte Brontë makes *Shirley* different from her other novels, and oddly close to *Wuthering Heights*. She has learned the device from Scott, but puts it to her own original uses. There is none of *Waverley's* romantic nostalgia in *Shirley*. Nor do the Napoleonic Wars and their influence ennoble Robert Moore by association as the Scottish religious struggles do Henry Morton in *Old Mortality*. Characters are hemmed in by the times in which they live and by the span of their own individual lifetimes. Robert Moore's business, and by connection his personal fate, depend on the actual historical time when events happen: his bankruptcy is barely averted by the repeal of the Orders in Council. Caroline in her misery thinks how she will get through the rest of her life – a question Jane Eyre never considers. Where Jane and those she encounters can look forward with reasonable assurance, if not with certainty, to what comes after death to comfort them, *Shirley* re-echoes with Caroline's question:

> 'What am I to do to fill the interval of time which spreads between me and the grave?' (Chapter 10)

This is a new view for a novelist to take. Eternity is quite left out. Even George Eliot, not Christian and with no faith in a hereafter, does not make her fictional characters so uncompromisingly mortal, so committed by their own actions, and so restricted by the history of their time. Death is present and inescapable, even for minor characters. The introduction so early in the novel (Chapter 9) of Jessie Yorke, whose death we are shown before we even have the chance to see her living, is characteristic of the whole, and suggests more the method of the historian or biographer than the novelist.

Though in many ways the all-seeing narrator, Charlotte Brontë reserves the right to withhold information, and so have the effect of mystery as well as of power. The main mysterious and only partly-revealed figures are Robert Moore, Shirley and Mrs Pryor. While concealing nothing about their essential personalities or the principles by which they are ruled, and while providing many clues to them and their situations, Charlotte Brontë never reveals to the reader anything that they themselves are concealing from all the other characters. Though we know all the principles on which Robert holds his mill, we are not told until afterwards those which bring him to propose to Shirley; and though we know the standards by which Shirley will *not* marry, we are not allowed to see those by which she will. The other characters range round these in treatment, from Caroline of whose mind the reader is made free, down to the Sympsons or the Sykes ladies, who, as Pope suggested of women, 'have no characters at all', only characteristics visible from the outside.

Charlotte Brontë creates yet another limitation for herself in *Shirley* out of her strengths in *Jane Eyre* and *Villette* – her sex. Being an author of courage, she faces in her very first chapter the problem (so notably avoided by Jane Austen) of portraying men when no woman is present, and in places where women's influence is at its least: she plunges confidently into bachelor curates' lodgings and a mill-owner's counting-house at night. All that can be got right by observation is accurate, the idiom is often excellent, and details of behaviour inspired: one of the finest instances is Malone at Moore's counting-house (Chapter 2) getting flown with punch – a condition Moore diagnoses to Helstone as 'He has been eating a mutton-chop'. What sometimes fails is the topic. We feel the incongruity in this same episode when hard-headed Moore and hot-headed Malone, uncongenial company for each other, expecting to be attacked by the frame-breakers, discuss the matrimonial prospects of Sweeting (a man neither of them cares about) and even of Moore himself. When Moore exclaims

'I believe women talk and think only of those things, and they naturally fancy men's minds similarly occupied.'   (Chapter 2)

we recognize that the author has unconsciously exposed herself.

In *Jane Eyre* plot and theme were closely connected, and were at many points almost the same thing. In *Shirley* they part company, and a résumé of the plot alone would virtually exclude the pre-occupations which the novel as a whole reveals. There are clearly several subjects: on the simplest level the novel is about the events leading to the marriages of the most intensely-observed heroine, Caroline Helstone, and of the one who gives it its title, Shirley Keeldar. It is also quite clearly in many ways a social novel and an historical one, concerned with the effects of the Napoleonic Wars and the Industrial Revolution in the West Riding clothing district of Yorkshire in 1812. The hero of this social side of the novel is Robert Moore. Charlotte Brontë's choice of material is sensible and well-judged; she has her setting in a district that is home to her (an advantage *Shirley* has over *Villette*); she has events of which she had heard eyewitness accounts, and which were in themselves of more moment than any in *Jane Eyre*, based on history but leaving room for invention, and she has thus the kind of retrospect she used rather peripherally in *Jane Eyre* (which opens, though the dating is confused, some thirty years back). She has therefore the advantages the '45 gave Scott in *Waverley* (while not in any sense borrowing or plagiarizing), and she is able incidentally and by chance, one feels, to make use of many of Scott's own techniques – probably unconsciously, since the Brontës had known Scott since childhood. Even so, she does not attempt the comprehensive, as Scott does. She knows her own powers are not his. She has learned from *Jane Eyre* not to attempt the upper-class when there is no single vision like Jane's to turn faults of perception into insights into personality; and her omissions show clearly that she knows she cannot, like Mrs Gaskell, depict justly the sufferings of the working class, or depict and analyse a whole society through its representatives, like George Eliot. She suggests, rather than exhibits, analyses, or judges. Her economic and social questions are firmly fixed to the fate of the individual. The troubles of only one mill-owner are retailed – Robert Moore who, half-Flemish, and the romantic hero as far as the novel has one, is not at all typical of his age or setting; the responsibilities of the landowner in a mixed industrial and agricultural society are embodied in Shirley Keeldar, who is equally the centre of romantic interest, and closely concerned with the other underlying themes of the novel also; the growing influence of the Methodists and nonconformity in general appears as the one-legged rogue Moses Barraclough, and its fanatical extreme in Mike Hartley, the antinomian weaver and would-be assassin. Charlotte Brontë claims, and we admit, her right to select from her material, and analyse in the greatest detail the aspects that concern her most. We admit as a corollary, at an early point in the story, her right to exclude, when she adverts to the child-workers in Hollow's Mill:

> though I describe imperfect characters (every character in this book will be found to be more or less imperfect, my pen refusing to draw anything in the model line), I have not undertaken to handle degraded or utterly infamous ones. Child-torturers, slave masters and drivers, I consign to the hands of jailers; the novelist may be excused from sullying his page with the record of their deeds.
>
> (Chapter 5)

> the children, released for half an hour from toil, betook themselves to the little tin cans which held their coffee, and to the small baskets which held their allowance of bread. Let us hope they have enough to eat; it would be a pity were it otherwise. (ibid.)

This is not sentimentality, or turning a blind eye to the sordid; it is her claim to the novelist's right to choose what he shall do. She refuses, as she says in a very significant juxtaposition, 'to harrow up the reader's soul, and delight his organ of wonder' (ibid.).

Yet the preoccupations which the action and characters of *Shirley* bring forth come near to harrowing the reader, with no delight to compensate. These preoccupations are contemporary, not historical. As always, Charlotte Brontë is deeply concerned with a woman's place in the world. What was individual and personal in *Jane Eyre* has become more detached, more explicit, more a matter of society and economics. Through Caroline and Shirley she examines the position and the difficulties of the single young woman, and how common life, the attitudes of men, and the accepted tenets of society, frustrate her. Again she selects, and limits herself to what she can do thoroughly and well. She does not try to consider the position of women in general, and is not at all what would later have been called feminist. The many difficulties of the married woman are barely touched on in Mrs Pryor, and those of the middle-aged or old are merely suggested in the minor characters of Miss Mann and Miss Ainley. On the other hand she is concerned with very much more than just the troubles of girls in love. Spiritual freedom rather than social or financial independence, or emotional satisfaction, is what is in question. Caroline suffers when Robert Moore neglects her, but her sufferings become intolerable to herself, and claim the reader's serious sympathy, because she is actually prevented from finding any purpose in life when, the role of wife and mother denied her, she is kept uselessly at home by her uncle, forbidden to seek work or financial independence, cut off even from any source of intellectual improvement, condemned to a life of idleness which may only be relieved by efforts at minor local charity, with the prospect in the future of literal penury when Helstone dies. As Caroline says 'it is scarcely *living* to measure time as I do at the Rectory. The hours pass, and I get over them somehow, but I do not *live*' (Chapter 21). The only view of woman's function offered her is to do what her servants can do for her:

> 'stick to the needle – learn shirt-making and gown-making, and pie-crust-making, and you'll be a clever woman some day.'
>
> (Chapter 7)

a bleak prospect at eighteen. The release Charlotte Brontë and her characters ask is very modest: they do not even ask for happiness:

> 'Caroline,' demanded Miss Keeldar abruptly, 'don't you wish you had a profession – a trade?'
>
> 'I wish it fifty times a day. As it is, I often wonder what I came into the world for. I long to have something absorbing and compulsory to fill my head and hands, and to occupy my thoughts.'
>
> 'Can labour alone make a human being happy?'
>
> 'No; but it can give varieties of pain, and prevent us from breaking our hearts with a single tyrant master-torture. Besides, successful labour has its recompense; a vacant, weary, lonely, hopeless life has none.'
>
> 'But hard labour and learned professions, they say, make women masculine, coarse, unwomanly.'

'And what does it signify, whether unmarried and never-to-be-married women are unattractive and inelegant, or not? – provided only they are decent, decorous, and neat, it is enough.'

(Chapter 12)

This is not at all revolutionary or unrealistic. Caroline, wishing to be a governess, implies that the order of things in the 1840's could provide enough scope for a woman, if only social pressures did not inhibit her. When she finds she has a purpose in life, she revives from the mental and physical breakdown which has crushed her: her health is restored by the claims of Mrs Pryor, and, even though Charlotte Brontë cannot handle the relationship, the point made is a sound one.

Shirley Keeldar by contrast has all the apparent advantages: financially and socially independent, with personal beauty and an original, robust and healthy personality. Yet she also suffers from the prevailing attitude to women when she is carefully and deliberately excluded not only from the defence of her own property Hollow's Mill, but even from knowing that it is likely to be attacked, or if attacked, defended; she has to find out by guesswork, using the wits the men refuse to recognize. Charlotte Brontë makes as many of her points through Shirley's words as through Caroline's situation. It is Shirley who provokes the abortive discussion in which the mill foreman Joe Scott refuses to talk politics to two young women, and asserts male superiority in the traditional terms:

'I think that women are a kittle and a froward generation; and I've a great respect for the doctrines delivered in the second chapter of St Paul's first Epistle to Timothy.'   (Chapter 18)

But this same conversation shows that Charlotte Brontë is not dogmatic, and can see all sides of the situation:

'Joe is well enough in his own house,' said Shirley: 'I have seen him as quiet as a lamb at home. There is not a better nor a kinder husband in Briarfield. He does not dogmatize to his wife.'

'My wife is a hard-working, plain woman: time and trouble has ta'en all the conceit out of her; but that is not the case with you, young Misses.'   (ibid.)

Another of Charlotte Brontë's close concerns is the effect of suffering on personality. She ensures in her own voice that we shall attend to her view, which is both realistic and unconventional:

> Sweet mild force following acute suffering, you find nowhere: to talk of it is delusion. There may be apathetic exhaustion after the rack; if energy remains, it will be rather a dangerous energy – deadly when confronted with injustice. (Chapter 7)

Again this theme mainly concerns the women, since the most helpless are the most likely to suffer. Caroline is the central example, but she is supplemented by Miss Mann, whose ill-health and penury make her sour, and by Robert Moore, whose financial straits make him hard. The novel examines both the immediate effect when Robert Moore, 'not far off the end of the plank' (Chapter 9) himself, antagonizes William Farren by being quite unable to show any sympathy for a man with a starving family; and also the final result in Miss Mann who, judging her neighbours, 'went to work at this business in a singularly cool, deliberate manner, like some surgeon practising with his scalpel on a lifeless subject: she made few distinctions; she allowed scarcely any one to be good; she dissected impartially almost all her acquaintance' (Chapter 10).

Whereas the material for *Jane Eyre* was primarily Jane herself and what happened to her, with a close identification between character and author, the material of *Shirley* is very obviously *other people*. Few characters in *Jane Eyre* can be conclusively identified with real persons; those in *Shirley* were lifelike enough to expose their anonymous author and were promptly identified by the originals and by their acquaintances. Leaving on one side the remarkable achievement of being able to produce such readily identifiable portraits in a work of fiction, and even admitting that the portraits from observation like Mr Yorke do not entirely harmonize with Caroline (still drawn largely from Charlotte Brontë) there is remarkably little discord or obvious difference in handling between the actual and the imagined personalities. Likewise there is never any sense of shock or disharmony when startlingly different types come together or change roles. The grotesque and wholly unsympathetic Mr Donne may be hunted into the bedrooms by Tartar as a subject for farce, and may very soon after be a fit object for Shirley's righteous wrath when demanding extortionate sums for charity (Chapter 15).

Characters, consciously and widely varied, seem more varied because they are not all seen through the responses of one character: they behave differently in different situations, and according to whom they affect. Matthewston Helstone is probably the most striking example of the various aspects of one nature: he is seen first as the sardonic and masterful rector in his dealings with the curates; he is then analysed as the man who has missed his vocation – 'he should have been a soldier, and circumstances had made him a priest' (Chapter 3); he next reveals himself as the High Tory political antagonist to the radical Yorke, as the insensitive husband of the woman Yorke loved, and as the insensitive uncle of the orphan Caroline. Charlotte Brontë thus gives herself more freedom and more power. Yet she seems at times to feel the weight of too much liberty, and is unequal to her task. Though characters are decisively differentiated, yet in like situations – especially crises – they tend to show like qualities. Excitement thrills them, and exceptional events stimulate them to exceptional action: the attack on the mill draws Helstone, Moore and Malone, and also Caroline and Shirley to similar excitement and similar impulses, despite their very different natures. They also tend to share the same language to an extent that class and region cannot account for. When not being Irish (Malone), French (Moore), or eccentrically. rustic (Yorke) they use a language very similar to their author's; and, as will be examined later, it would be difficult to tell from expression alone, without the aid of content and context, which of the main characters were speaking.

Though the origins of the characters vary, and though the author is deliberately working on different lines, she still sees the novel in terms of the separate individual and his perceptions – in terms of character – so that examination of individual personalities is much more useful in Charlotte Brontë's work than in *Wuthering Heights*. Of these separate characters the most important are women. This need not be a limitation, since theoretically a woman's perception of women may be as valuable as a man's of men. Jane Austen found it so, as did Charlotte Brontë herself in *Jane Eyre*. But Charlotte Brontë here has committed herself to a subject which demands, if it is to succeed, an at times equal perception of both sexes. In this she patently fails. The most notable disaster, Louis Moore, and the other lesser ones, will be examined in their place. The successes are generally characters who amuse, and those who are drawn from life, yet even here we meet with dissension, since many readers detest the curates, and fail to register the humour pervading the Yorkshire speakers in general, and appearing in many passing observations.

Charlotte Brontë wisely exercises great discretion and restraint in the bulk of the novel. She does not attempt to go deeply into the motives and impulses of her men. That she is not equipped to do so is amply proved by the journal of Louis Moore. Even though her restraint itself can be very effective, and Robert Moore can gain a power and interest from his chance remarks and ambiguous details of conduct that his uneasy beginning does not suggest, yet the men inevitably become secondary characters, even though the weight of the plot and most of the action belongs to them; while Caroline and even Shirley become the most important, though both are essentially passive, not initiating action but acted upon by others.

In creating and manipulating characters Charlotte Brontë wisely keeps clear also of relationships she does not comprehend. Her main characters are conspicuously parentless, depending for family ties on brothers and sisters, uncles and cousins. The exceptions are the Yorkes, who are as a family so eccentric as not to call on ordinary standards for judgement; and Caroline and her late-found mother Mrs Pryor, whose relationship, as far as possible removed by circumstances from any usual one between mother and daughter, somewhat disarms criticism. Some of the most successfully revealed relationships are unusual ones for a novelist to concern himself with. Charlotte Brontë has a sure hand with associations between different ages and sexes, often represented with delicacy and humour, and most successful where there is an element of rivalry or feud.[1] While

[1] They are unique to *Shirley* since neither *Jane Eyre* nor *Villette* offers scope for them, though their attraction for Charlotte Brontë was disclosed by the relations between Jane Eyre and Mr Rochester during their month's engagement.

Shirley herself alone often fails to convince, Shirley talking to the clergymen Hall and Helstone is a refreshing pleasure, revealing very convincingly the charm which Charlotte Brontë means her to possess, and disclosing sides of the clergymen hitherto unsuspected. Almost equally engaging are the scenes between Caroline and young Martin Yorke, whose behaviour, if not his actual thought-processes, impress the reader as being both original and true.[1]

Characters in *Shirley* offer themselves for classification. There is considerable patterning of an obvious kind: the active heroine Shirley with a congenial and diffident governess balances the passive heroine Caroline with an insensitive and dominant uncle; Shirley's ineligible lover is the brother of her spiritual sister Caroline's eligible one; Shirley's young, sensitive, intimate, crippled admirer Henry Sympson parallels Caroline's uninhibited, newly-acquainted, and robust one Martin Yorke; there is a radical landowner (Yorke) to contrast with a Tory parson and an independent mill-owner; there is a rigid continental housekeeper (Hortense) to balance a rigid indigenous one (Mrs Yorke), and there are three parsons, three curates, and three old maids. Classifications according to function produce different categories, and according to treatment different ones again, while within each group are characters both from life and from invention, and some characters may be in a different group at different points in the novel. The effect is one of variety, complexity, richness and truth. It becomes more profitable at this point to take major characters individually, and minor characters in appropriate small groups.

Caroline Helstone, despite the novel's title, is the most important: the most closely observed, the closest to the author, and the one whose fate concerns us most. She has many points of interest, uses she shares with Shirley, uses peculiar to herself, and a handling which provides a guide to her author's development.

With Shirley, Caroline reveals, as has been said, her author's

---

[1] Unfortunately the parallel situation between young Henry Sympson and Shirley is an embarrassing failure, chiefly because Charlotte Brontë has denied them any friction, and herself any humour in its representation, and has declined into falsity in the effort to avoid sentimentality.

concern with the position of women. Even though what we feel most keenly are the things Caroline lacks by contrast with Shirley, yet she is a proof of Charlotte Brontë's growing power since Caroline, unlike Jane Eyre, has a great many apparent advantages. She is pretty, and as a rector's niece has a safe place in the world – at least while he lives. Her sufferings touch us more for being first spiritual, and physical only as a consequence. She joins with Shirley also as a light on others – neither being fully informed about events, each supplements the other. Both are intelligent and perceptive, and the eyes of Caroline, a native of the district, supplement those of Shirley, the candid and unprejudiced newcomer. Caroline's own pleasantly mingled humour and seriousness make her an attractive guide, whose judgement we trust. Humour reveals itself in quiet irony:

> 'Put all crotchets out of your head [says Mr Helstone *apropos* the governess scheme], and run away and amuse yourself.'
> 'What with? My doll?' asked Caroline to herself as she quitted the room. (Chapter 11)

in delicate indulgence of the sentiment she diagnoses in the gentle bachelor rector Mr Hall:

> '*you* don't care for a bouquet, but you must give it to Margaret: only – to be sentimental for once – keep that little forget-me-not, which is a wild-flower I gathered from the grass; and – to be still more sentimental – let me take two or three of the blue blossoms and put them in my souvenir.' (Chapter 15)

and in the many acute perceptions of Robert Moore, about whom her love does not blind her, but increases her understanding – a useful and necessary state of affairs when what the reader sees of him in person (particularly with Shirley) is often both ambiguous and unattractive.

Louis Moore excepted, Caroline is her author's only assistant as a method of perception; she is sensibility at work in a cold and materialistic setting. She has the full power of Charlotte Brontë's sympathy behind her, and is necessarily the more interesting heroine, having a full ten chapters' start of her rival Shirley. Since the

workings of her mind are visible she is often seen moving towards
conclusions the author already holds and the reader already perceives, giving progression and development to themes which, without her, might well remain mere author's dicta, certainly unfelt,
probably static, and possibly unconvincing. She guides the reader
also to positions he would not reach unaided, that would seem
heterodox and even unacceptable if, with Caroline's feelings unknown, they were voiced by the narrator on the mere external
evidence of Caroline's plight. Such musings as this would certainly
come oddly from a narrator (and could well cause embarrassment
to one who was also daughter to a clergyman):

'Does virtue lie in abnegation of self? I do not believe it. Undue
humility makes tyranny; weak concession creates selfishness. The
Romish religion especially teaches renunciation of self, submission
to others, and nowhere are found so many grasping tyrants as in the
ranks of the Romish priesthood. Each human being has his share of
rights. I suspect it would conduce to the happiness and welfare of all,
if each knew his allotment, and held to it as tenaciously as the martyr
to his creed. Queer thoughts these, that surge in my mind: are they
right thoughts? I am not certain.

'Well, life is short at the best: seventy years, they say, pass like a
vapour, like a dream when one awaketh; and every path trod by
human feet terminates in one bourne – the grave: the little chink in
the surface of this great globe – the furrow where the mighty hus-
bandman with the scythe deposits the seed he has shaken from the
ripe stem; and there it falls, decays, and thence it springs again, when
the world has rolled round a few times more. So much for the body:
the soul meantime wings its long flight upward, folds its wings on
the brink of the sea of fire and glass, and gazing down through the
burning clearness, finds there mirrored the vision of the Christian's
triple Godhead: the Sovereign Father; the Mediating Son; the
Creator Spirit. Such words, at least, have been chosen to express
what is inexpressible, to describe what baffles description. The soul's
real hereafter, who shall guess?'   (Chapter 10)

In the actual personality created in Caroline, Charlotte Brontë
shows herself to have gained in assurance. Caroline is a pretty, sub-
missive heroine who thereby runs the risk of being a conventional

nonentity; she is a figure of pathos and misfortune, and thereby
risks sentimentality; small matters cause her suffering, so she risks
being trivial; and her situation, friendless and lovelorn, is a 'romantic' one, and so risks being neither solid nor real. Charlotte Brontë
makes it quite clear she knows what she is about; Caroline is treated
in a manner as down-to-earth, as anti-romantic, and as unsentimental as possible. Her looks are no mere ornament but an aspect of
her personality (epitomized in the 'little Rafaelle head' (Chapter 29)
which Louis Moore observes), and a barometer of her spiritual state:

> the hues of her complexion were paler, her eyes changed – a wan
> shade seemed to circle them, her countenance was dejected: she was
> not, in short, so pretty or so fresh as she used to be.   (Chapter 10)

She becomes pathetic by the most precise and Tennysonian details
combined with her own clear view of herself:

> for Moore's manly companionship, she had the thin illusion of her
> own dim shadow on the wall. Turning from the pale phantom which
> reflected herself in its outline, and her reverie in the drooped attitude
> of its dim head and colourless tresses, she sat down – inaction would
> suit the frame of mind into which she was now declining – she said
> to herself:–
> 'I have to live, perhaps, till seventy years. As far as I know, I have
> good health: half a century of existence may lie before me. How am
> I to occupy it? What am I to do to fill the interval of time which
> spreads between me and the grave?'
> She reflected.
> 'I shall not be married, it appears,' she continued. 'I suppose, as
> Robert does not care for me, I shall never have a husband to love,
> nor little children to take care of. Till lately I had reckoned securely
> on the duties and affections of wife and mother to occupy my
> existence. I considered, somehow, as a matter of course, that I was
> growing up to the ordinary destiny, and never troubled myself to
> seek any other; but now, I perceive plainly, I may have been mis-
> taken. Probably I shall be an old maid. I shall live to see Robert
> married to some one else, some rich lady: I shall never marry. What
> was I created for, I wonder? Where is my place in the world?'
>
>   (Chapter 10)

Pathos is never strained after; and mitigating details are constantly brought forward, as in Robert's passing remark that 'even at fifty you will not be repulsive' (Chapter 10), or Fanny the maid's genuine if limited sympathy, or Shirley's intelligent companionship. Sentimentality is entirely avoided. Charlotte Brontë is restrained in the presence of personal emotion, deliberately reducing it even by the context in which she places it, notably in Chapter 23, where Caroline's day –

> whose long, bright, noiseless, breezeless, cloudless hours (how many they had seemed since sunrise!) had been to her as desolate as if they had gone over her head in the shadowless and trackless wastes of Zahara –

breaks into momentary pleasure when Hortense invites her to the cottage, but is vigorously checked by the encounter with Mrs Yorke and her insults:

> 'Are you aware that, with all these romantic ideas, you have managed to train your features into an habitually lackadaisical expression, better suited to a novel-heroine than to a woman who is to make her way in the real world, by dint of common sense?'

Caroline has to act here and her passive state is broken, while the reader's own possible unspoken criticisms are destroyed when uttered so uncongenially. Emotions are always handled with precision, particularly where sloppiness is both the easy and the conventional thing – notably in Caroline's and Mrs Pryor's firm distinction between 'love' and 'forgiveness' (Chapter 34) for the drunken and not to be regretted husband and father. Charlotte Brontë deals as accurately with Caroline's physical struggles as with her mental ones – few novelists can suggest sleeplessness so well – showing (as she knows from experience) that distinction between them is difficult. She knows equally unsentimentally that recovery from mental and physical ills is not instantaneous or automatic when the cause of them is removed: Caroline's long hot summer of wishing to recover though not able to (Chapter 24) is as impressive as her long decline.

Caroline must in many ways recall Jane Eyre: small, neat, friendless, original, suffering in mind and body; probably because both are based on some aspects of their creator. Having less vitality, and being of less importance in the whole novel, she is of course less fascinating than Jane. This does not indicate a falling-off in Charlotte Brontë's powers, but a different role. The heart of Jane Eyre was her passionate and triumphant fulfilment of her emotional and her moral being. The heart of Caroline is her long and patient suffering under the frustration of all her possible sources of hope. This takes up much more of her story than her return to health and her final happiness, and is what makes, and is intended to make, the deepest impression on the reader. Caroline's career is deliberately less fantastic than Jane's: it has no sensational events except regaining her mother, and no startlingly unique tests or ordeals, while her final content rests in a clearly very imperfect husband with whom her relationship bears no comparison with Jane's and Rochester's.

Caroline's antitype is Shirley Keeldar, the eponymous heroine with the man's name and station. She is not, though the novel bears her name, the overwhelming interest, nor is there any reason why she should be, any more than Daniel Deronda is, or Nostromo, or, as an extreme example, Tristram Shandy. She comes second to Caroline. Some of her functions have been necessarily discussed along with Caroline's, which she complements either by resemblance or difference. Their romances are apparently very unlike, but oddly similar in that the two girls are the novel's only characters with much faith in either human nature or human affections, and in that both, though sure of the object of their affections, are unable to make the first matrimonial move. Unlike Caroline Shirley is active, both in the social and the emotional affairs of the novel. She is to some extent a mover of the plot, since it is she who saves Moore from bankruptcy by financing him after his first loss at the hand of the framebreakers. She is one of the reader's means of observing the Mill's affairs: it is Shirley's midnight escapade that conducts the reader to the attack on the mill in Chapter 19, and through her he observes the aftermath of confusion, arrests, care of the wounded, and local reaction in the chapter aptly entitled 'Tomorrow' (Chapter 20). She is also frequently the voice of the reader's own response at points where Caroline is inadequate, especially where Robert Moore is concerned, and especially at her idiosyncratic but essentially just outburst:

'He is a puppy – your cousin: a quiet, serious, sensible, judicious, ambitious puppy.'

(Chapter 14)

Shirley is presented as a figure whose mystery is part of her attraction. Charlotte Brontë tells of her nature, but not her thoughts, which we are left to deduce from her words and behaviour. As in a detective story, the clues are clear in retrospect, and noticeable enough at the time of reading to make the reader refuse to take her at her face value, and to realize that what she confides to Caroline is often ambiguous. Most of the ambiguity surrounds her relations with Robert. Charlotte Brontë has steered her course well here, since we must feel she has given Robert enough unwitting encouragement to make his proposal to her a reasonable (if self-seeking) act, while we must feel equally that she has not been acting immodestly. The greatest problem this ambiguity sets for author and reader is in Shirley's association with Caroline. She is clearly intended to understand Caroline's situation and sympathize with her, yet she must apparently be ignorant of how her friendship with Robert increases Caroline's misery; serious limitations are thus implied, in her perception and in the very sympathy we are supposed to admire. Since the reader sees very clearly how the supposed romance with Robert torments Caroline, cutting her off so soon from her new-found and only friend, we inevitably feel that Shirley ought to perceive it too, and we judge her for appearing to trifle, not with Robert's affections, but worse, with Caroline's.

Of Shirley's nature the aspect recognized by Mr Helstone as 'Captain Keeldar' is the most original and best. Shirley succeeds as a public rather than a private figure; memorable much more for laughing at an embarrassed Malone tying up his knees in a silk hand-kerchief, for discomfiting Sam Wynne and spilling her tea on purpose at the school feast, for rejecting the carving-knife in favour of a brace of pistols as a weapon against marauders, and for sending the entire contents of the Fieldhead larder and wine-cellar in hay-carts on the morning after the mill is attacked, as provisions for a mere six soldiers. Such incidents are far more vivid than her inti-mate conversations with Caroline, and still more intimate ones with

Louis Moore, or even her domestic interludes, making toast before
the school-room fire or practising French.[1]

The charm she undoubtedly exerts over the reader at the same
time as over the other characters consists in her mixture of the unconventional and the down-to-earth in speech and sentiment: here
for instance she is considering with Robert his possible supporters
in defence of the mill:

> 'Shall I speak to Mr Helstone? I will, if you like ... that is, if I
> can win him.'
> 'Whom can you not win?'
> 'Perhaps not the Rector; but I will make the effort.'
> 'Effort! He will yield for a word – a smile.'
> 'By no means. It will cost me several cups of tea, some toast and
> cake, and an ample measure of remonstrances, expostulations, and
> persuasions.' (Chapter 13)

Such unconventional and practical reactions on minor matters
prepare the reader to accept similar responses on graver events:
lightly though she speaks of the carving knife and pistols, we believe she could use both; and they in their turn prepare us to accept
later that she has indeed used a red-hot iron to cauterize the bite on
her own arm. But, since the representation of Shirley moves
steadily from the public to the private, she seems to fall off towards
the end of the novel, though defying her uncle Sympson gives her
some of her finest moments.[2]

Shirley seems to have several literary antecedents, all of them
linked in Charlotte Brontë's consciousness. She is professedly based
on Emily, *in posse* rather than *in esse*; she is also perceptibly an ex-

[1] It is notable that her clothes even, which Charlotte Brontë takes pains to
mention (though wisely not to detail) are for social rather than domestic wear:
her 'purple dress' of 'rich silk' with a 'deep embroidered scarf' (Chapter 17)
worn for the school feast, emphasized by the contrast with Caroline's white
muslin one with a white crape scarf, suggests a difference not merely of expense
and temperament, but of role.
[2] The failure may be explained (though not of course mitigated) by the connection between Shirley and Emily Brontë which, Emily being so recently
and dreadfully dead, may well have inhibited Charlotte, imposing a restraint
on her which impedes the reader, and which manifests itself in the sudden use
of Louis' 'journal' in place of the narrator.

pansion and re-working of Diana Rivers – handsome, lively, un-conventional – who was herself the Emily-figure in *Jane Eyre*; while both clearly owe something to Scott's Diana Vernon in *Rob Roy*, that early version of the unorthodox and active heroine who adopts a brotherly, manly tone to all about her, and whose name Charlotte Brontë has already borrowed, even in the very unusual spelling of the diminutive – 'Die'. Shirley also seems to be related – allowing, of course, for the vastly different context, theme, and treatment – to Catherine Earnshaw, which further brings out the connection with Emily: her young adviser Henry Sympson re-calls her schooldays in these terms:

'She was a wild, laughing thing, but pleasant to have in the room: she made lesson-time charming. She learned fast – you could hardly tell when or how. French was nothing to her: she spoke it quick – quick; as quick as Mr Moore himself.'
'Was she obedient? Did she give trouble?'
'She gave plenty of trouble in a way: she was giddy, but I liked her. . . .'
(Chapter 26)

There can be no doubt that Shirley, even though she is well-con-ceived throughout and in her early career skilfully handled, is a problem for her author and not, in the final estimate, a complete success.

With two heroines come two heroes, brothers who balance the spiritual sisterhood of the girls. They have not much else in com-mon, since their roles differ as widely as their treatment. Robert Moore is by far the more impressive, important, deeply-observed and surely-handled. He is the hero as far as the novel has one, not simply by being the man Caroline is to marry, but by being the man whose struggles and eventual success form the framework of the novel; the single and, at times, unsupported opponent of the forces of disorder the frame-breakers; the embodiment of the plight of the manufacturer in times of hardship; the centre of the economic and social plot, around whom all the examination of national and local politics rotates. He is also the embodiment of ambition, whose various forms are studied and judged in his career, particularly in his relations with Shirley, from whom he borrows money – uncon-ventionally and legitimately – and attempts to marry for her fortune

– conventionally and reprehensibly. His being part-Flemish is useful, since the state of Europe is an important background question.
Moore can reasonably hold views that are European rather than
English, and can thus provoke discussion of what is at stake in
disputes with Yorke and Helstone – discussion very necessary to
enlighten the reader. Just as Caroline is memorable in misfortune,
he is memorable and impressive when facing disaster, both in
general (he faces it, present or in prospect, for thirty-six chapters
out of thirty-seven) and in particular incidents. We recall Robert
at his most finely-observed when defying not only the mill-
breakers but his neighbours Yorke and Helstone; when wearing

> the smile a man of determined spirit wears when he reaches a
> juncture in his life where this determined spirit is to feel a demand
> on its strength: when the strain is to be made, and the faculty must
> bear or break.   (Chapter 2)

He is, as the sixth chapter makes plain, a Coriolanus in a cottage.
He is seen first of all as a public man, in relation to other men –
grilling chops with Malone, disputing over the Peninsular War
with Helstone, and exchanging abuse in French with Yorke; he is
therefore safe from seeming effeminate when seen thereafter chiefly
through the eyes of Caroline, who is the means whereby his private
nature is made as important as his public one. His motives are
detectable only from what his actions suggest, what he himself says,
and what Caroline can deduce. The author's summaries of him
only reinforce and render explicit one or other of the main sources.
She tells us nothing that Robert himself is concealing from other
characters. He must be somewhat of a mystery to the reader to
render it acceptable for him to puzzle and distress Caroline, but his
motives must equally be clear enough for his character to be judged.
Caroline is a fair guide to how he regards herself – affection over-
ruled by ambition – but is not of course able to guide us through his
courtship of Shirley, where detailed incidents and Shirley's own
reactions combine to suggest that the situation is not as straightforward as it seems. He becomes more attractive than his own role
permits by the force of contrast. Despite poverty, ambition, and
some rather reprehensible acts, he is clearly superior, not only to the

curates in drawing-room manners, but to Yorke or Helstone in political broadmindedness, to the young aristocrat Sir Philip Nunnely in intellect, and even in looks and initiative (if not intellect and sensibility) to his own brother. Despite his unpromising beginning Caroline's final dictum 'nowhere so perfect a gentleman as at your own fireside' (Chapter 37) rings true.

Robert Moore owes a good deal to St John Rivers: he too has features of 'a southern symmetry, clearness, regularity in their chiselling' (Chapter 2); he too might call himself like St John a 'cold, hard, ambitious man'; and he too is cousin to the heroine, whom he dominates and whose emotions he tramples on; but he is a great deal more subtle a creation, being another personality set up like Mr Rochester in opposition to the usual concept of a hero for a novel.

His brother Louis is a true novelist's problem: a character who does not even appear until the novel is two-thirds over, is unconnected with the main action, has nothing to do but wait for others to act, no one to whom he can talk, and emotions which must be concealed from everyone but the reader. His function, though, is well-conceived. He is an illuminating pair to his brother in appearance, career and personality. His emotional ambitions are clearly as high as Robert's worldly ones, and he is equally dogged and self-sufficient. As a potential partner for Shirley he is apt: mature, undemonstrative, unworldly and unhandsome; becoming even more convincing after we hear the terms in which she has rejected Robert. Louis' late arrival is a wise arrangement, since there is quite enough action in the early part of the novel; but, after Robert's disastrous proposal for Shirley and his near-assassination have brought him to his senses and reconciled him with Caroline, Robert's affairs must wait inactively for the repeal of the Orders in Council which allow him to trade and prosper, and therefore a new impulse is welcome.

It is in the treatment of Louis that the trouble lies. Charlotte Brontë prevents herself from using any of the obvious and mechanical ways of linking Louis to the main action: to allow him to be seen with his brother or his friend the clergyman Mr Hall, or to share in conversation with his sister or even with Caroline, would all do away with the isolation that Charlotte Brontë is at pains to preserve. It is in fact wise of the author to be drastic, and change her method entirely, and use the self-revelatory journal, even though the result is not a success. She had nothing to lose: by any other means she is absolutely certain to fail in producing the power of emotion needed if Shirley's courtship is to parallel Caroline's; by using the interior monologue and the journal – which she knew she could handle, having done so before – she had a good chance of succeeding, and indeed does succeed up to a point. She does rouse in the reader excitement and an impression of intense suppressed feeling when Shirley confesses her fear of hydrophobia, or when Louis finally declares his love; and it is most fitting that Louis, who understands and responds most keenly to Shirley, should be the reader's means of perceiving what she feels. But yet Louis Moore is neither convincingly related to the other characters, nor satisfactory in himself. The material that was adequate to create a Crimsworth is inadequate in the context of *Shirley*. The reader did not cavil when Crimsworth's teaching skill rested only on English and French translation, since this was all that Belgian school-children required. The same skill seems inadequate as the only one Louis can teach Shirley, especially when it was also the one Hortense taught Caroline. The personality that coped with Crimsworth's situation, with the inmates of a Belgian pensionnat, with a Mlle Reuter and with a Frances Henri, does not seem adequate either for the husband of Shirley or for the future landlord of a Yorkshire farming and manufacturing estate during the Industrial Revolution.

The rest of the dramatis personae range themselves round these main ones, their functions generally determining the degree of emphasis they receive, with the single exception of the Yorke family who overspread the bounds set for them by the story. The most successful are probably the ones where humour or local colour has the greatest play, such as Helstone and the curates; while the most important are those most closely influencing the two heroines, such as Helstone again, and Mrs Pryor.

It is easier to see what is wrong with Mrs Pryor than to do justice to her importance, or to realize how far she actually performs what is intended of her. She is a unique member of the group of middle-aged persons; as a widow she balances the married woman Mrs Yorke, and the spinster Misses Mann, Ainley, Hall and Moore. With them she is part of a dialogue about marriage (paralleled on another side by Mr Helstone) in which they set off their views against those of Caroline and Shirley. Though having little in common personally, both Mrs Pryor and Helstone are directors of the heroine's conduct, and both are disillusioned cynics about marriage. They thus make clear that Caroline's own bleak stoicism is not cynical. By her own deficiencies Mrs Pryor reveals those of others: her oddities do not make her repulsive to persons of real worth, while her inertia on one memorable occasion is a moral comment on Shirley's excessive zeal: her holding back from sending supplies to the mill turns out to be no less well-judged, and far less ridiculous, than Shirley's over-provisioning.

Unfortunately Mrs Pryor's main role is as Caroline's mother, in which she conspicuously fails, partly because Charlotte Brontë is attempting to create what she has no personal experience of (though this has not hampered her elsewhere) but mainly because the situation of the grown-up daughter meeting the never-known parent is an almost impossible one for any novelist to tackle as a secondary topic in a work which has many other preoccupations. Yet in many ways Mrs Pryor is well handled. Charlotte Brontë provides many hints to the relationship – Mrs Pryor's concern for Caroline's health and her story of her marriage – and takes good care to build up confidence and intimacy between Caroline and her mother before the relationship is known, so that their coming together is no mere sentimental convention.

Mr Helstone is almost her antithesis, the vehicle of Caroline's frustration, as Mrs Pryor is of her release; an active, self-assured man who is connected, unbeknownst, to a passive, diffident woman, of whom he has always disapproved and yet with whom he finally, and quite convincingly, learns to live. Helstone has other functions: as a type of cleric offsetting Boultby and Hall, as a fierce Tory contrasting with Yorke and Robert Moore, as an exposer of fools (notably the empty-headed Misses Sykes), and as a foil for Shirley. And he has more life than these functions would suggest. He impresses chiefly by his vigorous and characteristic speech, through which, being a fairly simple though original nature, he can display himself. He has two main traits: 'He should have been a soldier, and circumstances had made him a priest' (Chapter 3), and he has an inflexibly low opinion of women. His appearances are generally a delight for his vigour and wry humour; whether making easy prey of the curates:

'Davy, thou hast an enormous organ of Wonder in thy cranium; Malone, you see, has none; neither murders, nor visions interest him: see what a big, vacant Saph, he looks at this moment ... from a boy upwards, I have always attached a personality to Saph. Depend on it he was honest, heavy and luckless; he met his end at Gob, by the hand of Sibbechai.' (Chapter 1)

or ironically exposing his own deficient sensibility:

'Now, here is the very same little silver fork you used when you first came to the Rectory: that strikes me as being what you may call a happy thought – a delicate attention. Take it, Cary, and munch away cleverly.' (Chapter 24)

Opposing Helstone is Yorke; like him outspoken, politically-minded, sure of his position; unlike him a radical, cosmopolitan, secular head of a family. He and his family are interesting, original, and convincing,[1] and have a variety of uses: Yorke is a businessman to contrast with Moore, an exponent of clerical views opposing Helstone, and of political views at odds with both of them. Mrs Yorke, already mentioned as a type of womanhood, emphasizes Caroline's pathetic isolation. As a family they represent Yorkshire society, not least by being a set of jarring individuals; they are another social point of reference, Briarmains clearly assuming a place somewhere between the Mill and the Rectory, and Shirley's own Fieldhead; and they embody the claims of the individual, since all the children assert their separate independence and individuality. Parental love, though seen to exist (Yorke loves Rose and pets Jessie, while Mrs Yorke favours the dangerous oldest son Matthew), is yet not a powerful influence. They are split by dissension, and oppose at some point all the other characters. Through them in-

[1] And apparently also instantly identifiable, since once *Shirley* was published the identity of Currer Bell was no longer a secret.

dividuality, and consequently isolation and loneliness, seem to be a law of a life in which only the strong survive:

> 'Miss Helstone is not my mother's match [says Rose] – for she allows herself to be vexed: my mother would wear her out in a few weeks. Shirley Keeldar manages better. Mother, you have never hurt Miss Keeldar's feelings yet. She wears armour under her silk dress that you cannot penetrate.' (Chapter 23)

The family, more use to the themes than to the plot, has little to do, and makes its effect by dialogue and analysis. Their handling suggests the art of the biographer rather than the novelist. Each member of the family is dealt with fully and equally on the first united appearance in Chapter 9 in a way that seems to preclude development and do away with expectation – we hear that Rose will travel to New Zealand alone and that Jessie will die young abroad. Only Matthew, compared with Vesuvius, seems a possible source of action, while it is in fact Martin, contriving Caroline's visits to the invalid Robert, who is the one to re-enter and influence the story.

The curates by contrast are clearly designed to be of use, and have more purpose than their obviously amusing appearances suggest. They are a level of society in themselves, and by being from areas as remote as Southern England and Ireland they demonstrate that 'narrow' and 'parochial' are more than simply synonyms for 'stay-at-home'. They define their respective rectors: Sweeting, the best of the bunch, belongs to Mr Hall; the bellicose Malone to Helstone; and the uncouth Donne to Boultby. When Caroline declares she must be an old maid because 'I will never marry a Malone or a Sykes – and no one else will ever marry me' (Chapter 12) we, knowing Malone, acquit her of over-strained sentiment. They provoke self-revelation in others: Donne arouses Shirley's rage by demanding her charity, Malone provokes Helstone's humour – a quality without much chance to show itself. Yet they are primarily a source of easy and felicitous comedy, of situation allowing the author's strong sense of fun one of its few outlets in this novel: Donne, fleeing in terror from Shirley's bulldog Tartar, holding the door of Mrs Pryor's bedroom against the onslaughts of both dog and the fleeing Malone (Chapter 15), is as memorable as Malone in his own difficulties, 'left entirely to his own resources, on a large sofa, with the charge of three small cushions on his hands' (Chapter 7).

By contrast with the characters of action like the curates are those like the spinsters who do their part simply by existing. Miss Mann, Miss Ainley, and Miss Hall say nothing and advance the action not at all. Their business is to exist for our consideration and Caroline's, rather than to impress or move us in themselves, bearing out (like the refusal to discuss child workers) that Charlotte Brontë's pre-occupations are personal and interior rather than social. By contrast yet again come the occasionally appearing Yorkshire-speaking workers, who exist mainly by speech. Joe Scott and William Farren are both types, one the uneducated but canny overseer, the other the indigent and helpless victim of social depression. Both are done with decorum and restraint; witness the sure hand at humour and the absence of caricature of Mr Yorke's story:

> 'I said, "Is there aught wrong anywhere?" – "'Deed is there," somebody says, speaking out of the ground, like. "What's to do? be sharp, and tell me," I ordered. – "Nobbut four on us ligging in a ditch," says Joe, as quiet as could be. I tell'd 'em, more shame to 'em, and bid them get up and move on, or I'd lend them a lick of the gig-whip; for my notion was, they were all fresh. – "We'd ha' done that an hour sin'; but we're teed wi' a bit o' band," says Joe.'
>
> (Chapter 3)

The way in which characters are organized and their settings enhance them – the parishes of Nunneley, Briarfield, and Whinbury, the manors of Fieldhead, Briarmains and de Walden Hall, the simpler houses of the rectory and the cottage, and of the landscape of Stilboro' Moor and of Nunnwood – all bear witness to the care for structure that has gone into *Shirley*. As far as conscious planning can make a novel succeed, *Shirley* does. Its more complex plot is as coherent as *Jane Eyre's*, and even better contrived. The first six chapters skilfully deal all the cards with which the hand is to be played, only excepting Shirley, the ace up the author's sleeve. We are in possession of Moore's financial difficulties, the state of his relations with his workpeople and his neighbours, of the nature of the Yorke family, who are to advise Moore, shelter him in sickness, and alternately separate and unite him and Caroline, we have met Mr Helstone who separates them, and the supposed orphan Caroline who is to be the emotional centre of the story. Charlotte Brontë never loses any of the threads of her plot (though the reader may well do) even though several of them drop out of sight as more apparently unconnected events supervene.

Attention to detail is unobtrusive yet unflagging. The necessary coincidences are anticipated and prepared, though their essential nature is not glossed over. The two most important are that the brother of Shirley's tenant Robert Moore should be tutor in the family of Shirley's uncle Mr Sympson; and that Shirley's own governess Mrs Pryor should be the eighteen years lost mother of Caroline Helstone. There are plenty of clues – of the intellectual kind from which deductions can be made – to what is to happen, producing a sense of suspense and mystery. Shirley's liking to talk of Robert Moore with Caroline for instance, contrasting with her outburst against him as a 'quiet, serious, sensible, judicious, ambitious puppy' (Chapter 14); or her list of those whom she would consult on a man's character:

> 'the little Irish beggar that comes barefoot to my door; the mouse that steals out of the cranny in the wainscot; the bird that in frost and snow pecks at my window for a crumb; the dog that licks my hand and sits beside my knee.' (Chapter 12)

and her comment, when Caroline applies the definition to Robert, that 'I was well inclined to him before I saw him' (Chapter 12). When Louis arrives, and is seen feeding sparrows and able to entice Tartar away from Shirley, suspicion is certainty. Intellectually clear it may be that Shirley, though interested, does not love Robert, and that Robert may be acting upon the hints Yorke gave him about marrying for money (at the end of Chapter 9) and the imminent opportunity to do so –

> 'if you are sound both in heart and head, there is no reason why you should not profit by a good chance if it offers . . . I promise ye naught and I advise ye naught; but I bid ye keep your heart up, and be guided by circumstances.'

yet since Robert's and Shirley's emotions must necessarily be concealed, the situation cannot be an experience shared by author, character and reader, like Mr Rochester's wooing of Blanche Ingram; nor does the situation gain much additional power in retrospect when we know all, like that (to use another author) between Emma and Jane Fairfax and Frank Churchill. Jane Eyre declared that had Miss Ingram been a worthy object of Mr Rochester's affection ·

> I should have had one vital struggle with two tigers – jealousy and despair: then, my heart torn out and devoured, I should have admired her – acknowledged her excellence, and been quiet for the rest of my days. (*Jane Eyre*, Chapter 18)

This is the situation Caroline sees: but because Moore and Shirley have not impressed us so strongly nor been seen so clearly, Caroline's sufferings do not move us like Jane's. Mrs Pryor is similarly managed, but her attentions to Caroline and their natural affinity soon leave little room for doubt, when reinforced by Shirley's casual remarks:

> 'Mrs Pryor there sometimes talks of leaving me, and says I might make a more advantageous connection than herself. I should as soon think of exchanging an old-fashioned mother for something modish and stylish.' (Chapter 13)

In detail the action is most professionally handled. Charlotte Brontë is well aware that she has more, and more complex, material here than in *Jane Eyre*, and is a conscious and considerate storyteller. Simple evidence is that here for the first time she gives titles to her individual chapters, suggesting their thematic relevance as much as their content: 'Coriolanus', the episode in which Caroline spends the evening at the Cottage and reads Shakespeare with Robert, 'Tomorrow', recounting the effects of the attack on the Mill on all those concerned with it, and the ironically named 'Communications on Business' in which Caroline is the observer of one of Robert's calls on Shirley. Chapter divisions here contain and separate incidents from what precedes and follows, unlike those in *Jane Eyre*, which were used for an emphasis which advanced rather than impeded the flow.

As in *Jane Eyre* action, dialogue, and self reflection are balanced and interwoven, and seriousness is alternated with humour. However the transitions here are more clearly marked, by having an author-narrator, whose reflections have more weight and are more detached from events. This is necessary in work involving the public as well as the private, where Caroline is parted from Robert, for instance, because Helstone is outraged by Moore's politics. Charlotte Brontë's assurance as an author has increased, enabling her to interpolate her own dicta:

> All men, taken singly, are more or less selfish; and taken in bodies they are intensely so. The British merchant is no exception to this rule: the mercantile classes illustrate it strikingly. These classes certainly think too exclusively of making money: they are too oblivious of every national consideration but that of extending England's (*i.e.* their own) commerce. (Chapter 10)

The paragraph continues to condemn and exhort, only returning to Moore with the prayer:

> Long may it be ere England really becomes a nation of shopkeepers!

Comedy too is the narrator's prerogative; the humorous eye is usually hers, and comedy is embodied in secondary persons only, notably the curates and the unforgettable Mr Sympson.

Where she has a clear sense of her emotional purpose, not merely of the story, Charlotte Brontë succeeds as well, and by the same means, as in *Jane Eyre*. The events which drive Caroline to her breakdown are almost as well handled as those at Thornfield. The movement and material are unobtrusively and expertly managed, though full appreciation of them can only be had in retrospect. The visit of the Sympsons in Chapter 22 (significantly entitled 'Two Lives') deprives Caroline of her only remaining friend Shirley, prevents her from realizing – as closer contact would certainly have done – what Shirley felt for Robert, and leaves her weakened in spirit for her last evening at the cottage where, instead of peace and refreshment with Hortense, she finds she has to exert her last energy to refute Mrs Yorke's hints that she cultivated Hortense merely to angle for Robert. The excellence of the management here only becomes clear when it is realized that the Sympsons are introduced to bring Louis Moore into the story, an arrival superbly managed amidst burning black cherries and treacle, the circumstances being, at the time, almost more impressive than the man, like Mr Rochester's fall on the ice.

Time and the weather play their part as essentially as in *Jane Eyre*; though their symbolic relevance has vanished, the sense of history (already noted) has replaced it. The seasons dictate people's acts on a scale as small as Caroline's clothes, or as large as the School Feast at Whitsuntide; while the weather is all-pervasive. The twilight of a late October evening hangs over Robert and Yorke when Robert is shot on Rushedge. The feverish west wind of Chapter 25 is our means of perceiving Caroline's sickness, just as the varied weathers of Chapter 28, which do not prevent Shirley from riding on the moor, or walking when she thinks the weather too rough for her mare, signify her tormenting fear of hydrophobia. Yet taken as a whole the novel in retrospect does not feel as though it has a proper development. It seems to *stick* on each episode. The splendid impulse that drove *Jane Eyre* up to, through, and beyond its big scenes, which prepared for each other, and never rested for a moment even after ecstasy or disaster, is gone. There are great scenes, but it is not easy to remember the order in which they happen, or which grows out of or leads into the next. There is no discernible artistic reason why the attack on the Mill must necessarily follow the Sunday-school Feast, or why Caroline's attempts to see Moore, lying ill at Briarmains, should alternate with Louis' courtship of Shirley.[1]

Yet despite the obvious technical skill of *Shirley*, despite memorable scenes of a kind different from those in *Jane Eyre* or *Villette*, despite a worthy subject and a serious purpose, this remains Charlotte Brontë's least successful novel. While one may bear in mind

[1] This is a Thackerayan method, and clearly owes something to the alternating of Becky Sharpe's and Amelia Sedley's affairs in *Vanity Fair*; but whereas theirs are always mutually illuminating by running parallel and presenting satiric juxtapositions, neither illumination nor satire is in question in *Shirley*.

that it was written at the worst period of its author's life, that the deaths of her brother and sisters had exhausted its author, one may well, putting biography aside, and working only on internal evidence, feel that the novel was wrongly conceived, demanding powers its author did not own, and inhibiting the full use of those she demonstrably possessed.

5

VILLETTE

Charlotte Brontë's *Villette*, by being her last novel, tempts one to consider it the culmination of her career – 'Heaven's last best gift'. The three surviving chapters of another novel, *Emma*, prove that she herself did not think so. *Villette* itself puzzles greatly the reader who expects her to be not only different from what she has been before, but better. It is at first sight plainly not only less realistic than *Shirley*, but much less well constructed mechanically than either it or *Jane Eyre*. Its obvious affinities are with the early and imperfect *Professor*. Even though it returns to the freer, less demanding method of the single vision of the narrator-heroine, it abounds with inconsistencies and loose ends, while Lucy is clearly a less comprehensive, less vital, less appealing, and therefore less satisfying narrator-heroine than *Jane Eyre*. Yet that one reads and admires *Villette* must prove that it is no failure, and its having been preferred even to the undoubtedly great *Jane Eyre* indicates that it has qualities not to be found elsewhere.

Charlotte Brontë is here, as usual, a much more self-effacing – or rather self-concealing – author than she seems. Though it has always been plain that she has made use of more of her own experiences, and more of her nature, in Lucy's story, and Lucy herself, than in any other novel, yet it is a ridiculous oversimplification (just as it is in *Jane Eyre*) to assume that the heroine is the author, that how Lucy feels and judges her situation is how Charlotte Brontë does, or intends the reader to feel and judge. If Lucy were Charlotte Brontë's rendering of herself, the novel would be fascinating biographical quarry (and as such it has often been used), it might be useful as a psychological document in which its author 'wrote out' her own troubles, or as a social one in which she expounded her beliefs and conclusions; but it would not thereby be a good novel. However, *Villette* very soon makes plain that Lucy is a very much more limited nature than her author;[1] while the novel itself is even ridiculous considered as an examination of the position of the indigent English-woman in Brussels, or as a treatise on education in the 1840's. *Villette* is very close, not to the real-life basis of its own material, but (as will be examined later) to the same material as it was employed in the other novels. Thus *Villette*'s value must be, if anything at all, that of a conscious literary creation. On the other hand, it is almost equally unsatisfactory to think that in this novel Charlotte Brontë's innovation is to detach herself and the reader from the narrator, not permitting the reader to accept Lucy's responses as the valid ones (as he accepts Jane's), but to judge her by them, and to see the book as an interior study of an extraordinary personality whose conflicts are the novel's central preoccupation.[2] Charlotte Brontë's own remarks may be relevant here, if only to show what she thought she was about. She did not like Lucy, as her letters to her publisher proclaim, and the remarks bear out the sense we have of a different relationship between author and character from that in *Jane Eyre*.

> You say that she may be thought both morbid and weak, unless the history of her life be more fully given. I consider that she *is* both morbid and weak at times; her character sets up no pretensions to unmixed strength, and anybody living her life would necessarily become morbid. It was no impetus of healthy feeling which urged her to the confessional, for instance; it was the semi-delirium of solitary grief and sickness.[3]

(Letter to W. S. Williams, 6 November 1852)

A third hypothesis, that the opening chapters of the novel seem to suggest, where the girl Lucy observes the child Paulina, is that of

---

[1] Being certainly a great deal less able to write Charlotte Brontë's novels than David Copperfield to write Dickens, or Stephen Dedalus James Joyce's.

[2] The view is a fairly popular reaction from the one that reads *Villette* as autobiography and wish-fulfilment.

[3] Such violent expressions may nevertheless rouse the suspicion that Charlotte Brontë, afraid of how close what she has created has come to making public what might well be taken for her own most personal feelings, is sheltering herself behind rather overstated distaste.

an even greater degree of detachment between author, narrator, reader and material, that Lucy may not even be the heroine, but only an observer – a suggestion made again when Paulina re-enters the story. Plainly if this ever was a plan, it is soon abandoned, and Lucy, from being the frigid observer of others, becomes, as soon as she sets foot in Labassecour, the protagonist. As soon as Lucy begins to respond to life, Charlotte Brontë's methods are such (as they have always been) that we must respond with her, and detachment is lost – no bad thing. A plausible variant of this hypothesis is that Charlotte Brontë intended Lucy to be the central one of a group of instances of fortune and misfortune in life, set forth in Chapters 1–6, where we meet Lucy, Paulina, Miss Marchmont and Ginevra, all exhibiting different kinds and degrees of responses to life, and of awareness of their responsibilities. Again, however, this pattern, though it is felt intermittently throughout the novel, is clearly not the main one.

Yet a fourth interpretation offers itself of the relation between the author and her heroine: that Lucy is, more than Charlotte Brontë at first intended, an expression of Charlotte Brontë herself, not in her experiences merely, but in her own nature; the original intent being to advocate repressing feeling, and obeying the dictates of reason; but that Charlotte Brontë's passion, overwhelming her, is recreated as Lucy's.

Only one of these hypotheses – the second, that the author here stands apart from her narrator-heroine – can, if it come near to being demonstrably true of the whole work, make *Villette* the entire and achieved masterpiece, without fairly radical deficiencies of conception and performance, that *Jane Eyre* is. While it is tempting to think the best, and regard *Villette* as that new departure, the work in which Charlotte Brontë detaches herself and the reader from the heroine, yet still presents her with the deepest understanding, one yet must feel that the best things in this novel, though not the same as those in *Jane Eyre* or *The Professor*, yet call for the same quality of response from the reader, and do so by most of the same means. One can only conclude, when the novel's materials, structure, and techniques have been studied, that *Villette* is, in part, misconceived, but that the originality, and still more the quality, of what is best in it are such as to outweigh in a final judgement the obvious blunders.

Like Emily's in *Wuthering Heights*, Charlotte Brontë's ultimate purpose must be perceived – felt rather than deduced – from the preoccupations with which she concerns herself, and the light in which she presents them to the reader.

Villette is clearly more about people for their own sakes, rather than for what they represent, than is *Shirley*. It is clearly less about the progress of a single soul than is *Jane Eyre*. Though firmly placed in mid-nineteenth century Brussels it is less instantly recognizably everyday life and experience than is either. It is an extraordinary mixture of the romantic and the grotesque with the commonplace. Charlotte Brontë is occupied with the extreme. Lucy's predicaments are not straightforward, still less her solutions to them. Her perils are not temptation nor penury, like Jane's; one cannot find society culpable for her agonies, like Caroline's. Lucy is lonely and unfortunate, by temperament and by what fate sends her; she deliberately chooses isolation;[1] and she believes herself destined to misfortune. The novel's most moving scenes are its loneliest and most inward: Lucy's dreadful long autumn vacation and her confession, and her delirious wandering in the festive Park. Yet the novel has a most prosaic setting – a bourgeois pensionnat in a very small and bourgeois capital; it has events unsensational in themselves – though what Charlotte Brontë makes of them is another matter; an unattractive heroine – while Jane Eyre was plain, she was young and frank and full of life, while Lucy (at 24) is no longer young, doggedly self-repressing, and constitutionally unhopeful; and a hero, Paul Emmanuel, who is both comic and grotesque. Charlotte Brontë has thus cut herself off from much of her own strength and much of a novelist's material, and done so apparently deliberately. She cuts herself off even further in her choice of extremes. Whereas in *Jane Eyre* the extremes are of both kinds – happiness as well as misery, shared and felt alone, the ecstasy of Thornfield as well as the agony of Morton – *Villette* lives for what

---

[1] She need not have left England for a country whose language and religion were both alien, and when there she need not have rejected the opportunity to be sister and companion to Paulina de Bassompierre.

it tells of the agony that is experienced alone. This is a much tougher topic than any of the other novels ventures on. Charlotte Brontë makes no easy concessions to her reader's liking for the pleasanter emotions. The stress is always on pain. Lucy says very early 'the negation of severe suffering was the nearest approach to happiness I expected to know' (Chapter 8). Pure joy, still less ecstasy, is never offered to the reader, even on the one occasion when it is to Lucy. We look before and after, and the happiness is only the memory of Lucy the old woman telling the tale, whose hair is 'now at last white, under a white cap, like snow beneath snow' (Chapter 5), who has good reason for her belief that she is not one of those chosen to be happy in this life. With the single exception of the climax, Paul Emmanuel's proposal, and the three years following it spent waiting for his return from Antigua, the degrees of happiness experienced are all qualified in some way. Pleasure of life is for Lucy as for the Duchess of Malfi's Antonio, merely 'the good hours of an ague'. It is overshadowed by the well-grounded fear that it is illusory or, at best, transitory. The fear colours the whole of Lucy's association with Graham and extends to the smallest details. Her precious letter is snatched away from her as soon as got. Her single evening's pleasure alone with him, at the performance of Vashti, is the one when he meets Paulina. Paul Emmanuel himself is never to be the ideal lover: Charlotte Brontë emphasizes that the joy he offers her is of a modest order:

> I envied no girl her lover, no bride her bridegroom, no wife her husband; I was content with this my voluntary, self-offering friend. If he would but prove reliable, and he *looked* reliable, what, beyond his friendship, could I ever covet? But, if all melted like a dream, as once before happened —? (Chapter 35)

The hyperbole here depresses rather than elevates. He causes her indeed as much pain as the unreliable friend, being separated from her by ill-temper, misunderstanding, and his Roman Catholic faith, almost as soon as they come together. Even as her fiancé, Lucy does not forget, nor allow us to forget, his limitations.

Once – unknown and unloved, I held him harsh and strange; the

low stature, the wiry make, the angles, the darkness, the manner,
displeased me.
(Chapter 41)

They never change.

The attitude to these sufferings is not one that allows the indulgence of pity. The coldness of the young Lucy, who 'remained calm'
while witnessing the child Polly's 'dedful miz-er-y' (Chapter 3)
remains as self-repression. It does not occur to Lucy to hope to find
sympathy or to feel that the reader's response will be pity for one
in her situation:

> How strange it was to look on Mrs Bretton's seven weeks and con-
> trast them with my seven weeks! Also, how very wise it is in people
> placed in an exceptional position to hold their tongues and not
> declare how much a position galls them! The world can understand
> well enough the process of perishing for want of food: perhaps few
> persons can enter into or follow out that of going mad from solitary
> confinement.
> (Chapter 24)

Her hardness to herself is clearly not mere masochism, or even self-
righteous satisfaction in denying herself, brutal though her self-
denials and their expression sometimes are; it is rather her only
method of managing a lonely life. This theme of the lonely life
appeared in *The Professor* and *Jane Eyre* and loomed large in *Shirley*,
and here it is not easy to be certain how far the attitude is Lucy's
alone, or her author's. The resentment, and weariness of intense
passion, of the teenage Lucy for instance:

> it was a scene of feeling too brimful, and which, because the cup did
> not foam up high or furiously overflow, only oppressed one the
> more.
> (Chapter 2)

or the frighteningly mature comment on choosing to go to Miss
Marchmont,

> I had wanted to compromise with Fate: to escape occasional great
> agonies by submitting to a whole life of privation and small pains.
> (Chapter 4)

such as these suggest a strong weight of author's agreement. There
is no doubt, however, that the organic unity here is far greater than
in *Shirley*, and equally certain that, however much the modern
psychologically-enlightened reader may dislike both the position

163

and the conclusion, he cannot deny Charlotte Brontë the right to make an artistic use of it, nor can he condemn the novel on that account.

Though Lucy's position is a moral, as much as an emotional and personal one, there is not only no easy certainty that right is might, that virtue will triumph and achieve happiness, and that vice will be vanquished; there is not even a sense of universally applicable standards of right and wrong, or of the individual's feeling any satisfaction in doing what is, for him, right. Lucy's religion does not help her in personal crises; she is never able to say, with Jane Eyre's confidence,

> I care for myself. The more solitary, the more friendless, the more unsustained I am, the more I will respect myself.
>
> (*Jane Eyre*, Chapter 27)

Nor does Lucy have the same kind of moral growth as Jane – she is morally grown up at the beginning. Nor is there a social 'moral' as there is in *Shirley*. Lucy is not tempted to do wrong; her sufferings (when she loves Graham) are no one else's fault. She cannot cry out on society for making her suffer, as Caroline and Shirley can. Her suffering is through the nature of things, of herself and others, and is the more painful because we recognize that there is no help for it. Lucy does not choose between right and wrong in how she treats Graham, but chooses the way that will in the long run lead to the least hurt and shame, as she does also, until almost the end, with Paul Emmanuel.

She may often seem therefore to be acting according to the Victorian conventions which Jane so obviously flouts, but she is, like Jane, and like Catherine and Heathcliff, acting in fact according to the necessities of her own nature, whose impulse the reader feels to be right, though he cannot cite the rules that make it so. She grows wiser like them about her own soul and the souls of others in a way the reader recognizes and acknowledges. Thus the ending of the story hardly matters – again in direct contrast with Jane Eyre, whose final union with Mr Rochester is essential; whether Lucy marries Paul Emmanuel or loses him, the wisdom she has gained and the experience she has undergone cannot be taken from her. To borrow from her own summary of Paulina's happiness with Graham:

> if such perfect happiness is once felt by good people (to the wicked it never comes), its sweet effect is never wholly lost.
>
> (Chapter 37)

What matters is what Lucy's own individual soul has come to be. So stern a view of the individual woman's relation to her own life and her God is, judging from the nineteenth-century novel, a feminine trait, evinced by George Eliot and Mrs Gaskell, since no male writer of the time can be so unemotional about a woman's emotions. Thus *Villette* is the most 'modern' of the Brontë novels, looking forward to Forster, or to Lawrence.

Whatever doubt one may feel about how the author's intentions for her novel may have changed as she wrote, there is no doubt that the main outlines of its plot are not only most coherently followed through, but have been clearly seen from the first, for the hints of the course it takes are carefully and early placed. Graham and Paulina are those we meet first, closely followed, after the interlude with Miss Marchmont, by Ginevra Fanshawe. Plainly the strong close passion Polly has for Graham is a foretaste of what is to come, and plainly he is not the man to immediately appreciate her, as his passion for Ginevra later proves. Lucy responds so sensitively to him that she also must be his victim, though with no hope of success. One expects there will be action of which Lucy is not the centre, that it will exemplify different degrees and kinds of fortune and happiness, worked out through the events leading to marriage. All this, guessable before Chapter 4, is exactly what comes to pass. Only two things can change, therefore, as the novel goes on: firstly the emphasis and the handling which draw Lucy from her position as an outsider to heroine, whose love for Graham becomes, instead of one concern among those of Paulina, Graham, and Ginevra and her Colonel, the centre of the novel: and secondly, the view of the characters of the others, notably Paulina and Graham: the former becoming the recipient of happiness instead of the sufferer, as Lucy fears, of 'the shocks and repulses, the humiliations and desolations, which books, and my own reason, tell me are prepared for all flesh'

(Chapter 3); and the latter, Graham, becoming her lover, rather than the bringer of misfortune by the 'faithlessness' which is so much stressed in his boyhood. The plot in fact indicates a mistaken aim. It has too much material for what Charlotte Brontë does best – to concentrate on the spiritual trials of a single nature – even though it is not much elaborated compared with Thackeray, still less Dickens.

To recognize the plot is to understand and accept what can seem to be ineptitudes. Since the purpose of the opening is to present Graham and Paulina quite as much as Lucy, the coincidences involved in reuniting them all in Brussels become not only acceptable but structural. They do not happen because they are vital to Lucy, but because she, as the medium of the narrative, must come again into contact with the persons whose history she is to relate. The story really begins in Brussels; what comes before is introduction and prologue, enabling the reader to understand the story. Coincidence indeed is a method rather than a device, and decrees that Lucy, fainting after her confession, shall be restored by the Dr John who visits the pensionnat, who aided her when she first came to Villette, and who is Graham, the son of her godmother; it also decrees that the profligates who molested her on her first arrival (Chapter 7) shall be the scholars who torment her into writing her essay on Human Justice (Chapter 35), and that the priest to whom she makes confession (Chapter 15) shall be M. Paul's spiritual adviser, to whom she is reintroduced by a storm convenient and coincidental to Mme Beck's purposes, whereby she can hear M. Paul's past history (Chapter 34). It even determines that the insignificant bunch of violets given to Lucy, but we are not told by whom (Chapter 13), shall have come from Paul Emmanuel (Chapter 31). Coincidences happen so often – in matters both trivial and momentous – that they seem a necessary and credible part of life as *Villette* sees it. Such extremes of coincidence, while yet fewer than Fielding's or her immediate master, Thackeray's, prove, with the multiple plot, that Charlotte Brontë had no intention of allowing *Villette* to be merely a sadder and a wiser *Jane Eyre*.

The material on which the plot works is obviously very often

what she has used before.[1] Common to all her novels is the lonely
heroine, now at her most isolated, having not even hostile relations
like Jane Eyre's, nor uncertain financial support like Caroline's.
Even much of what is new has been glanced at before. Lucy, who
loses her beloved Graham to a truly worthy rival Paulina, faces the
situation Jane fears when Mr Rochester courts Blanche, or that
Caroline faces temporarily when Robert Moore courts Shirley.
Caroline sees no way out but a lonely life and eventual death. In
Villette Charlotte Brontë faces the much more mature fact that
second love follows first, and that Lucy, having learned to respond,
will do so again, for a different, a better, and a more testing object:
her love is now grown strong enough

To feed on that, which to disus'd tasts seemes tough.

Wholly new material on a minor scale are the English episodes
of the opening chapters, done briefly because they are only preliminary. No such household as Mrs Bretton's or Miss Marchmont's has been handled before, nor anything comparable with
Lucy's stay in London. A wholly new topic in *Villette* is a heroine
who rises gradually in the social scale by her own exertions. The rise
is a modest one, but the Lucy of the last chapters could not be mistaken for a servant by a chambermaid, as she is during her stay in
London (Chapter 5). She begins quite destitute, and is by turns
nursemaid, teacher, intimate of the flourishing professional man
Dr John, and the aristocrat Comte de Bassompierre, and finally
directrice of her own flourishing school. The movement might be
compared to that in *The Professor*, but that Crimsworth comes from
a family with some social pretensions, while we never hear that
Lucy's had any; and is the opposite of Jane Eyre, who is even, she
feels, degraded by becoming a village schoolmistress. *Villette* is
impressive for the new and valid artistic results achieved with such

---

[1] The most obvious quarry being the unpublished *Professor*, from which comes
in some form all the Brussels material: the girls' school, the Belgian characters,
Mme Beck herself, the landscape, food, and weather. *Villette* is more an imaginative re-working of *The Professor* than of Charlotte Brontë's own two years in
Brussels, the ultimate source of its matter, as structure and treatment of material
bear out.

apparently limited and much-used material, so that incidents or situations from each novel, however closely allied, are not inter-changeable, but serve different ends. Miss Marchmont, for instance, is very like the invalid spinster Miss Mann in *Shirley*, but where Miss Mann is a moral touchstone, and a threatened future for Caroline, Miss Marchmont is Lucy's temptation to retreat from life's challenge, and indulge her emotional cowardice. All such uses show an advance. The English material in *The Professor*, for instance, is quite separate from continental (except for Yorke Hunsden's odd visits); in *Villette* the Brettons and the Homes and Ginevra intermingle, supplying refreshing changes of scene and atmosphere, a society for Lucy such as Crimsworth lacks, and an English-speaking group, whose idiom contrasts fruitfully with that representing a foreign language.

Carefully detailed though so much of the material is – references abound to food, clothes, furnishing, weather, topography – natural-ism seems not to be the main intention. There are many violations of what we know to be either actual or possible. Though we can visualize the schoolrooms, the garden and the long dormitory, what happens in them could not happen in a real school of the 1850's. Lucy has all sorts of intimate conversations with Paul Emmanuel, apparently in full view and earshot of a class of sharp-eared, in-quisitive, adolescent girls, the most extraordinary perhaps being that in which she manages to break his spectacles (Chapter 38). Nor are the personal relationships likely, when taken out of their place in the novel, notably odd being Lucy's various ironic exchanges with Ginevra Fanshawe. The material is often autobiographical, yet no school on earth could run like this one. These centrally im-probable situations are often supported by brilliant and meticulous detail – the rats and beetles in the stuffy *grenier* where Lucy learns her part in the play, or the enchanting furniture from Bretton that Lucy sees when she revives at La Terrasse. Some opportunities for realistic *tours de force* are actually rejected, such as the acting of Vashti, which is done entirely by imagery, when Charlotte Brontë could well have depicted the real Rachel acting the real Athalie, as she herself saw her. The result is that *Villette* convinces as hallucina-tion or delirium convinces: it is at times even more real than the

actual. The disproportion between a situation and the response to
it, or between what observations tell us it is, and what it is for Lucy,
allow Charlotte Brontë to make new and fitting novel material out
of states of mind hitherto only the province of poetry or poetic
drama. Hence material affects method, since the most significant
events are not necessarily the most naturally important. The end of
the year examinations for the students at Mme Beck's school pass
over undetailed even though one would expect the withdrawn
Lucy to be apprehensive of conducting an examination (Chapter
15); the narrative rests rather upon Paul Emmanuel's outburst of
jealousy the evening before, at having to share with Lucy his glory
as sole examiner. The whole association between Lucy and Paul
Emmanuel is built out of small extraordinary happenings, which
bear a relation to common life, but could never be documentary
evidence of life in a Brussels pensionnat. They are the plausible
doings of unique and extraordinary beings. Dr John is not odd, like
Paul Emmanuel, but the association with him moves in the same
way: propelled at first by his finding Lucy with the mysterious
billet-doux dropped in the *allée défendue* and the conversation which
follows, and developed when he picks her up off the steps and
carries her home in her illness, it short-circuits, just as *Jane Eyre*
does, all the conventions which Charlotte Brontë neither will nor
can handle. Whereas *Jane Eyre* harmonized the important events
and the significant ones, *Villette* achieves its effects by the contrast
between them. Yet her themes here are as far as possible removed
from such as can be revealed by the 'accurate daguerrotype' of the
'carefully-fenced, highly cultivated garden with neat borders and
delicate flowers', which so little appealed to her in Jane Austen.[1]

Characters, like other material, draw heavily on life and yet are
never seen by the light of common day. As in *Jane Eyre*, they are all
transformed by being seen through the narrator's eyes. Since Lucy
is a stranger and more complex person than Jane, the people she
interprets are stranger and more complex also; since she is less self-
absorbed than Jane, and the novel in any case concerns not only her
individual fate, the rest of the characters are more fully observed

[1] Letter to G. H. Lewes, 12 January 1848.

than in *Jane Eyre*, and have more life independent of their observer.
The sense of their strangeness increases accordingly. It is all-pervasive. *Villette*'s grotesques – Mme Walravens, three feet high,
bejewelled and hunch-backed, the teacher Mlle St Pierre, reptilian
in appearance and propensities, or the healthy barrel-shaped Labas-
secourien singers – are not, like Dickens's grotesques, different in
kind and function from the main characters, nor are they figures of
farce and satire like Thackeray's. They are of the same stuff as the
most central: Mme Walravens is less detailed, but no odder or more
comic than Paul Emmanuel.

Several conclusions thus suggest themselves. Firstly Lucy Snowe's
vision obviously colours all that comes within it, indicating a great
achievement in an author who can so consistently present so strange
a vision of life. The trite phrase 'eternal triangle' for instance, is
utterly inapposite for Lucy, Ginevra and Dr John, or Lucy, Paulina
and Graham; while her reason for not letting herself love Graham
is essentially, to borrow from *Jane Eyre*, that she is 'not of his kind'
or, to borrow from *Wuthering Heights*, that they are as different 'as
a moonbeam from lightning, or frost from fire.'[1] Secondly, the
vision may be as much the author's as the character's. Undoubtedly
this may be partly true, yet it is clear from her other novels that
Charlotte Brontë is capable of seeing life very differently. Thirdly,
and most importantly, there may be signs of a new purpose in the
novel, making use of hitherto unacceptable material – moving to
the centre what has hitherto been only peripheral, and shifting to
the periphery what has usually been central. Lucy and Paul
Emmanuel are the oddest hero and heroine in the history of the
eighteenth- and nineteenth-century novel, while John Graham and
Paulina, now secondary, would make quite conventional ones. It
is as if Dickens had written *Great Expectations* from the point of view
of Biddy, with Pip thus performing Graham's part, and with Joe
Gargery – grotesque and worthy – her reward, just as the grotesque
and worthy Paul Emmanuel is Lucy's.

Characters are all not only strange but imperfect. They all embody different degrees of ignorance and misunderstanding. Lucy

[1] But the parallels reveal that the human relationships in both *Jane Eyre* and
Wuthering Heights are much less complicated than those in *Villette*.

herself is only partly wise, though she grows wiser as her experiences teach her. The other characters, none of whom fully sympathizes with or understands her, range themselves according to how well they can appreciate her. The one who does best is Paul Emmanuel, but even he falls far short of Mr Rochester's understanding of Jane Eyre. The other extreme is Ginevra, who is invariably ridiculously wrong. Mme Beck is dangerous because, while unsympathetic, she does understand both Lucy and Paul. Such degrees of misunderstanding apply to so many of the characters that they form a motif: even the elementary Ginevra is misinterpreted by an infatuated Graham, and by an inexperienced Paulina. Graham himself is one of the main objects of misunderstanding. Lucy, Mme Beck and Paulina all, in their ways, love him and attempt to pluck out the heart of his mystery. Mme Beck tries least, and gives up soonest; Lucy gives the fullest portrait of him, but consciously stops herself thinking of him, and leaves some contradictions unresolved; and, while we are given to understand that Paulina succeeds, by changing him through his love for herself, yet it does not happen while the reader or Lucy is looking on. The one delightful exception to universal misunderstanding is Paul Emmanuel, who has no disguises, reticence, or dignity. Nobody mistakes him in essentials, yet even he is not clear from the beginning, since Lucy withholds some of what she knows about him, so that he seems to grow as her feeling for him grows. Such degrees of misunderstanding suggest the complexity and richness of real life, while they impress the harsh truth that man is an island. Charlotte Brontë with Matthew Arnold is certain that a God their severance ruled

> And bade between their shores to be
> The unplumb'd, salt, estranging sea.

Loneliness is felt, not just as Lucy's doom, but as a condition of life.[1]

Characters generally appear more complicated than in the other novels. Whereas in *Jane Eyre* they were all primarily connected with

[1] There is not even a single complete family in the novel: Graham and Paulina have one parent, Mme Beck is a widow, and Ginevra's family never appears.

the heroine, and in *Shirley* were to be neatly related to a theme, here they exist for other reasons as well. Though Lucy is the heroine and the medium, Paulina is a second reason for characters' existence, nature, and interpretation, affecting our view of Mr Home, Mrs Bretton, Ginevra, and, of course, Graham. Characters can therefore usefully receive more than one interpretation. Lucy, the silent recipient of (often unwanted) confidences, is the reader's means of seeing not only the various misreadings of herself, but of Paulina. Furthermore, since Lucy herself changes as the novel develops, so her interpretation of characters changes. Since Lucy stays in Villette, with no change of milieu and company as in *Jane Eyre*, such changes are seen in detail. One of the most impressive and justly-treated instances is Mme Beck, who, from the being whose 'cool native impudence' Lucy and the reader detachedly enjoy, becomes the woman admired for overcoming her predilection for Graham and recognizing that her youth is past, who becomes in turn the cousin whose manipulation of Paul Emmanuel's generosity makes her a danger and a torment in the closing chapters. The most complicated personality is Graham, rendered so by how he is presented, as well as how he is conceived. Lucy's feelings towards him change. She comes to know him only gradually, he concerns Paulina as well as herself, and he is the object of more comment by others – Ginevra, Mrs Bretton, Mr Home – than any other man in the whole work.

Villette seems thus to present a more complex world than Charlotte Brontë's other novels, and is aided in doing so by two devices used in the early *Professor*. *Villette* like that novel allows numbers of transitory beings who are seen only briefly, often only once. The Irish, whisky-drinking Mme Svini for instance, or Paulina's companion and chaperone Mrs Hurst, or the bookseller whose daughters are Lucy's first pupils, or even the spaniel Sylvie, have the same kind of attention paid to them as those who return for more important roles. The novel thus becomes as rich and uncertain as would befit the genuine autobiography. Secondly, *Villette* frequently suggests the nature of whole groups of people, in the mass. The school, and the classes of pupils in it, have a corporate personality:

They were to be humoured, borne with very patiently: a courteous though sedate manner impressed them; a very rare flash of raillery did good. Severe or continuous mental application they could not, or would not, bear: heavy demand on the memory, the reason, the attention, they rejected point-blank. (Chapter 9)

they act as one in more trivial matters as well – when the hairdresser comes, or they get the chance to loiter about *en déshabille* for a morning. A few individuals may represent the mass, like the 'three titled belles in the first row' (Chapter 8) who try to prevent Lucy from teaching her first class, or the rebellious Catalonian Dolores, whom she conquers by flinging into the cupboard. These representative yet vivid types made their debut in *The Professor*, but were there not nearly so well worked into the structure of the whole.

Lucy Snowe, a heroine ultimately more impressive than Jane Eyre, is yet not uniformly so. The reader only gradually comes to have confidence in her. In the opening Bretton chapters, where Lucy holds herself apart from what she narrates, the reader holds himself apart from Lucy. But even when, in Villette, confidence is established, Lucy, defensive and reticent, is clearly a much harder proposition than any novelist has undertaken before, or any after, until Henry James writes *What Maisie Knew*. She is less attractive than Jane because she is less vigorous and less happy: she early remarks 'the negation of severe suffering was the nearest approach to happiness I expected to know' (Chapter 8); grief and despair constantly threaten her; even in her joyful moment (Chapter 21) she calls her joy 'sweet insanity'; on receiving Graham's letter she quarrels over it with Paul Emmanuel, almost loses it in the *grenier*, and refuses to write impassioned answers, or to hope that Graham will become fond of her.

She is painfully and obtrusively self-conscious and full of observations about herself:

though I forced myself to *realize* evils, I think I was too prosaic to *idealize*, and consequently to exaggerate them. (Chapter 4)

The Villette chapters abound in comments on her from others, from

Graham, Mrs Bretton, M. Paul, down to Mr Home and Ginevra. Such references not only show how others misinterpret Lucy, they show how painfully she is aware of it. She gets comfort for her lack of personal attraction only in the penultimate chapter, from Paul Emmanuel's reply to her question 'Do I displease your eyes *much*?'; but while his 'short strong answer' 'profoundly satisfies' Lucy, the reader does not hear what it was, and it comes too late to correct the impression left by the whole work. Lucy faces and makes the reader face the truth that self-knowledge is not self-help.

Lucy is, however, an apt narrator in that Charlotte Brontë can use much of her own nature quite legitimately in realizing her. Lucy is harsh to herself, hurrying back to school from the Brettons and La Terrasse:

> I could have cried, so irritated and eager was I to be gone. I longed to leave them as the criminal on the scaffold longs for the axe to descend: that is, I wished the pang over. (Chapter 21)

with her author's mixture of strong passion and strong will. One may hear Charlotte Brontë's voice as much as Lucy's when

> No Mause Headrigg ever felt a stronger call to take up her testimony against Sergeant Bothwell, than I – to speak my mind in this matter of the popish 'lecture pieuse'. (Chapter 13)

and may well feel that Lucy's defensive attitude may be shared with her author, and that Lucy's hedgings and concealments may relate to Charlotte Brontë's loss of trust in her reader. Charlotte Brontë, having lost faith in life, uses her loss of faith to create Lucy. Such use of self is far from self-indulgent.

Lucy is conceived like Jane Eyre in a spirit both romantically idealistic, and down-to-earth; she combines what she herself terms Reason and Passion. She will not compromise in her essential demands upon life. She is most herself in moments of extreme testing, which rouse her from her usual self-imposed calm. Action is always her response to both the legitimate challenge – of Mme Beck asking her to teach an English lesson – and to the excessive demand – to spend her whole vacation caring for an idiot child. On the other hand she seems very unromantic in recognizing the dangers of passion and in repressing it. Indeed she seems even afraid of it and the suffering it brings, and tries to avoid it. When in its grip she tries never to give way to it, answering Graham's letter even less warmly than propriety permits. But the violent and hyperbolical style which expresses how she both acknowledges and hates the power of reason is very far from classical restraint:

> Reason is vindictive as a devil: for me, she was always envenomed as a stepmother. If I have obeyed her it has chiefly been the obedience of fear, not of love.
>
> (Chapter 21)

Such allusions are frequent, and Lucy herself is very much her own interpretation of the actress Vashti:

> To her, what hurts becomes immediately embodied: she looks on it as a thing that can be attacked, worried down, torn in shreds. Scarcely a substance herself, she grapples to conflict with abstractions.
>
> (Chapter 23)

One of Lucy's most striking characteristics is also a striking and even puzzling part of the novel's method. She often conceals, or only partly reveals, vital information to the reader. She knows that Dr John is both the man who helped her when she arrived in Villette, and also the Graham Bretton she knew as a child, long before she ever lets the reader know or even guess.[1] Such concealments happen too often and too structurally to be dismissed as carelessness, or condemned as a tiresome device of Charlotte Brontë's for producing artificial excitement and surprise. Restraint and concealment are innate in Lucy, and it is even artistic decorum to have her conceal not only from all the other characters, but at times even from the reader. Properly read, she must seem by this device, as by others, more like an autobiographer than a novel's heroine. Reservation often expresses itself in hints and in figurative language, a mode present as soon as the adult Lucy appears in Chapter 4:

[1] She hides innumerable other things, many of them only trifles; we find out in Chapter 31 that the little knot of white violets mentioned in Chapter 13 as having been 'once silently presented to me by a stranger' came in fact from Paul Emmanuel.

It will be conjectured that I was of course glad to return to the bosom of my kindred. Well! the amiable conjecture does no harm, and may therefore be safely left uncontradicted. Far from saying nay, indeed, I will permit the reader to picture me, for the next eight years, as a bark slumbering through halcyon weather in a harbour still as glass.

The withdrawal occurs at intervals throughout, and in the strikingly ambiguous end, whose likeness to this passage absolutely forbids us to interpret as a 'happy' one.[1] Though the reader may feel repulsed by such a fobbing-off, it is clearly structural, and is reinforced by another of Lucy's habits, that of occasionally telling more than she could know at the time, sketching in a whole character or state of affairs which she has only just encountered, as she does, conspicuously, with Mme Beck. The effect of such knowledge, greater than the narrator could have had at the time of the event, is to distance what happens, to prevent it striking on the reader's nerves as it does in *Jane Eyre*, to cause the reader to see the present, like that of *Wuthering Heights*, as already among 'old unhappy far-off things' in the past. Just as Gibbon had to find his style first in order to write his *Decline and Fall of the Roman Empire*, so Charlotte Brontë has to find and establish her central consciousness. In *Shirley* she did not find it, and so failed. In *Villette* she has found one, akin to Jane Eyre's, but more sophisticated and less frank, more suited to a more mature writer, and to an older heroine.[2]

[1] The parallel here remains valid even though we know that the ambiguous ending was a concession to old Mr Brontë, who did not want an unhappy one. The art shown in its handling is far from casual, and it is difficult to conceive of an ending more in keeping with the method of the whole.

[2] As a narrative medium in fact Lucy sometimes fails. This is not the fault of the character, but of the wrong kind of material. The failure is Graham Bretton, who must come to be more subtle than Lucy can comprehend, and whose motives must be seen before he is in a position to reveal them to Lucy. Hence he thinks aloud like Mr Rochester.

'If I knew you better, I might be tempted to risk some confidence, and thus secure you as a guardian for a most innocent and excellent, but somewhat inexperienced being.' (Chapter 13)

But what will do for the open and unconventional Mr Rochester speaking to Jane is unsuitable for Graham (who even enjoys deceit) speaking to the stranger

Lucy, close in circumstances to Crimsworth, and in nature to Jane Eyre, suggests an even earlier prototype in the private juvenile epics, where Charlotte Brontë used Lord Charles Wellesley as the cold, cynical observer of the affairs of his brother, the real hero, the Byronic Marquis of Douro. There the purpose was to allow an escape route from the depths of emotional indulgence. Here a connected device is a safeguard against sentimentality and self-pity, for an author whose subject lies in great danger of it. But the passion that always comes to Charlotte Brontë when she writes has to find its release. So the cold, detached Lucy becomes herself the unwilling embodiment of passionate feelings, and so becomes the most complex and subtly realized of Charlotte Brontë's women.

After Lucy, those who concern the reader most are those who concern Lucy most. While John Graham Bretton must always puzzle the reader, Paul Emmanuel has never been a problem. He is the only character who is wholly Lucy's concern, having no relevance to the secondary part of the novel concerning Graham and Paulina. While he is an engaging creation, he is not a particularly subtle one. His public character can be reduced to a few essentials: a fiery temper, kindness, eccentric habits, and an odd undignified appearance. We remember him reducing big girls to tears, sharing his bread roll with little ones, hissing insults in public, and appearing everywhere with shaven head, bonnet-grec and paletôt. His importance is as much what he denotes – Lucy's gradually growing understanding of what is truly valuable in a man, and the religious conflict that almost separates them – as what he actually is.

Lucy. Worse, Lucy cannot suggest what she does not know, that Graham is really not so besottedly in love with Ginevra as he seems, information the reader ought to have to appreciate him. An awkward remark in Chapter 18, rather late in the affair, is one of the few useful clues:

'Dr John,' I began, 'Love is blind!' But just then a blue subtle ray sped sideways from Dr John's eye: it reminded me of old days, it reminded me of his picture; it half led me to believe that part, at least, of his professed persuasion of Miss Fanshawe's naïveté was assumed.

He is the ultimate in the unheroic hero. Unromantic, even unobtrusive, in the early sections, where Lucy is absorbed in Graham, he gradually looms larger as he occupies more of Lucy's thoughts. He contrasts with Graham, not only in character, but in presentation. Where Lucy is conscious of the effect of every one of Graham's doings, Paul Emmanuel's begin almost casually: he forces her to learn her part and act, with some distinction, in a play he has produced (Chapter 14); he makes an impressive appearance before royalty at the concert (Chapter 20), and with the savants at the Hôtel Crécy (Chapter 27), on all of which occasions Lucy feels herself to be wholly absorbed in what is happening to Graham Bretton. Nevertheless Charlotte Brontë ensures that the reader shall feel the link with Lucy, since he is the man whose cryptic character-reading in Chapter 7 gets her her place with Mme Beck, whose idiosyncrasies are revealed through what he says to her and does in her presence, who has always had a hand in her affairs – he is even the one who delivers her precious letter from Graham (Chapter 21) – who takes the trouble to understand her – discovering that she is not in fact learned, that this apparently 'colourless shadow' has 'a passionate ardour for triumph' (Chapter 15) – and whose style when speaking to her has echoes of her own when thinking: 'I see on your cheek two tears which I know are hot as two sparks, and salt as two crystals of the sea. . . . You look like one who would snatch at a draught of sweet poison, and spurn wholesome bitters with disgust' (Chapter 21). He rouses amusement in Lucy and the reader, at the same time as he reveals his worth. He is thus an apt hero, unideal to suit the unideal heroine, and able to be developed by the material which develops her. Being often comic, at times near grotesque, and always unorthodox, he can appear at his best in the unconventional, even improbable situations that best suit Lucy, in a way that Graham cannot – reciting a play in a dusty rat-and-beetle-ridden attic, reading Corneille under a tree, sharing stewed apples by a schoolroom stove, and conversing outrageously before a whole class of schoolgirls. His very lively nature is provoked by Lucy's still one, which he rouses in his turn, again and again, until the final outburst against Justine Marie which brings them together. Lucy understands and trifles with him (holding

back the watchguard she has made for him) as Jane trifles with Mr
Rochester, with results as entertaining, and of even greater consequence in advancing the relationship.

He is a most successful creation. Known of course to have much
in common with M. Héger, he is often cited as an instance of
Charlotte Brontë's power to use the material of real life. But he is
clearly no mere transcript. Paul Emmanuel, comic and faulty, is
handled in a way that recalls other figures in the novels, not only
Mr Rochester, but Yorke Hunsden in *The Professor*. If Mrs Gaskell[1]
had not told us, it would be impossible from the fabric of the novel
to tell where life takes over from imagination: that M. Paul, im-
petuously demanding Lucy's approval of his speech (Chapter 28)
is drawn straight from Thackeray speaking to Charlotte Brontë
after a public lecture. He is a remarkable and uniquely successful
mixture of fact and fancy. As a comic hero, it is salutary to compare
him with Thackeray's Captain Dobbin in *Vanity Fair*, another
grotesque who eventually marries a heroine. Whereas Dobbin's
gaucheries – big feet, stammer and awkwardness – are gradually
dropped, Paul Emmanuel's never cease to be stressed, his finest
moment, defying Mme Beck, being a far from dignified one:

> 'Femme!' cried the professor, not now in his deep tones, but in his
> highest and most excited key, 'Femme! sortez à l'instant.'
>
> (Chapter 41)

In technique and sophistication, he is an advance on Mr Rochester,
since we are allowed to see M. Paul with our own, as well as Lucy's,
eyes. Whereas it is disastrous to judge of Mr Rochester other than as
Jane does, it does no harm to Paul Emmanuel. One delights in him
at the end as one delights in the worth of another woman's husband.

The most absorbing character after Paul Emmanuel is probably
Modeste Maria Beck, like him a close concern of Lucy's. She is the
first extensive study Charlotte Brontë has made of a woman not her
heroine, not young, and neither wholly good nor bad. Correct and
controlled as she always is, she embodies the 'convenance' without
feeling to which Paul and Lucy are the antithesis. In the earlier
stages of the story the measure of Lucy's rise in prosperity is the way

[1] *The Life of Charlotte Brontë*, Chapter 33.

she is treated by the socially assured Mme Beck, who knows the social value of everything, from pupils of rank to the presence of young men at a school dance. She promotes Lucy from nursery-maid to schoolteacher, trusts her with the privilege of walking in *l'allée défendue*, and finally excepts her from the régime of universal *surveillance*. Lucy, by growing to seem Mme Beck's equal, seems also on a level with her former superior, Professor Paul Emmanuel. Mme Beck concludes as the ultimate hardship Lucy has to suffer, the woman who understands her but is quite incapable of sympathizing. Being the main instrument of keeping Paul and Lucy apart, she also, by opposing them, tests and ripens their feelings for each other, as, in a much more elementary way, Blanche Ingram does Jane's.

Formidable though she is, she is yet attractive, interesting, and entertaining. Her attaction is revealed in qualities which please without being virtues: the good health which gives her a complexion able to wear a '*chapeau vert tendre* – hazardous, as to its tint, for any complexion less fresh than her own, but, to her, not unbecoming' (Chapter 13); the calm with which she helps the Doctor to set her daughter's broken arm; and which elicits his praise:

'Voilà un sang-froid bien opportun, et qui vaut mille élans de
sensibilité déplacée.'   (Chapter 10)

and the neatness Lucy admires:

some people's movements provoke the soul by their loose awkwardness, hers satisfied by their trim compactness.   (Chapter 13)

– even when she is spying into someone else's workbox. Charlotte Brontë takes pains to make her less repulsive and reprehensible than the reader, left to himself, would judge her. Her first appearance at espionage, for instance, occurs just after we have encountered the grotesque Mme Svini – '*Anglicè* or *Hibernicè* Sweeny', 'the heroine of the bottle' (Chapter 8) – snoring in her drunken sleep; it draws from Lucy only fascinated curiosity, and the pleasantly neutral comment 'All this was very un-English' (ibid.). She can even, for a moment, be not only impressive but moving, when facing the truth that she cannot charm Dr John, and is no longer young:

One single white hair streaked her nut-brown tresses; she plucked it out with a shudder. (Chapter 11)

Her most obvious precursor is Mlle Reuter, in *The Professor*, whom, although older, she resembles physically and temperamentally. Both are generally agreed to have their original in Mme Héger. Mme Beck is obviously the subtler and less pleasant recreation. If the hatred were simply Charlotte Brontë's for Mme Héger (the jealous wife of the man she reputedly loved) one would have expected it to be least disguised in the earlier portrait, written quite soon after the incidents in Brussels, presumed to have provoked it. In fact Mme Beck shows more signs of being a novelist's mature re-working of her own earlier attempt, than a return to the common original. Whatever the origin of Mme Beck, however, the disapproval she arouses is never in excess of what her conduct demands, so that she seems, like Paul Emmanuel, a legitimate fusing of life with fancy. Charlotte Brontë presents her as impartially and fairly as she did Mrs Reed in *Jane Eyre*, or Mr Helstone in *Shirley*, both of them, like her, harsher than they realize to a helpless victim; but Lucy's intelligent perceptions, and humorously balanced attitude, are both an advance and a sophistication.

The rest of the school characters range themselves round these two, Mme Beck and Paul Emmanuel, to whom they must seem linked by the fact that they are all French-speaking, and that their language must be rendered, rather than reproduced. Rosine the portress, Goton the cook, Zélie St Pierre, the various pupils, are are mainly felt for their foreignness rather than their individuality. They must be there to emphasize Lucy's loneliness in their midst. The exception is Ginevra Fanshawe, who is the only link beside Lucy herself (and Graham during the brief period of his infatuation, and his attendance as a doctor on Mme Beck's children) between the world of the pensionnat and the English world of La Terrasse and the Hôtel Crécy.

Ginevra is, as Lucy calls her, 'small-beer' (Chapter 24). Coincidence it may be that makes her the niece of Mr Home and cousin of Paulina, but she is a credible niece of the frivolous 'empty-headed butterfly' wife who has deserted her husband and child at the opening of the novel. Though neither natural nor very interesting in herself, she is a useful character and an original one. She is the instrument of the mystery of the 'nun' (her lover, whom Lucy sees at three crucial moments), and the object of Graham's first love (possibly indicating that she was intended to have more importance than the novel actually permits), a contrast therefore with Paulina as well as Lucy. But she mainly serves to make points about social values. By scorning Graham for the empty-headed colonel she indues him with more force than his devotion suggests – he is plainly too good for her. Lucy utters many of her most characteristic remarks to her, condemning her love of finery and pleasure, and she is therefore both powerful and entertaining when she scores in her turn, summarizing Lucy at the concert in the controversial pink dress as being 'dressed, actually, like anybody else' (Chapter 21). Her existence proves that Lucy, even at her loneliest and most withdrawn, is not incapable of inspiring friendship.

The rest of the characters belong structurally to Paulina as well as to Lucy, even though, as Paulina does not appear until Chapter 23, the connection is not immediately obvious. She is herself undoubtedly a failure. In the opening chapters she seems intended as the heroine of the future, whose divided loyalties, between her father and the young Graham who unconsciously neglects and ill-treats her, foreshadow her fate as a woman. She is intended to be absorbing and moving for her situation, her deep feelings, and her noble and mature restraint. The situation, like those in *Shirley*, is well conceived. The execution fails. Her small size, intended to emphasize the intensity and maturity of her feelings, is no more than a substitute for personality. The passionate speech, that rang true in the context of the child's own story of herself in *Jane Eyre*, rings false against Lucy's detached and adult tones. When she returns to the story as a young lady and as the Countess de Bassompierre, her original role has become submerged. Charlotte Brontë deals with her rapidly, almost cursorily, creating sympathy for her by reminiscence, and by the same means she had used for Lucy, observing how she is disturbed by Graham, and withdraws from him, how she receives a letter from him which she is afraid to open, and which she answers coldly 'with a morsel of ice flavoured with ever so slight a zest of fruit or sugar' (Chapter 23). But Paul Em-

manuel is now in the ascendant, so Paulina – the topic of loyalties
divided between father and husband being briskly disposed of –
may be satisfactorily married off to Graham, and become the being
whose fate moves in the way opposite to Lucy's:

> so guided from a soft cradle to a calm and late grave, that no exces-
> sive suffering penetrates [her] lot, and no tempestuous blackness
> overcasts [her] journey.   (Chapter 37)

Her father, Mr Home (Count de Bassompierre, as he becomes)
partners Graham's mother Mrs Bretton, the one Scottish, the other
English. Neither is vital; both are agreeable, cheeful, and robust.
Both as devoted parents heighten Lucy's loneliness, both by goodwill without understanding cause her pain. Both, because slight,
succeed. Both show Charlotte Brontë on unsafe ground in attempting to handle the relation between parent and child, though clearly
she has realized the dangers of Mrs Pryor, and here eschews sentiment and resorts to irony, which, if not impressive, avoids the
embarrassing.

The last and most awkward personality is John Graham Bretton's,
intended to be complicated, and made more so by the change of
direction it takes at Villette, and by Charlotte Brontë's failure to
realize what she originally conceived. The key to his early personality is the word 'faithless', which foretells the future quality
that is to mar the pleasant personality of the boy. In fact he is not
'faithless' to anyone, although the events at Villette follow a course
which could have been that of the male jilt, rousing disappointed
hopes in Ginevra, Mme Beck, and Lucy. The idea of a subtle, misleading man remains; the varied opinions on him – Ginevra's,
Mme Beck's, his mother's, and Paulina's, make him puzzling, but
Lucy's withholding moral judgement makes him finally unattractive. He is mysterious in treatment rather than in essence.[1] Hints of

---

[1] He has three names, all of which are used as surnames, to signify different
aspects of himself. It is a device Charlotte Brontë has always enjoyed, but has
never before used as more than ornament: 'Isidore' is Ginevra's name for him,
'Dr John' signifies consistently the person connected with the pensionnat and
Ginevra, whereas 'Graham' belongs to the English world of La Terrasse, the
milieu of his mother and Paulina.

duplicity recur at Villette, when he visits the pensionnat, in hopes of seeing Ginevra, on the pretext of visiting the sick child. Lucy mentions his 'shrewdly sparkling eye' and his 'supple' and 'pliant' manner (Chapter 10), terms which suggest something other than Ginevra's devoted swain. The idea of the jilt gives way, but he remains both a mystery to Lucy and a character to be thought of as less worthy than Paul Emmanuel. Mystery as he is, Lucy makes him the more so to the reader by refusing to tell, not only when she discovers that Dr John is the Englishman who helped her when she arrived, but that he is the boy she knew at Bretton. Charlotte Brontë makes several attempts to suggest to the reader that he should perceive more than Lucy; successfully, when Graham fails the test offered him by the acting of Vashti, watching her

> not with wonder, nor worship, nor yet dismay, but simply with intense curiosity. (Chapter 23)

unsuccessfully when, on Lucy's remarking that 'love is blind',

> a blue, subtle ray sped sideways from Dr John's eye: it reminded me of old days, it reminded me of his picture. (Chapter 18)

No doubt thereafter we believe, as Lucy, that 'his persuasion of Miss Fanshawe's naïveté was assumed'; but it is too late, and there has been no such suggestion before. Likewise when Graham finds Lucy's letter on the attic floor and keeps it, we have no reason to feel the truth of Lucy's exclamation 'Curious, characteristic manoeuvre' (Chapter 22).

If Graham Bretton has any literary antecedent in Charlotte Brontë's own work, it is the boy Martin Yorke, who also is pleased to torment all the women round him, and to tease the one he admires. The closest outside connection is with Edgar Linton,[1] and the terms in which Charlotte Brontë renders him recall those of *Wuthering Heights*:

> to bright, soft, sweet influences his eyes gave bright, soft, sweet welcome, beautiful to see as dyes of rose and silver, pearl and purple, embuing summer clouds; for what belonged to storm, what was

[1] Although the name John Graham suggests a link with the John Grahame of Claverhouse, Viscount Dundee, of Scott's *Old Mortality*.

wild and intense, dangerous, sudden, and flaming, he had no sympathy, and held with it no communion. (Chapter 23)

For the first seven chapters, moving from Bretton, to London, to Villette, and from childhood to maturity, *Villette* seems to repeat the movement and structure of *Jane Eyre*. On the other hand, having apparently two heroines with interwoven stories, it recalls *Shirley*. However, as soon as the action has moved to Villette, this novel has a new and more elaborate structure than either. Judged by the rules applying to *Jane Eyre*, *Villette* often looks shapeless; there seem to be discrepancies, loose ends, and some very casual use of detail. But recollected in tranquillity, the whole feels more coherent than the examination of its parts suggests. The coherence derives from mood rather than material; it is brought about by the regulation of tone, and by the handling of the progression and juxtaposition of material. Events are often just as important for the way they prepare the reader for what follows, as for themselves. Their real importance is only felt later. A good example is Lucy's stay with Miss Marchmont (Chapter 4). It is not at all necessary to the plot, yet structurally it is indispensable. Loneliness (the motif of *Villette*) has been Miss Marchmont's life, as it is to be Lucy's, she also living on after her lover's death. Much of the mood of the Villette story begins here, Miss Marchmont's death being heralded, like Paul Emmanuel's, by a storm and a wailing 'Banshee' wind. The section itself is a fine prelude for what follows: after the 'two close rooms' and the 'steam-dimmed lattice of this sick-chamber', the comparative confinement of Villette impresses the reader, like Lucy, as freedom and life. It could not conceivably do so if it immediately followed the childhood at Bretton.

Events continue to plant associations in the reader's mind, and prepare him to accept an unforeseen future, not only by significant material in a significant context, but also by apparent structural awkwardness. Lucy, arrived at the pensionnat, is interviewed by Mme Beck, who calls in M. Paul to advise her, thus effectively presenting the two most vital characters, in a most characteristic way, at the first possible moment, and beginning the story with the same trio as will end it. But Lucy has then to report a conversation in a language she does not know, so Charlotte Brontë has her bluntly state:

> I shall go on with this part of my tale as if I had understood all that had passed; for though it was then scarce intelligible to me, I heard it translated afterwards. (Chapter 7)

The reader may well wonder who was the translator – it could be only Mme Beck or M. Paul. Retrospect tells (what could fairly be suspected, though it is not) that Lucy heard it from her fiancé. Charlotte Brontë has at once roused and lulled our suspicions, by using what looked a trite and awkward narrative device, for quite novel ends.

Lucy's great experiences being mainly inward, involving, not great happenings, but the significance of things, events must be presented so that their importance is not the obvious one, but the underlying one, which may be quite incongruously disproportionate. In Chapter 12, Lucy, walking alone in the *allée défendue*, sees thrown a casket containing violets and a *billet-doux*. It is a stale situation, and a silly letter, very fit for the foolish colonel de Hamal to send to the foolish Ginevra. The reader must not be allowed for a moment to think of it as romantic, or as embodying romance for Lucy. So Charlotte Brontë holds back the contents of the letter, while Lucy resents intrusion on her peace, scorns romantic notions, and voices her own robust common sense:

> If the other teachers went into town, or took a walk on the boulevards, or only attended mass, they were very certain (according to the accounts brought back) to meet with some individual of the 'opposite sex' whose rapt, earnest gaze assured them of their power to strike and to attract. I can't say that my experience tallied with theirs in this respect. I went to church and I took walks, and am very well convinced that nobody minded me. (Chapter 12)

She goes on to say that Dr John, the idol of the school, has taken no notice of her either. The windy and sentimental letter, when it at last comes, is thus bathos, turning to ironic fun at the abuse of 'that dragon the English teacher', Lucy herself. Dr John's arriving immediately afterwards is unexpected but not incredible, since he has already been mentioned. The excitement has thus shifted away from the apparently exciting event, the vapid letter, to the genuine object, the representative of true feeling, Dr John. The handling here not only shows how to regard events, it suggests character. Dr John may at present be the genuine lover, in contrast with de Hamal, but we are surprised to find so worthy a man in so trivial a situation, just as we shall later be surprised to find him in love with so trivial a girl as Ginevra. Both surprises prepare us in turn for his cure, and his finding the true object of his affections in Paulina. We have also learned considerably more about Lucy herself, notably her ironic humour, revealed in the sustained, quietly self-mocking image of Dr John's blue eyes, whose conventional 'admiring beam' is for Lucy 'calm as the sky, to whose tint they seemed akin' (ibid.); and revealed even more in the remark which follows the letter's abuse of her:

> the reader will excuse my modesty in allowing this flattering sketch of my amiable self to retain the slight veil of the original tongue.
>
> (ibid.)

The whole incident springs from false, conventional, and empty relationships – Ginevra's and de Hamal's, and Dr John's with Ginevra – and itself sets on foot a genuine and extraordinary one – between Dr John and Lucy herself.

The whole series of events involving the ghostly nun works in the same way. The nun (the amorous de Hamal's disguise for visiting Ginevra) is never in itself an object of mystery to the reader, or indeed of much interest. It would be intolerable if the phantom that is to resolve itself into a bolster in fancy dress lying on Lucy's bed, were to suggest any real power of doing harm. Like the *billet-doux*, a phantom nun is too trite for serious consideration, a fact Charlotte Brontë (who has already created Bertha Mason) knows very well. She has to preserve a rational balance between Lucy, whose already overstrained nerves are terrified, and Graham, who never even considers the possibility that the nun may be palpable to feeling as to sight. Charlotte Brontë does not cheat; the 'nun' is delineated quite accurately by what the colonel is wearing:

> a figure all black or white; the skirts straight, narrow, black; the head bandaged, veiled, white.   (Chapter 22)

the rustle of the boughs that precedes her later rush past Paul and Lucy in the *allée* (Chapter 31) is actually the colonel making a hasty descent from the attic. But, as with the casket, what really concerns Charlotte Brontë and the reader is the emotional effect of the event on others, not the emotional power inherent in the thing itself. Lucy is clearly over-susceptible to nervous shock when she rushes from the attic to Mme Beck's sitting-room; Graham is equally clearly not treating Lucy right, and proving himself inadequate, when he does not even consider that she may have seen something to cause her fears. Paul Emmanuel unites himself to Lucy by taking the figure seriously, and resolving as he says 'to follow up the mystery'. His words

> Whether this nun be flesh and blood, or something that remains when blood is dried and flesh wasted, her business is as much with you as with me, probably.   (Chapter 31)

are proved true on one level when the nun immediately afterwards is seen by both of them. On another they lead forward to the next chapter but one, in which Lucy hears that Paul Emmanuel is self-devoted to the memory of a girl who took the veil when they were unable to marry. The phantom nun, like the unexplained translation of the conversation (already mentioned) between Mme Beck and Paul Emmanuel, is a stock literary device, an apparent gaucherie whose awkwardness is deliberately exploited to regulate the reader's response. It is the means to highly unconventional and original ends.

This sense that events are not important in themselves, but only for the effects they have on the mind and soul, fundamentally influences the structure and the handling, from major scenes down to the smaller details. The major scenes in *Villette* are not so much those in which things happen, as those in which we observe reactions and responses, not only Lucy's, but those of others. Hence the interesting recurrence of situations which form touchstones for worth. The two most notable are the painting of the 'Cleopatra' and the acting of Vashti. They are a device, quite new to Charlotte Brontë, which enables her to reveal the moral and spiritual worth of Lucy and others which Lucy herself cannot assess. Lucy's view of the painting of Cleopatra in the Art Gallery reveals her as robust, candid, and with a sense of comedy that rarely finds an outlet:

> She lay half-reclined on a couch: why, it would be difficult to say; broad daylight blazed round her; she appeared in hearty health, strong enough to do the work of two plain cooks; ... she ought likewise to have worn decent garments; a gown covering her properly, which was not the case: out of abundance of material – seven-and-twenty yards, I should say, of drapery – she managed to make inefficient raiment. Then, for the wretched untidiness surrounding her, there could be no excuse. Pots and pans – perhaps I ought to say vases and goblets – were rolled here and there on the foreground; a perfect rubbish of flowers was mixed amongst them, and an absurd and disorderly mass of curtain upholstery smothered the couch and cumbered the floor.   (Chapter 19)

Lucy's response is a non-aesthetic, even a philistine one; but it is a reaction to Rubens[1] that any reader can acknowledge and share with delight. It does not matter whether it is a good or bad painting, for through Cleopatra we can assess Ginevra's Count de Hamal, who sees her as 'le type du voluptueux'; Graham, who exposes himself by two remarks 'my mother is a better-looking woman' and 'compare that mulatto with Ginevra!'; and Paul Emmanuel, whose comment (though still wholly unaesthetic) is, of the three, the most analytical and the best sense:

> 'Une femme superbe – une taille d'impératrice, des formes de Junon, mais une personne dont je ne voudrais ni pour femme, ni pour fille, ni pour sœur.'   (ibid.)

Such tests are not all such set-pieces. Ginevra fails as Graham's idol because she does not recognize Mrs Bretton's worth, and quizzes

[1] To whom Lucy attributes the picture, along with 'all the army of his fat women'.   (Chapter 23).

her at the concert; Graham himself is inadequate beside Paulina, because, while she remembers every detail of what passed between them at Bretton, he remembers only vaguely.

Just as events themselves are handled in *Villette*, with an emphasis very different from what they had in *Jane Eyre* or *Shirley*, so also is the movement. *Jane Eyre* was straightforward in chronology, and its intervals of retrospect looked back to what the reader had seen for himself. *Shirley* was rather more elaborate in that it had to chronicle events in more than one place, so tended occasionally to go back on its tracks, to collect and bring up to date matters that had fallen out of sight. This is true also of *Villette*, where, for instance, the action pauses to resume and narrate the fortunes of Paulina, when they have not been Lucy's. Yet there are greater variations in the way time is treated. Charlotte Brontë refers often to happenings in the recent past that have not been mentioned before; many of the happenings retailed represent a continuous state of affairs, not individual incident; and some separate incidents are narrated out of their chronological place. The first type is more frequent in the latter part of the action, and generally supplies new detail about Paul Emmanuel:

> There was M. Emmanuel, bent over the soil, digging in the wet mould amongst the rain-laden and streaming shrubs, working as hard as if his day's pittance were yet to earn by the literal sweat of his brow.
> In this sign I read a ruffled mood. He would dig thus in frozen snow on the coldest winter day, when urged inwardly by painful emotion, whether of nervous excitation, or sad thoughts, or self-reproach. He would dig, by the hour, with knit brow and set teeth, nor once lift his head, or open his lips.
>
> (Chapter 36)

We hear also of his gifts of books, his habit of 'pruning' them, of searching Lucy's desk, and leaving presents of sweets, all of which, had this been a novel like *Jane Eyre*, would have been mentioned the first time they occurred. A striking instance of the scene told out of place occurs in Chapter 38. Charlotte Brontë tells us first of Lucy's bitter shock on hearing that Paul Emmanuel has left the school and

is going to Guadaloupe, and only afterwards of the delicate, interrupted exchange between them:

> One evening, not ten short days since, he joined me whilst walking
> in my alley. He took my hand. I looked up in his face; I thought he
> meant to arrest my attention.
>
> 'Bonne petite amie!' said he, softly, 'douce consolatrice!' But
> through his touch, and with his words, a new feeling and a strange
> thought found a course. Could it be that he was becoming more than
> friend or brother? Did his look speak a kindness beyond fraternity
> or amity?
>
> His eloquent look had more to say, his hand drew me forward, his
> interpreting lips stirred. No. Not now. Here into the twilight alley
> broke an interruption: it came dual and ominous: we faced two
> bodeful forms – a woman's and a priest's – Madame Beck and Père
> Silas.   (Chapter 38)

So passes briefly and in retrospect what was almost their coming
together. Clearly Paul Emmanuel has been about to tell Lucy of
his plans; they must be interrupted if the public announcement is
to be a shock to Lucy as to the reader. But the reason why the whole
incident is told so much later than it occurred is a more essential one.
The events at this point reveal a thematic design, rather than a
narrative, which Lucy's incident in its place would obscure and
break up. Lucy's shock and despair must immediately follow and
counterbalance the account of Paulina's married happiness in the
two juxtaposed chapters entitled 'Sunshine' and 'Cloud'.

The claims of the design are what rule the other narrative in-
novations also. When a novelist can be so precise as to give Mme
Beck's maiden name – Kint – in Chapter 8, and take it up again and
use it for her brother Victor Kint in Chapter 38, one must hesitate to
convict her of forgetfulness or carelessness of detail in general.
Were Lucy to recount at an early point those details she introduces without preparation – like borrowing Paul Emmanuel's
books or eating his chocolates – the reader would soon be so much
wiser than Lucy about her own affairs that he would cease to pay
the proper attention to her relations with Graham, which are
thematically still the more important. We hear of events only as
they impinge on Lucy's consciousness as significant. Charlotte

Brontë is concerned with verisimilitude, not apparent historical accuracy.[1]

What is true of events is true also of their setting. Charlotte Brontë tells only what is required, at the point at which it is needed. The novel moves gradually from the vague to the intensely detailed, as Lucy grows, from inertia, to respond to life, and, through her sufferings, moves to a painful and hypersensitive perception of what is around her. The Bretton of her childhood is without detail; London is much more impressive; Villette the most vivid of all. The details of the pensionnat – the *classes*, the *berçeau,* the dormitory, the attics – all have their atmosphere affecting what happens in them. The garden has a personality of its own – a mixture of health, life, and peace, with espionage and mystery (in the *billet-doux*, and Paul Emmanuel's spying from his window at the boys' college) – all permeated with a sense of *lacrimae rerum*, since it contains the actual grave of the pitiful and authentic nun, and the figurative one of Lucy's love for Graham, after she has buried her letters there. Lucy's moments of most intense suffering are her moments of hypersensitive response to her surroundings, whether of pleasure or agony. In her long vacation illness

> The solitude and stillness of the long dormitory could not be borne any longer; the ghastly white beds were turning into spectres – the coronal of each became a death's head, huge and sun-bleached – dead dreams of an elder world and mightier race lay frozen in their wide gaping eye-holes. (Chapter 15)

Her bewildered state when she recovers consciousness at La Terrasse reveals itself through her recognizing, not the place, but what it contains:

[1] There are however undoubtedly some imbalances in the latter sections of the novel; the gradual stages of Paulina's and Graham's courtship, which Lucy, we know, observes, are dealt with cursorily; and worse, the whole of Paul Emmanuel's serious attempts to convert Lucy to Roman Catholicism are disposed of in part of one short chapter (36). Charlotte Brontë almost certainly feels the pressure of length on a plot with too many threads to it, and may well feel, as she did in *Shirley*, exhaustion from forcing herself to write when she is both ill and unhappy.

I knew – I was obliged to know – the green chintz of that little chair; the little snug chair itself, the carved, shining-black, foliated frame of that glass; the smooth milky-green of the china vessels on the stand; the very stand too, with its top of grey marble, splintered at one corner; – all these I was compelled to recognize and to hail, as last night I had, perforce, recognized and hailed the rosewood, the drapery, the porcelain, of the drawing-room. (Chaper 16)

Her delirious and drugged wanderings through the festivities in the Park express themselves through the details she observes:

the iron gateway, between the stone columns, was spanned by a flaming arch built of massed stars ... a land of enchantment, a garden most gorgeous, a plain sprinkled with coloured meteors, a forest with sparks of purple and ruby and golden fire gemming the foliage; a region, not of trees and shadow, but of strange architectural wealth – of altar and of temple, of pyramid, obelisk, and sphinx ... no matter that I quickly recognized the material of these solemn fragments – the timber, the paint, and the pasteboard – these inevitable discoveries failed to quite destroy the charm, or undermine the marvel of that night. (Chapter 38)

Her greatest happiness transmits itself by her intense sensitive and sensuous response, not to Paul Emmanuel himself, but to the house he gives her:

Opening an inner door, M. Paul disclosed a parlour, or salon – very tiny, but I thought, very pretty. Its delicate walls were tinged like a blush; its floor was waxed; a square of brilliant carpet covered its centre; its small round table shone like the mirror over its hearth; there was a little couch, a little chiffonière; the half-open, crimson-silk door of which, showed porcelain on the shelves; there was a French clock, a lamp; there were ornaments in biscuit china; the recess of the single ample window was filled with a green stand, bearing three green flower-pots, each filled with a fine plant glowing in bloom; in one corner appeared a guéridon with a marble top, and upon it a workbox, and a glass filled with violets in water.[1] (Chapter 41)

[1] Setting like action has apparent ineptitudes. It is revealed as it is required, not prepared in advance; particularly effectively when Lucy recognizes the Bretton furniture at La Terrasse – the excitement would be quite destroyed if the reader

Charlotte Brontë's style, even though it is recognizably the voice and idiom of the other three novels, is more emphatic and idiosyncratic in *Villette* than it has ever been. It is in many ways 'dated', rather than 'old-fashioned', and antipathetic to present-day readers: her rhetoric and worked-up imagery are less to modern taste than the brutal datelessness and the allusive, thematic, near-symbolic mode of *Wuthering Heights*. Charlotte Brontë cannot be expected to write a standard Southern English, spending as she did her formative years isolated in the West Riding of Yorkshire with an Irish father and a Cornish aunt, receiving only intermittent formal schooling, reading literature of the turn of the century, in particular that of two other non-English men – Scott and Byron. The only regular training she had in composition was in French, and she thus tends to think consciously in terms of the *mot juste*, rather than the felicitous phrase or the easy idiom. She has indeed many styles, varying between extreme simplicity and extremely heightened rhetoric, by way of the vigorously naturalistic, the choice epithet, the elaborated image and the consciously heightened and unlikely idiom. She draws freely and allusively on other writers, especially on the Bible, Shakespeare and Scott, putting their effects to work to produce her own. Though her expression may be accused of being inappropriate or misconceived, it can never be called slipshod or merely showy. Her methods always reveal a purpose, and move to a predetermined effect. It is usually an emotional or atmospheric as well as a rational one, whose method is usually cumulative, so that details, striking in themselves, all work together to make the whole. Hence the oddities one observes when quotations appear out of context: a part of their function is instantly lost, and hence their effect is easily misjudged.

The various ends served by a novelist's prose, notably narrative, description, reflection and dialogue, are not easily separable here;

---

could identify it for himself before Lucy does; but more awkwardly in the case of the fountain in the school garden, which comes to exist only when it is wanted, or the study where the *lecture pieuse* takes place, whose seating plan is only recounted when Paul Emmanuel is about to upset it. Again the effect is more like autobiography than the novel.

since so much of the story is what happens inside Lucy, to which what she observes contributes; the first three categories often merge, while dialogue (as will be seen shortly) has its own problems. As in *Wuthering Heights*, the response to an event is often so greatly at odds with the reader's own natural response to it, that speech, thought, and narrative have to be greatly intensified for the character's response to be shared. When the action carries its own effect, as when Lucy gains control of her unruly schoolgirls by tearing up the essay of one, and thrusting another into the cupboard, simplicity carries the day:

> All I could do now was to walk up to Blanche – Mademoiselle de Melcy, a young baronne – the eldest, tallest, handsomest, and most vicious – stand before her desk, take from under her hand her exercise book, remount the estrade, deliberately read the composition, which I found very stupid, and as deliberately, and in the face of the whole school, tear the blotted page in two.
>
> This action availed to draw attention and check noise. One girl alone, quite in the background, persevered in the riot with undiminished energy. I looked at her attentively. . . . She seemed both tall and wiry; but, if the conflict were brief and the attack unexpected, I thought I might manage her.
>
> Advancing up the room, looking as cool and careless as I possibly could, in short, *ayant l'air de rien*, I slightly pushed the door [of a small closet where books are kept] and found it was ajar. In an instant, she occupied the closet, the door was shut, and the key in my pocket.
>
> (Chapter 8)

The slight over-formality of diction here ('remount', 'deliberately', 'as deliberately') and the carefully-constructed sentences, reveal Lucy's ironic balanced self-regarding. When this balance is overthrown the imagery surges in; here Mme Beck, having spied on Lucy's letters from Graham, approves of her behaviour:

> 'les Anglais ont des idées à eux, en amitié, en amour, en tout. Mais au moins il n'est pas besoin de les surveiller,' she added, getting up and trotting away like the compact little pony she was.
>
> 'Then I hope,' murmured I to myself, 'you will graciously let alone my letters for the future.'

Alas! something came rushing into my eyes, dimming utterly their vision, blotting from sight the schoolroom, the garden, the bright winter sun, as I remembered that never more would letters, such as she had read, come to me. I had seen the last of them. That goodly river on whose banks I had sojourned, of whose waves a few reviving drops had trickled to my lips, was bending to another course: it was leaving my little hut and field forlorn and sand-dry, pouring its wealth of waters far away. The change was right, just, natural; not a word could be said: but I loved my Rhine, my Nile; I had almost worshipped my Ganges, and I grieved that the grand tide should roll estranged, should vanish like a false mirage.

(Chapter 26)

No doubt here the parallels come perilously near the comic (Rhine, Nile, Ganges) but the passage has a force not felt in extract, for the essence here is not the incident – Mme Beck's remarks – but the revealing of how Lucy is suffering under Paulina's fast-growing hold on Graham. The imagery is a powerful way of denoting what Lucy never lets herself think explicitly – she quite honestly rejects the imputation of 'warmer feelings'. It reproduces her suppression, but not denial, of her love.

Lucy's spiritual crises and the conflicts they cause within her are reproduced dramatically in terms of personified abstractions. They reveal the force of involuntary impulses that are neither intellectual nor rational, but have far more power than impulse or emotion. They render universal a private conflict, and reduce the egotism of a self-centred one. They are often neither virtues nor vices, but neutral qualities that may be either, according to events. They grow more frequent and elaborate as the novel proceeds. Early instances are notable mainly for their characteristic mixture of humorous self-awareness:

Into the hands of common-sense I confided the matter. Common-sense, however, was as chilled and bewildered as all my other faculties, and it was only under the spur of an inexorable necessity that she spasmodically executed her trust. Thus urged, she paid the porter: considering the crisis, I did not blame her too much that she was hugely cheated.

(Chapter 5)

Lucy's drugged sufferings in the park, thinking Paul Emmanuel is about to marry his young ward Justine Marie, are represented by a whole troop of abstractions, which rush upon Lucy and the reader in grotesque numbers, reproducing her drugged state, and her habitual self-control now turned, grotesquely, almost to an indulgence.

> I invoked Conviction to nail upon me the certainty, abhorred while embraced, to fix it with the strongest spikes her strongest strokes could drive, and when the iron had entered well my soul, I stood up, as I thought, renovated.
>
> In my infatuation I said, 'Truth, you are a good mistress to your faithful servants! While a Lie pressed me, how I suffered! Even when Falsehood was still sweet, still flattering to the fancy, and warm to the feelings, it wasted me with hourly torment. The persuasion that affection was won could not be divorced from the dread that, by another turn of the wheel, it might be lost. Truth stripped away Falsehood, and Flattery, and Expectancy, and here I stand – free!'
>
> (Chapter 39)

They later collapse themselves into a single pair:

> They had boasted their strength loudly when they reclaimed me from love and its bondage, but upon my demanding deeds, not words, some evidence of better comfort, some experience of a relieved life – Freedom excused herself, as for the present, impoverished and disabled to assist; and Renovation never spoke; he had died in the night suddenly. (Chapter 41)

This return is deliberately sardonic and deflatory, the register of Lucy's return to a rational though still hopeless state of mind.

Such self-consciousness produces its own kind of wit. Charlotte Brontë can exploit even her own mannerisms:

> This said 'lecture pieuse' was, I soon found, mainly designed as a wholesome mortification of the Intellect, a useful humiliation of the Reason; and such a dose for Common Sense as she might digest at her leisure, and thrive on as best she could. (Chapter 13)

and she can borrow effectively from others: the schoolgirls are a '*swinish multitude* not to be driven by force' (Chapter 9); Ginevra determines to rid herself of 'a *bread and butter-eating*, school-girl air' (ibid.); Rosine helps Lucy to dress 'like the *neat-handed Phillis* she could be when she chose' (Chapter 23); Mme Beck's children 'drew her into no deviation from the *even tenor* of her stoic calm' (Chapter 10); while the Comte de Bassompierre '*the grave and reverend signor* looked down on her as men do look on what is the apple of their eye' (Chapter 25); these are instances of drawing deliberately, in the italicized phrases, on the reader's memories of Burke, Byron, Milton, Gray and Shakespeare, to produce valid effects of her own. Less easy to accept are her more serious uses of Biblical allusion:

> This longing, and all of a similar kind, it was necessary to knock on the head; which I did, figuratively, after the manner of Jael to Sisera, driving a nail through their temples. Unlike Sisera, they did not die: they were but transiently stunned, and at intervals would turn on the nail with a rebellious wrench; then did the temples bleed, and the brain thrill to its core. (Chapter 12)

This, startling in its context, and even distasteful out of it, attempts to impress personal, and present, spiritual torment, in terms of past physical agony, a device she has used in her other novels.

She can also create precise felicities of her own. Many of the descriptions of details have even a Tennysonian sensuous accuracy:

> The rain-laden and streaming shrubs. (Chapter 36)

> pale walls over which a slight but endless garland of azure forget-me-nots ran mazed and bewildered amongst myriad gold leaves and tendrils. (Chapter 16)

while she can transfix a situation with a well-chosen word, as when Ginevra, aboard the channel ferry scorns 'the flaunting silks and velvets, and the *bears* which thereon *danced* attendance' (Chapter 6, my italics); or the hairdresser, fixing his quarters in the oratory, 'there, in the presence of "bénitier" candle, and crucifix, solemnized the mysteries of his art' (Chapter 14); or when Paul Emmanuel 'paid Mademoiselle de St Pierre a very *full-blown* compliment on the superiority of her bouquet' (Chapter 29); or, looking enraged at Lucy, 'he turned on [her] his spectacles', the symbol of his easily-shattered unapproachability (Chapter 38).

One power from which Charlotte Brontë cuts herself off in *Villette* is in dialogue. She has again the same disadvantage as in *The Professor*. A foreign setting entails a foreign language, French, so that what French-speaking characters say cannot be coloured by how they say it, nor can their mode of speech enrich our understanding of them. Of all the dialogues between Mme Beck and Paul Emmanuel and Lucy, supposed to be in French, the reader does not recall actual phrases, as he remembers those of Jane and Mr Rochester, or even Shirley, Caroline, Robert and Louis. What he may remember is in French: 'me voilà veuf de mes lunettes' (Chapter 38), 'oubliez les anges, les bossues, et surtout les Professeurs – et bon soir' (Chapter 34). But again Charlotte Brontë has the virtues of her defects. She has always had the urge to break into French, even inappropriately or superfluously,[1] but the habit is most useful here to give the foreign flavour. Her rendering of foreign speech is strikingly good: no speaker ever appears ridiculous merely for being foreign, and indeed the novel's most moving moment is when Lucy herself charms by her broken French:

> 'All these weary days,' said he, repeating my words, with a gentle, kindly mimicry of my voice and foreign accent, not new from his lips, and of which the playful banter never wounded, not even when coupled as it often was, with the assertion, that however I might *write* his language, I *spoke* and always should speak it imperfectly and hesitatingly. '"All these weary days," I have not for one hour forgotten you.' (Chapter 41)

Elsewhere, she rightly makes very little of Lucy's language problems, which would make a quite superfluous difficulty in the narrative.

Villette conceals rather than exposes its author's limitations. She cannot write polite conversation; not only has Jane Austen's power to make neutral, formal, exchanges significant never been hers, she can rarely render it naturalistic. But she can here circumvent situations which require it, since the language of half the characters is

[1] The worst example must be the landlady in *Shirley*, exasperated by the curates: '"Ç'en est trop", she would have said, if she could speak French.'
(Chapter 1)

purportedly French, while Lucy, by nature inarticulate even in her own tongue, is rarely present at formal or conventional meetings. The hiatus is quite plausible, and Charlotte Brontë's limitation, somewhat notable by the ineptitude of what filled it in *Jane Eyre*, or by the deliberately eccentric conversation in *Shirley*, is no longer a matter of concern. When Paulina re-enters the story, Lucy can report their unconventionally frank reminiscences of Bretton, and the strange whims of the elfish daughter welcoming her father, dancing, and tasting 'old October' in the old Dutch kitchen of La Terrasse, but can appropriately avoid hearing any of the speeches by which Paulina impresses the savants and literati (Chapter 27), or any of the exchanges between Paulina and Graham.

A notable change in *Villette* is that dialogue often ends, or gives way to, reported speech and résumé, at just the crucial moments for which she has habitually depended upon it. Almost all the exchanges between Lucy and Paul Emmanuel break down thus, most conspicuously the last, in which Lucy, passionately refusing Paul Emmanuel's ward Justine Marie for her pupil, though she 'lacked not words now' when her tale 'streamed on her tongue' (Chapter 41) not only passes rapidly over her experiences in the Park, but holds back the words that cause Paul Emmanuel to make his declaration. This scene stops where the corresponding one in *Jane Eyre* begins to take life. It may be said that Charlotte Brontë is again showing ruth to emotion and recollection, rather than to fact: it is much more natural for Lucy to forget the words used at the moments of greatest feeling, than for Jane Eyre to remember them.

Even though the apparent awkwardnesses of *Villette* frequently have a discoverable and legitimate purpose, one must conclude that it is not so perfect as a whole as *Jane Eyre*. Even though its scope breaks new ground for the novel, and uses it as no other novelist has done, it is restricted in that it takes in less than the full range of human experience. Charlotte Brontë has grown older and wiser since she wrote *Jane Eyre*, and can breathe life into an older and wiser heroine. She has learned more of the professional business of writing a novel, and grown more aware of her reader's part in what she does. She has taken entirely new material – whether she realized that her own Brussels school life was so or not. But much has been lost. Wisdom has not brought joy, and the young writer's *élan* has gone with the young heroine. *Villette* brings the sense that Lucy, calmly resilient, is not the only one worn down by her plight; Charlotte Brontë herself has grown, not only painfully lonely, but tired. The faults of carelessness of finish are not loss of skill, but loss of power.

It is impossible to speculate on what Charlotte Brontë might have done, had she lived. The fragment of a last novel (published as *Emma*)[1] is too short for evidence, even if her remarks to her husband did not prove that she expected to revise it out of recognition. With Charlotte Brontë, unlike most writers, the first published work is also the greatest and most perfect in conception and achievement. The charge that she is never a major novelist will not stand, since so many of the marks of greatness are upon her. She is unlike anyone else; she never repeated herself; no sensitive reader is impervious to her (though many resent and repel a power they cannot account for); and (a simple contributory point) she is read and relished by many who, though readers of the classics, are not readers of novels; by those who are not readers of literature; and even by those who do not class themselves as readers at all. It is tempting to say that Charlotte Brontë wrote one good, one outstanding and one great novel – *Shirley*, *Villette* and *Jane Eyre*; and that all three would stand higher than they do had their author's anonymity never been penetrated, her own life thus been prevented from colouring the reading of them, and had *Wuthering Heights* never seen print.

[1] In the *Cornhill Magazine*, April 1860.

6

AGNES GREY

No one could call Anne Brontë's two novels masterpieces; but she deserves neither to be ignored, nor to be regarded only as a pale copy of her sisters. She is absorbing on at least three, though not equal, counts: as the first novel writer of the family, using material later used by Emily and Charlotte; as a norm from which to judge the powers of her sisters in using such material; and as a novelist in her own right with a mode and flavour of her own – worthy of attention, original and good. She resembles Charlotte in having similar experiences to draw upon, and in feeling in her second novel a moral duty to write of an uncongenial topic; she resembles both her sisters in finding man's inhumanity to man a fitting element in a love story; and in being startlingly unconventional, unsophisticated, and candid. She uses some of the methods of both in organizing her material. But her own personality, her way of considering the experiences she puts before her heroines, and the idiom in which her heroines present them, are not so much akin to her sisters as to the eighteenth century. If the reader goes to Anne Brontë for what either Charlotte or Emily offers, he is disappointed. If he takes pleasure in Fanny Burney or Maria Edgeworth – or, to name a greater, Jane Austen – he will find her manner congenial and her writing attractive. While I propose to relate her novels to those of Charlotte or Emily where the connection is useful to either sister, I intend also to assess them on their own terms, for what they attempt and achieve.

Anne Brontë has suffered like her sisters from the Brontë legend. She has also suffered from the sisters themselves. One thing that is best forgotten is the image of the 'gentle Anne', as she is termed by Charlotte and Arthur Nicholls, since without the legend and the comment one would not see much 'gentleness' in her, even in *Agnes Grey*. One thing well remembered however is that *Agnes Grey* is probably the first prose for publication written at Haworth Parsonage, and would be read and absorbed by her sisters before *Wuthering Heights, The Professor,* and the story it most resembles, *Jane Eyre,* were written. If any credit for conception is to be claimed it must be by Anne. The attempt must therefore be made to think of her with a mind reasonably uncoloured by *Jane Eyre* and *Wuthering Heights,* while not yet forgetting the juvenile fantasies that themselves colour all three.

Agnes Grey is an unpretentious work about an unpretentious heroine. It is probably a recasting of the work mentioned in the 'Birthday Note' of 1845, where she remarks: 'I have begun the third volume of *Passages in the life of an Individual*': a title more apt to what is now *Agnes Grey* than the one it possesses, which, like the story, is unassuming, and does not adequately suggest what is actually offered. One would summarize the main story as one in which a clergyman's younger daughter, compelled by her father's fallen fortunes to earn her living as a governess in two middle-class country families, and later, at his death, to help her mother run a small school, meets, while in her second place of employment, a worthy young clergyman whom she later marries. The other plot concerns the young and beautiful pupil, a coquette, who marries a degenerate young landowner for his money and position. Few plots could be less sensational; even *The Professor,* by contrast, seems a heady brew. Of the few exciting moments Anne Brontë offers herself, she makes very little, reducing them by covering them briefly – as Agnes' father's death, which is comprised in a few words at the end of Chapter 18 – or by a calm literal manner of telling – like her meeting with Mr Weston on the sands (Chapter 24) – or by a dash of astringent or sardonic humour – as when she suppresses her reply to Mrs Bloomfield:

> 'You seem to have forgotten,' said she calmly, 'that the creatures were all created for our convenience.'
> I thought that the doctrine admitted some doubt.
>
> (Chapter 5)

Clearly her aim is not excitement or sensation, and, as will later be examined, is not indicated properly by such a summary, which is actually misleading. One does not, in fact, read *Agnes Grey* for the story, and its importance does not lie in the story, a matter which immediately sets Anne Brontë apart from her sisters. Like Jane Austen, Anne Brontë, working her way through it without excitement or sensationalism, produces some unique incident, pungent characters, and, above all, a serious, penetrating and new exposure of society.

Also like Jane Austen, she keeps to what she knows. The material is plainly drawn from her own life. Anne Brontë herself is a clergyman's daughter, the youngest of the family, compelled to teach to earn her living, employed in the families of the gentry, while Agnes Grey's eventual modest though happy marriage is what Anne Brontë could without impropriety envisage for herself. Like Charlotte, she draws on more than herself. The loathsome Bloomfield children in her first post are the Inghams of Anne's first post at Blake Hall; the Murray household resembles closely that of the Robinsons, with whom she stayed some years, as Agnes stays with the Murrays.[1] Some of the most telling incident also is from life, notably the one that most readers remember best, in which Agnes destroys the nest of young birds to prevent a brutal child from torturing them.

It is as tempting therefore with Anne Brontë as with Charlotte to identify the narrator with the author, to consider that what is revealed of Agnes must also be true of Anne. It is not necessarily any more true of Agnes Grey than of Jane Eyre. While the narrative stance adopted in *Agnes Grey* is very much more simple than that of *Jane Eyre*, it is no mere autobiographical fantasy. Considerable degrees of detachment may be seen between the 'I' at different points in the narrative, and the 'I' who comments on them. Quite clearly the childish eighteen-year-old girl of the opening chapters is greatly below the narrator and also the

[1] Mrs Robinson is better known as the object of Branwell Brontë's ill-founded passion than as the original of Anne's portrait, which is considerably more cooly damning than anything in Branwell's history, though that also indicates a true mother of the daughter figured forth in Rosalie.

reader, not only in quietly accepting that she is fit only to 'go and practise [her] music, or play with the kitten' (Chapter 1), but in thinking that

> the clear remembrance of my own thoughts in early childhood would [in training children] be a surer guide than the instructions of the most mature adviser. (Chapter 1)

As Agnes grows up the gap narrows, as it does as Jane Eyre grows up. But it never closes. Quite clearly the Agnes of the closing section is not only older but wiser than the young self narrating the events; yet at twenty-three, she still asks her mother's permission before accepting Mr Weston's invitation to a walk (Chapter 25). There is no suggestion, despite the moral and instructive tone of parts of the narrative, that this is the proper, or accepted, way to act for a woman of twenty-three (only a year younger than Lucy Snowe), as there is for instance in the works of Charlotte M. Yonge. Anne Brontë always represents Agnes as someone younger and less experienced than herself or the reader, who is much less often on terms of wholehearted sympathy with her than with Jane Eyre. As a narrator, she has more in common with Esther Summerson in *Bleak House*.

She has in common with Esther that she also is not the absolute centre of interest. She is what makes the action cohere, but she is not necessarily the protagonist. She is the means by which the novel progresses, the author's purpose in it is achieved, and the events and characters are connected. But unlike *Jane Eyre's*, the important events concern others, notably Rosalie Murray, as much as herself, and the personalities she delineates are almost as clearly seen, and as interesting, as her own. One remembers Rosalie's flirtation with the rector Mr Hatfield better than Agnes's meetings with the curate Mr Weston, remembers the Bloomfield children's revolting habits more than the horror they inspire in Agnes; one sees the horse-loving Matilda or her mother 'who required neither rouge nor padding to add to her charms' (Chapter 7) quite as clearly as the quiet, plain, little heroine. Anne Brontë, while clearly showing, and expecting to elicit, sympathy for the hard-pressed Agnes, is not primarily concerned with her responses.

Agnes does not actually create the reader's reaction to those with whom she comes into contact, nor do Anne Brontë and the reader judge them by how they treat her, as one judges those who come into contact with Jane Eyre. The whole of Rosalie's flirtation with Mr Hatfield proceeds without Agnes being moved by it at all, except to detached moral disapproval. Yet it is fully as significant and absorbing as Rosalie's next attempt, to flirt with Mr Weston, from which Agnes suffers considerable pain. What makes the second flirtation a graver matter than the first is what it reveals about Rosalie, that she is so taken up with coquetterie that she must descend from the willing and socially acceptable vicar to the unmoved and socially impossible curate. Agnes's feelings have very little to do with the artistic purpose here.

Agnes indeed as a personality can be effaced for quite long stretches. There are several points at which a secondary narrator supersedes her: as in Chapter 11, where the cottager Nancy retails the contrasting visits and behaviour to her of the two clergymen, or in Chapter 14, where Rosalie tells her own story. These, and scenes in which the story is told to Agnes, who merely comments, bear a resemblance to the method of *Wuthering Heights*. There are also many points at which the scene proceeds by way of dialogue in which Agnes takes no part and passes no comment. If so neutral a narrator has a precedent, it is found in Scott's *Redgauntlet*, which opens with the letters to and fro of Alan Fairford and his friend Darsie Latimer, the bulk of the narrative being that of Fairford, who is no more the all-absorbing hero than is Agnes. Scott has soon to abandon the method; Anne Brontë can continue in it. It is clear that her purpose in using her material, and adopting the first-person narrator, is an original and largely self-taught one; it is not a tentative movement towards either Charlotte Brontë's or Emily's. She is attempting an examination of a section of society, which, seen from the unusual view that a governess enjoys, exposes itself, its standards, its follies, and its failings for the reader's assessment, not necessarily so that an unusual judgement may be passed, but so that long-held opinions may be rescrutinized, refreshed, and confirmed.

Such a purpose affects the relationship between author, narrator and reader. Anne Brontë never forgets either herself, her creation, or her reader. Identification with Agnes is impossible, because of the childishness already noted, nor can one ever lose oneself in the action, since it is usually either comic or reprehensible. Emotional response is called up for a purpose, so that understanding and appreciation shall, as with Jane Austen, lead to moral judgement, the way to which is pointed by a whole variety of means, all befitting Agnes, but all making the detachment between herself and the reader very clear. Anne Brontë assumes a reader as rational and reasonable as Agnes's most mature self. Sometimes her tone is of serious straightforward utterance of dicta known to both, and given because they summarize what has gone, or prepare what is to follow:

> Habitual associates are known to exercise a great influence over each other's minds and manners. Those whose actions are for ever before our eyes, whose words are ever in our ears, will naturally lead us, albeit, against our will – slowly – gradually – imperceptibly, perhaps, to act and speak as they do. (Chapter 11)

It is with such well-grounded fears of her own deterioration in bad company that Agnes welcomes Mr Weston. Frequently she is much more oblique, as in her closing reply to Rosalie's wish

> 'to enjoy myself thoroughly, and coquet with all the world, till I am on the verge of being called an old maid; and then, to escape the infamy of that, after having made ten thousand conquests, to break all their hearts save one, by marrying some high-born, rich, indulgent husband, whom, on the other hand, fifty ladies were dying to have.'
>
> 'Well, as long as you entertain these views, keep single by all means, and never marry at all, not even to escape the infamy of old-maidenhood.' (Chapter 9)

The story begins

> All true histories contain instruction; though, in some, the treasure may be hard to find, and, when found, so trivial in quantity that the dry, shrivelled kernel scarcely compensates for the trouble of cracking the nut. Whether this be the case with my history or not, I am hardly competent to judge; I sometimes think it might prove useful to some, and entertaining to others, but the world may judge for

itself: shielded by my own obscurity, and by the lapse of years, and a few fictitious names, I do not fear to venture, and will candidly lay before the public what I would not disclose to the most intimate friend.
(Chapter 1)

It never loses sight of its opening. The purpose revealed – to establish moral standards, whether those of Agnes or others, to measure their conduct against them, and thus establish the worth of both the conduct and of the standards on which it is based – is plainly Anne Brontë's own, not her character's, since Agnes modestly disclaims what her whole history is designed to reveal – the possession of the 'treasure' of instruction. Agnes is plainly rather a mask behind which her author may retire, than a means by which, in Agnes's words, Anne Brontë herself can 'candidly lay before the public what I would not disclose to the most intimate friend'. She is showing herself ironically and wittily aware of the illusions of the fictional memoir which involves so improbable a laying before the public, and so establishes the terms on which she uses it. Anne Brontë, intending to be moral, avoids, again like Jane Austen, ever alienating her reader by instructing him in person. Agnes is her mouthpiece, a creation whose judgement the reader can always trust, but who is yet sufficiently his inferior in years and experience to make an appealing guide. The form of the candid, unsophisticated, unprofessional memoir is one very suited both to such a purpose and such a narrator. It makes the direct addresses to the reader acceptable and even desirable. They are frequent:

As I cannot, like Dogberry, find it in my heart to bestow *all* my tediousness on the reader, I will not go on to bore him with a minute detail of all the discoveries and proceedings of this and the following day.
(Chapter 7)

A few more observations about Horton Lodge and its on goings, and I have done with dry description for the present.
(Chapter 7)

As I am in the way of confessions, I may as well acknowledge that, about this time, I paid more attention to dress than ever I had done before.
(Chapter 17)

The diffidence that provokes these remarks makes Agnes an engaging guide, and prevents her from being a pontifical or priggish one. While one may suspect that the author also is diffident, she is proved to have chosen her form well, since it turns what could have been a defect to good use.

The narrative method and the form are, indeed, more cunning than they seem. The story is basically in two main sections, one comprising Agnes's experiences with the appalling Bloomfield family at Wellwood (Chapters 2–5), the other her several years' stay with the Murrays at Horton Lodge (Chapters 7–20). The sections are preluded by an account of her home life and the circumstances leading to her becoming a governess (Chapter 1); they are interrupted by several returns home for holidays (Chapter 3), for her sister's wedding (Chapter 8), and for her father's death (Chapter 18); and they are concluded by the brief account of her stay in her mother's school at A—(Chapters 21, 24, 25), and by her visit to the married Rosalie, Lady Ashby (Chapters 22, 23). The proportions of the material indicate clearly enough that this is not merely the chronicle of Agnes's life in these years. A minority of it is devoted to matters most touching her in her home life; her sister's marriage is passed over in a brief conversation with Rosalie:

> 'Who is she to be married to?'
> 'To Mr Richardson, the vicar of a neighbouring parish.'
> 'Is he rich?'
> 'No – only comfortable.'
> 'Is he handsome?'
> 'No – only decent.'
> 'Young?'
> 'No – only middling.'
> 'O mercy! what a wretch!'   (Chapter 8)

An exchange whose prime purpose is to display Rosalie's views on marriage, and reveals nothing of the relationship between Agnes and her sister. Similarly Agnes's father's death is dwelt on less than the callous behaviour of Mrs Murray, who

> concluded with saying I might have the phaeton to take me to O—.

'And instead of *repining*, Miss Grey, be thankful for the *privileges* you enjoy. There's many a poor clergyman whose family would be plunged into ruin by his death; but *you*, you see, have influential friends ready to continue their patronage, and to show you every consideration.' (Chapter 18)

Anne Brontë's business in the novel is with the society and attitudes she can examine through Agnes, rather than with Agnes herself. The examination becomes more subtle and complex (though one would never call it deep), as the novel goes on. The moral weight clearly regulates the shape not only of the whole but of its parts. Agnes's troubles with the Bloomfields occupy three chapters only; her stay with the Murrays, thirteen. What looks like disproportion results in balance, and shows the modest discretion of the author, as well as the purpose guiding her. Anne Brontë begins with the straightforwardly preposterous standards of the Bloomfields, who see no wrong in allowing a frustrated child to 'spit in the faces of those who incurred her displeasure' (Chapter 3); in encouraging a seven-year-old boy to kick not only the dog, but his governess; and who consider tormenting animals a child's legitimate amusement. Even with the Bloomfields, however, the rendering of character is convincing:

'Damme, but the lad has some spunk in him too! Curse me, if ever I saw a nobler little scoundrel than that! He's beyond petticoat government already: – by G— he defies mother, granny, governess, and all!' (Chapter 5)

and the reasoning perversely ingenious:

'I think,' said she, 'a child's amusement is scarcely to be weighed against the welfare of a soulless brute.'
'But, for the child's own sake, it ought not to be encouraged to such amusements,' answered I, as meekly as I could, to make up for such unusual pertinacity. 'Blessed are the merciful, for they shall obtain mercy.'
'Oh, of course! but that refers to our conduct towards each other.'
'The merciful man shows mercy to his beast,' I ventured to add.
'I think *you* have not shown much mercy,' replied she, with a

210

short, bitter laugh; 'killing the poor birds by wholesale, in that shocking manner, and putting the dear boy to such misery, for a mere whim!'   (Chapter 5)

The events at the Bloomfields' are so startling, and often shocking, that three chapters spent on them are enough; to continue or elaborate them would be to repeat, and to dull the effect. Once Anne Brontë has supplied an instance of the selfish and stupid father

'remember that, in future, when a decent dish leaves this table, they shall not *touch* it in the kitchen. Remember *that*, Mrs Bloomfield!'
(Chapter 3)

and of the consequences in a selfish and stupid son; and once she has made her point about the suffering that can be inflicted by both upon the helpless and the dependent, their use is over. Anne Brontë recognizes also that the grotesque is incapable of growth, and so moves her heroine away forthwith from a household of grotesques.

The transition to Horton is both smooth and artistic. Mood and themes are carried over. When Agnes first arrives at Horton, she is in charge of a family whose two youngest members are barbarians of a larger growth; John is 'rough as a young bear, boisterous, unruly, unprincipled, untaught, unteachable' and Charles 'only active in doing mischief, and only clever in inventing falsehoods' (Chapter 7). Though Anne Brontë wisely wastes no time on Agnes's tussles with them, which must repeat her tussles with the Bloomfields, their unpleasing presence connects Horton with the earlier section, while their speedy departure prepares for something new.[1]

The Murray girls are more mature and consequently more complex. Through them the novel moves on to consider not only the effects of negligent upbringing on behaviour, but the young person's own application of the deficient principles he has been

[1] The two girls also are mere schoolgirls at first, Matilda only thirteen, and Rosalie, at sixteen, still 'something of a romp' (Chapter 7), who has yet to grow up into the accomplished coquette.

given. The young boys having gone to school, the story concentrates on Rosalie, the most brilliant of the family, and the greatest disaster. The truths she exemplifies require a series of events, not mere isolated anecdotes, hence the greater length devoted to the telling. The story follows her 'coming-out' into society, her successes, her admirers, her betrothal to Sir Thomas Ashby, her encouragement and rejection of the clergyman Mr Hatfield, her attempt to captivate the curate Mr Weston, her wedding, and finally her married life. Anne Brontë firmly follows her on her career even after it has effectively ceased to be Agnes's, and drives home her message dramatically when Agnes visits Rosalie a year after her marriage (Chapter 22), to see the frustration and boredom to which her ambitions have led her. With this episode the social wheel has come full circle, Agnes Grey's function as narrator has been fulfilled, and the novel has completed its course. Rosalie has now become the parent, in her own household ruined by false values, with an unwanted child about to grow up to become, inevitably, another victim of its circumstances, as its mother has been. The situation is now seen from the mother's view:

> 'What pleasure can I have in seeing a girl grow up to eclipse me, and enjoy those pleasures I am forever debarred from? But supposing I could be so generous as to take delight in this, still it is *only* a child; and I can't centre all my hopes in a child; that is only one degree better than devoting oneself to a dog. And as for all the goodness and wisdom you have been trying to instil into me – that is all very right and proper, I dare say; and if I were some twenty years older, I might fructify by it; but people must enjoy themselves when they're young – and if others won't let them – why, they must hate them for it!'
> (Chapter 23)

The final episode, which settles Agnes in the situation she merits, drives home by contrast the points made at Ashby Park, and gains its power as much from this function, as for the happiness it brings to Agnes.

By contrast with her sisters', Anne Brontë's characters seem unsubtle. Though remarkably vigorous and memorable (considering how concisely they make their effects), they undoubtedly lack the strong flavour of Charlotte's, or the sublimity of Emily's. They are much closer to common life than either, and, equally, much further from any easily identifiable literary influence. They all have the rather simple force and the conviction of the documentary, the kind of personality that emerges from the sociological survey rather than the literary imagination. Excluding Mr Weston, they are of two separate kinds: those who form Agnes's family, and those whom she encounters away from home. The differences are of attitude as well as function and treatment, and indicate once more where Anne Brontë's interests lie. She wastes little time on the Grey family, large though it must figure in Agnes's mind. Clearly she could, without destroying the balance of the book, delineate the elder sister Mary more clearly, or spend more time on the mother, but to do so would alter the tone, since these characters are conceived in a different spirit from the rest. Their purpose also is different. They are the first on whom the candid Agnes exercises her judgement for the reader's benefit, thereby gaining the reader's confidence in her. Since we recognize how justly and acutely she assesses those who are virtuous in themselves, in circumstances we can readily enter into, whom we can readily recognize for ourselves, we are prepared to trust her summings-up of strangers, whose actions might well seem close to incredible. Agnes's family are not so much the stuff of nineteenth-century fiction, as of the eighteenth-century essay:

> my father was completely overwhelmed by the calamity – health, strength, and spirits sunk beneath the blow; and he never wholly recovered them. In vain my mother strove to cheer him by appealing to his piety, to his courage, to his affection for herself and us. That very affection was his greatest torment: it was for our sakes he had so ardently longed to increase his fortune – it was our interest that had lent such brightness to his hopes, and that imparted such bitterness to his present distress. (Chapter I)

The eighteenth-century note is no disadvantage: Agnes analysing her father is as reliable as Fielding analysing Squire Allworthy, or Dr Johnson summarizing Rasselas. The note persists when the analysis is more acute and verges on the humorous:

My mother like most active, managing women, was not gifted with very active daughters; for this reason – that being so clever and diligent herself, she was never tempted to trust her affairs to a deputy, but on the contrary, was willing to act and think for others as well as for number one. (Chapter 1)

Like the essayists, she reveals no more of the character than is perceptible to the intelligent observer, and has no occasion to go deeper. Her father's sufferings, even though they hasten his death, receive no more analysis than the above. Anne Brontë is happy, however, to allow dialogue to suggest relationships and underlying characteristics, and can do so economically and pleasantly, though she has no intention of using it, like Emily Brontë, for characters' deliberate self-revelation. The suggestion of cross-purposes, and modes of thought, is neatly done when Mrs Grey suggests that Mary should try to sell some of her drawings, while Agnes is preoccupied with her own plan to become a governess:

'I wish *I* could do something,' said I.
'You, Agnes! well, who knows? You draw pretty well too; if you choose some simple piece for your subject, I dare say you will be able to produce something we shall be proud to exhibit.'
(Chapter 1)

The atmosphere at home is admirably created, providing the settled existence behind Agnes which makes her resilient in the face of her astonishing experiences, so much more realistic than those in *Jane Eyre* or *Villette*, whose heroines Charlotte Brontë deliberately deprives of the refuge of a safe home. Economically, Anne Brontë continues to epitomize Agnes's home in her mother. She is the main speaker in the opening chapters, and the one who remains at the end, when, elder sister married, Agnes resigns her post to help her now widowed mother run her school. She represents a norm of good sense and right feeling, little emphasized but impressive, which prevents the disproportion of a world full of vice and folly, which would result from dwelling wholly on the families who employ Agnes.

Edward Weston, curate of Horton, on the other hand, is possibly the shadowiest hero ever invented by a woman novelist.

If Agnes were the all-absorbing heroine, this would be a very serious charge. In fact, though he cannot rouse much interest in the reader, or demand long consideration, he does adequately what he is called upon to do. He is primarily the doer of good deeds in a naughty world, the only well-principled person of her own class, other than her family, whom Agnes meets. He functions always as a moral force. He is the immediate contrast to the worldly and careless clergyman Mr Hatfield, and, even as the man Agnes loves, what are stressed are his moral qualities:

> I could think of him day and night; and I could feel that he was worthy to be thought of. Nobody knew him as I did; nobody could appreciate him as I did. (Chapter 17)

Lack of information is a dramatic asset when he is marked down by Rosalie as her last victim. The reader, like Agnes, knows his virtue, but has no way of knowing his emotional temperament, or how he will respond to Rosalie's advances. While the end of the story is certain – by the convention of the novel he will marry Agnes – there is no way of telling whether he will succumb to Rosalie and then, disillusioned, recover, or whether he will be acute enough to resist her.[1] A modest originality of Mr Weston's is to be an early instance of the unhandsome hero. The man 'a little, a very little, above the middle size' with 'his face too square for beauty', eyebrows 'too projecting' and eyes 'brown in colour, not large, and somewhat deepset, but strikingly brilliant' (Chapter 11) is the counterpart of a heroine with 'marked features, pale hollow cheek, and ordinary dark brown hair', just as Mr Rochester is the counterpart of Jane.[2] Anne Brontë does here, calmly, without any

[1] Any treatment of Weston such as that of Mr Rochester and Blanche Ingram would, though possibly creating more absorbing personalities, be to no useful end, since the movement at this point cannot turn away from Rosalie herself (the 'Blanche Ingram' of the episode) who is being swept on to uncongenial wedlock.

[2] He and Mr Rochester may well have a similar source, sharing as well as looks a fine voice, while at one point Mr Weston even uses a Rochester image

'The human heart is like india-rubber; a little swells it, but a great deal will not burst it. (Chapter 12)

continued on next page

sense in the writing that she is being novel, what Charlotte Brontë afterwards does with panache – a man who has no charms save in the eye of the narrator.

All the other characters are knaves or fools in some degree, even the children. Their failings are what justify their literary existence. Such a statement suggests that *Agnes Grey* must be either a satire, or a work of very limited interest. The nature of Agnes herself prevents it being the first, while the functions of the other characters prevent its being the second. Like the Grey family, the rest are seen only from outside, by the intelligent observer Agnes, whose author never allows her to guess at or speculate on the variety of impulses and motives which produce the behaviour she observes. Anne Brontë never causes the reader to worry what there can have been in common between Mr and Mrs Murray, for example, to cause them to marry, nor suggests how they may behave to each other in situations where Agnes herself could not observe them. She does not resolve the difficulty of how a selfish woman can endure the company of her own intolerable children. But she chronicles with such precision that the immediate incident rings so true as not to invite such speculation. Anne, like Emily, observes personalities, and allows them to expose themselves; she does not analyse or dissect; a feature which reveals that she is closer to Emily in this matter than to Charlotte, who is as much concerned with interior causes as with effects. The purpose of Anne Brontë's characterization is not psychological, but social. Actions and attributes are selected to lead the reader to consider their social and personal consequences, not their causes.

It is therefore wise of her to begin with the inhabitants of Wellwood. The reader's natural tendency with a child is to consider it as a being with a potential, but no past, who is very much the direct consequences of the influences it feels. The distasteful Bloomfield brood – Tom, Mary Ann, and Fanny – are presented firmly as the results of irresponsible overindulgence,

---

anticipating Mr Rochester's declaring himself as 'hard and tough as an India-rubber ball: pervious, though, through a chink or two still, and with one sentient point in the middle of the lump.'   (*Jane Eyre*, Chapter 14.)

to be judged themselves for conscious vices, and to cause judgement to be made both on their parents, and, by extension, on the grossly deficient moral and social standards by which the parents live. Good care is taken that they shall not be pitied as victims, either of the system or each other: Tom Bloomfield, enjoying brutality and torment, is his uncle Robson in miniature; Mary Ann, whom he bullies, is deliberately, systematically and inflexibly perverse, and the bad habits of both, and of the even younger Fanny, are such as to rouse more revulsion in the reader than in the narrator. Agnes herself and the nurserymaid Betty (who puts in a brief appearance in Chapter 3) prevent the reader from supposing that the children suffer from lack of affection, since it is offered and rejected. Anne Brontë clearly believes in original sin, as well as natural good, and in training as the very necessary force that will turn a child into a good man. The Bloomfield children's purpose, since they occupy only four hair-raising chapters, is to prepare the way for the Murrays, a more subtle and exhaustive study of the corruption of the individual, and the effects of wrong training on a faulty nature. Agnes, brooding on her charges, remarks:

> the children would, in time, become more humanized: every month would contribute to make them some little wiser, and, consequently, more manageable; for a child of nine or ten, as frantic and ungovernable as these at six and seven would be a maniac.   (Chapter 3)

The Murrays, in their early teens, bear her out, and the reader, when he meets them, is prepared to regard them in the same way as the Bloomfields, looking only to the consequences they bring about, not to what caused them to become what they are.

The parents of these unhappy offspring are revealed with the same documentary precision, though, because they impinge less on Agnes, and are less to the purpose, more briefly. Again the eighteenth-century note is heard, and the characters of Mr and Mrs Bloomfield, the Grandmother, and Uncle Robson seem true to type without ever seeming trite. They are revealed through the individual, small, significant encounter, and usually through dialogue. Mr Bloomfield suddenly and arbitrarily interrupts the narrative, just as he suddenly and arbitrarily descends on Agnes and his children, to abuse them and her and depart; Uncle Robson, a more positive evil though a temporary one, makes his devastating comment on his nephew, Tom, raging over the loss of his birds' nest, and departs likewise:

> 'Curse me, if ever I saw a nobler little scoundrel than that! He's beyond petticoat government already! – By G— he defies mother, granny, governess, and all! Ha, ha, ha! Never mind, Tom, I'll get you another brood tomorrow.' (Chapter 5)

Mrs Bloomfield on the other hand makes an impressive first appearance doing nothing; all the while Agnes wrestles with tough, cold, meat, with her hands numb from five hours' exposure to the bitter wind, what is being sensed is the tough, cold, numb Mrs Bloomfield silently watching her.

The handling of the convincingly unreasonable characters here leads forward to Horton, where the characters are to be unreasonable in ways more elaborate, and seemingly more like what usually appear in a novel. In the background are the neglecting father, and the worldly mother, seeing only what is to her daughter's social and financial advantage, bending all her efforts to an early and profitable marriage; in the foreground the two contrasting young women, the hoyden and the coquette; and attending on Rosalie an assortment of suitors, amongst whom the brutish and successful landowner contrasts, in his turn, with the aspiring social climber, the rector. Here also Anne Brontë successfully imposes her own tone, and, while using the stuff of convention, sees it not at all in the conventional way, contriving never to slip into the merely grotesque on the one hand, or on the other to allow herself or the reader to be seduced by the charm of what is inescapably reprehensible. The personality and position of Agnes herself imposes proportion, since what looms largest to her is also what matters most to the story and theme. The method is economical in itself, and performed with natural economy. The characterization here has the same verve as at Wellwood, but is far more varied in its methods. The least significant personalities are suggested with splendid precision. The setting, the kind of character, the cool justice which is accorded them, the humane partly-involved narrator, the mingling of humour with instruction, all suggest, not another of the Brontës, but Trollope. While it is clear that his handling of elaborate ecclesiastical politics and the edges of high society is beyond her, so are her just proportioning of means to her end, her impulse to understate rather than elaborate her points, beyond Trollope. Mr Murray for instance is only of concern as the father figure for an unsatisfactory family in general, and as the one who authorizes and condones Matilda in her hunting and swearing. Agnes never see him 'to speak to' (Chapter 12) as she says, but 'the figure of a tall stout gentleman with scarlet cheeks and crimson nose' (Chapter 7), precisely noted at the beginning of her account of the family, remains firmly fixed in the reader's mind. Mrs Murray, more important since her influence is upon the more important daughter Rosalie, is permitted to impress herself by speech, by quietly devastating self-exposure:

> 'I have hitherto found all the governesses, even the very best of them, faulty in this particular. They wanted that meek and quiet spirit which St Matthew, or some of them, says is better than the putting on of apparel – you will know the passage to which I allude, for you are a clergyman's daughter.'   (Chapter 7)

Her moral values, her self-satisfaction, her relationship to her governess need no more explanation. On the rare occasions when it is necessary to suggest her motives, the method is equally laconic:

> having notwithstanding the disadvantages of a country life so satisfactorily disposed of her elder daughter, the pride of her heart, [she] had begun seriously to turn her attention to the younger.
>   (Chapter 18)

'satisfactorily' suggests her own opinion, 'disposed' suggests Agnes's; while the conventional phrase 'pride of her heart' takes on a new richness applied to a relationship which has displayed all too much 'pride' and a total lack of 'heart'.

The younger daughter Matilda contrasts with her sister (her main function in the novel), demonstrating that, while to be sophisticated like Rosalie is unadmirable, to lack the quality may be, not admirable, but merely uncouth; to be deceitful like Rosalie is wrong, but merely to be frank in admitting is but little better:

'I pretended to want to save it, [a leveret killed by her dog] as it was so glaringly out of season; but I was better pleased to see it killed.'
(Chapter 18)

Anne Brontë's art shows in Matilda, as so often elsewhere, in her discretion and. restraint. Though Matilda is reportedly foul-mouthed, the reader hears very little of her, since to do so would make her too uncouth to be an impressive opposite to Rosalie. Her stable language is heard no more once its comic point has been made:

'I'll never say a wicked word again, if you'll only listen to me, and tell Rosalie to hold her confounded tongue.'
(Chapter 9)

Rosalie is almost as much the heart of the novel as Agnes herself. She embodies the most serious moral preoccupations, she is the most closely-observed, her career is the most complete, she is the most self-exposing, and she is the object of the most serious and complete concern not only of the narrator but of the author. Whereas Agnes understates her own affairs of the heart (out of diffidence and modesty), Anne Brontë allows no such considera-tion to prevent the reader from observing Rosalie at all the most memorable points in her career. This career extends from the childhood period, when she is the product of her environment and education, through that when, as a young woman, she chooses her course for herself, to her married life when she experiences the consequences of her conduct. The account of a governess is the ideal one for mapping such a course. Agnes is intimate enough for her pupil to confide in her, but not enough respected either to influence or repress her. Hence Rosalie explains herself as does no other character, laying bare her opinions (she has very few feelings) on what she has already done, and her plans for what she proposes to do. Frequently these opinions and plans loom larger than the events connected with them: for instance, the reader has Rosalie's account of her coming-out ball (Chapter

9), not the ball itself; her words immediately after being married (Chapter 18), but not the wedding. The disproportion between the events and the importance they assume in her career (the coming-out ball takes more space than the wedding), allows the moral point to make itself, with very little help from Agnes as commentator. Equally pertinent is the disproportion between characters, revealed through how Rosalie regards them. Her husband, Sir Thomas Ashby, is mentioned no more than is essential for the reader's benefit – he is 'the greatest scamp in Christendom' and 'any woman of common decency' is 'a world too good for him' (Chapter 14) – but the rector Mr Hatfield looms large in the narrative, both in her conversation and account of her thoughts, and in events in which they both take part. Rosalie is indeed the main reason why events and characters appear, even when she is not present.[1]

The ways in which Rosalie is presented show considerable assurance and unobtrusive skill. Since Anne Brontë's purposes do not include psychological development and interpretation, an opening description which fixes permanently the main features of a personality serves her well. Rosalie receives the most comprehensive and significant one in the novel. Her looks, the obvious beginning of a description, are a significant one here, revealing that this young lady's face is her fortune. Though such a character is not unusual, the account is far from conventional, and has the astringent edge of truth, which renders vivid both the subject and the speaker:

> on a further acquaintance, she gradually laid aside her airs, and in time, became as deeply attached to me as it was possible for *her* to be to one of my character and position: for she seldom lost sight, for above half-an-hour at a time, of the fact of my being a hireling, and a poor curate's daughter.   (Chapter 7)

---

[1] A striking instance is in Agnes's visit to the old blind woman Nancy Brown, where Nancy's long account of her religious doubts dwells as much on Mr Hatfield's deficiencies as on Mr Weston's excellences; the former need to be known in order to gauge the falseness of his sentiment to Rosalie, the latter to create anxiety about her attempts, as she herself says, to 'fix' him (Chapter 15), though it also obviously reveals him as a fitting husband for Agnes.

Once she is thus established, she makes most of her effects by speech, of which she has more than any other single person (excluding Agnes herself and the other temporary narrator, Nancy Brown). Like so many of Anne Brontë's effects, her speech is successful in context, being completely appropriate and exactly serving its purpose; but it contains much less that is immediately striking in extract. Self-exposure, by a frankness that ironically reveals more to Agnes and the reader than she intends, is its most frequent feature:

> 'Brown said that she was sure no gentleman could set eyes on me without falling in love that minute; and so I may be allowed to be a little vain. I know you think me a shocking, conceited, frivolous girl, but then you know, I don't attribute it *all* to my personal attractions: I give some praise to the hairdresser, and some to my exquisitely lovely dress – you must see it tomorrow – white gauze over pink satin ... and so *sweetly* made! and a necklace and bracelet of beautiful, large pearls!'
>
> 'I have no doubt you looked very charming; but should that delight you so very much?'
>
> 'Oh, no! ... not that alone: but then, I was so much admired; and I made so *many* conquests in that one night – you'd be astonished to hear —'
>
> 'But what good will they do you?'
>
> 'What good! Think of any woman asking that!'
>
> 'Well, I should think one conquest would be enough, and too much, unless the subjugation were mutual.'   (Chapter 9)

The hints here of the maid Brown's idiom which opens the speech, the limited wit in Rosalie which acknowledges the hairdresser's and costumier's help, but entertainingly misunderstands Agnes's question 'should that delight you?', and cannot save her from the vulgarism of 'conquests' (emphasized by Agnes's literal and polysyllabic periphrasis, 'subjugation' – recalling Charlotte Brontë's humour); all these are neatly and unobtrusively suggested without either idiosyncratic diction or unnatural idiom.[1]

The method which serves the Rosalie of the early chapters

---

[1] Such success with plain language is one outside the power of either Charlotte or Emily Brontë, and places Anne rather with Mrs Gaskell or Trollope.

works just as well for the dissatisfied married woman as for the pleasure-loving girl. Absence of proper feeling shows itself in her letter to Agnes (Chapter 21), where she speaks in the same offhand tone of her child, her dog, and her pictures:

'I forget whether you like babies; if you do, you may have the pleasure of seeing mine ... the most charming child in the world, no doubt ... and you shall see my poodle too, a splendid little charmer imported from Paris, and two fine Italian paintings of great value ... I forget the artist.'
(Chapter 21)

Her acute, though faulty, reasoning is obvious again in her confidences, where this time Agnes's comment is an unspoken one:

'as soon as he heard we were there, he came up under pretence of visiting his brother, and either followed me, like a shadow, wherever I went, or met me, like a reflection, at every turn. You needn't look so shocked, Miss Grey; I was very discreet, I assure you; but, you know, one can't help being admired.'
(Chapter 22)

Though static, the character is by no means elementary. Anne Brontë, having established the deficiencies, allows the considerable charm of youth and high spirits, and gives Rosalie all the assets deriving from doing what the reader longs to have done – putting the pretentious Mr Hatfield in his place. Similarly she can let Rosalie infuse some transitory excitement into the story by attempting to charm Mr Weston: her charm and intelligence have been just enough to make Agnes's anxiety seem justified, and the chance that Mr Weston may succumb seem one worth considering.

Mr Hatfield himself is a small but thoroughly adequate piece of work. His purposes as the foppish, ambitious clergyman, with no sense of his calling, are easily fulfilled by lively details of his behaviour:

[Mr Hatfield] would come sailing up the aisle, or rather sweeping along like a whirlwind, with his rich silk gown flying behind him, and rustling against the pew doors, mount the pulpit like a conqueror ascending his triumphal car; then sinking on the velvet cushion in an attitude of studied grace, remain in silent prostration for a certain time.
(Chapter 10)

But such details as this, and kicking Nancy Brown's cat out of his way, do not suggest the power and originality of the scene, reported verbatim by Rosalie (Chapter 14), of his astonishing proposal to her, which proceeds by way of conventional protestation, through astonishment and chagrin, to repressed rage and a direct *tu quoque* and threat of blackmail to protect wounded pride.

The principles of economy and the strong sense of means to an end that dictate the personality and role of the narrator, the shape of the whole, and the handling of characters, determine also the selection and manipulation of material within the individual scenes, and the style. It is even more plain here that Anne Brontë is an author whose effects are made by accumulation and inter-relation of simple details, very simply expressed, whose power is largely lost when they are seen in isolation. Her greatest single asset, apart from the handling of Agnes herself, is, as has already been examined, her use of dialogue. As well as revealing person-ality and exposing standards and lapses, speech is often used as an economical and dramatic means to other ends. There are occa-sional intrusions of transitory characters like Mr Smith 'the draper, grocer and tea-dealer of the village' (Chapter 1) whose gig takes Agnes to her first post. His comment:

> 'It's a coldish mornin' for you, Miss Agnes, and a darksome un too; but we's, happen, get to yon' spot afore there comes much rain to signify.'

and the laconic little dialogue that follows, create an accurate and atmospheric vignette without holding up the narrative, and create variety between the author's account of her home, and that of the Bloomfields which is to follow. Nancy Brown's long account of her spiritual troubles in Chapter 11 is another instance of speech whose end is structural. It again forms a welcome break in Agnes's story, and provides information it is not in her power to give, in a novel, compact, and racy way. While so long an account is not naturalistic, Anne Brontë balances most professionally the demands of easy reading with keeping up a convincing dialect, wisely relying more on idiom than on phonetic reproduction:

'After he was gone, Hannah Rogers, one o' th' neighbours came in and wanted me to help her to wash. I telled her I couldn't just then, for I hadn't set on th' potaties for th' dinner, nor washed up th' breakfast stuff yet. So then she began a calling me for my nasty, idle ways. I was a little bit vexed at first; but I never said nothing wrong to her: I only telled her, like all in a quiet way, 'a I'd had th' new parson to see me; but I'd get done as quick as ever I could, an' then come an' help her. So then she softened down.' (Chapter 11)

One hears Yorkshire speech as effectively here as in the much less decipherable Joseph of *Wuthering Heights*.

Scenery, setting, and the weather are plainly elements of situation as important to Anne Brontë as to her sisters. Like them she feels a whole scene through its central emotion, without ever suggesting sentimentality or the pathetic fallacy. Frequent and delicate notice of details of setting, of the weather, the seasons, or the passage of time, all vivify both the action and the subdued personality of Agnes herself. Here Anne Brontë rightly feels confident that mere allusion will evoke a response, without relying on description. She can be vivid and oddly moving with the most commonplace materials, precisely because what she uses is so familiar that she can depend upon the reader's response. Agnes, arriving exhausted at Horton Lodge after a winter day's travelling, where she gets no proper welcome, goes up to her room:

Then, having broken my long fast on a cup of tea, and a little thin bread and butter, I sat down beside the small, smouldering fire, and amused myself with a hearty fit of crying. (Chapter 7)

Anne Brontë always thus underplays rather than overplays her hand, marking the story's most moving moments by bringing some small detail into sharp focus, as in this brief account of Agnes's first journey from home:

We crossed the valley, and began to ascend the opposite hill. As we were toiling up, I looked back again: there was the village spire, and the old grey parsonage beyond it, basking in a slanting beam of sunshine – it was but a sickly ray, but the village and surrounding hills were all in sombre shade, and I hailed the wandering beam as a propitious omen to my home. With clasped hands, I fervently implored a blessing on its inhabitants, and hastily turned away; for I saw the sunshine was departing; and I carefully avoided another glance, lest I should see it in gloomy shadow like the rest of the landscape. (Chapter 1)

There is a deliberate rejection here of the significant or symbolic, for the sunshine moves naturally with the clouds; the significance is only what Agnes imagines, while what she describes has all the charm of reality. Like her sisters, Anne Brontë has also a strong sense of time passing. Each event in the story is precisely placed in its season, usually by its month.[1] In a story where the most significant happenings will almost certainly take place on Sundays – when going to church involves meeting the clergyman – such care might be imposed rather than voluntary. But Anne Brontë can delineate time passing like a prose Tennyson; the passage where Agnes at Ashby Park waits and muses in her sitting-room is almost her *Mariana*:

I sat musing on Lady Ashby's past and present condition; and on what little information I had obtained respecting Mr Weston, and the small chance there was of ever seeing or hearing anything more of him throughout my quiet, drab-colour life, which, henceforth, seemed to offer no alternative between positive rainy days and days of dull, grey clouds without downfall.

At length, however, I began to weary of my thoughts, and to wish I knew where to find the library my hostess had spoken of, and to wonder whether I was to remain there, doing nothing till bedtime.

As I was not rich enough to possess a watch, I could not tell how time was passing, except by observing the slowly lengthening shadows from the window, which presented a side view, including a corner of the park, a clump of trees, whose topmost branches had been colonized by an innumerable company of noisy rooks, and a high wall with a massive wooden gate, no doubt communicating with the stable yard, as a broad carriage-road swept up to it from the park. The shadow of this wall soon took possession of the whole

[1] Rosalie's 'coming-out' ball takes place on 3 January, Agnes visits Nancy in the third week in February, Mr Weston gives her primroses at the end of March, Mr Hatfield's courtship, refusal, and Rosalie's change to Mr Weston proceed day by day, and she is married on 1 June.

of this ground as far as I could see, forcing the golden sunlight to retreat inch by inch, and at last take refuge in the very tops of the trees. At last, even they were left in shadow – the shadow of the distant hills, or of the earth itself; and, in sympathy for the busy citizens of the rookery, I regretted to see their habitation, so lately bathed in glorious light, reduced to the sombre, work-a-day hue of the lower world, or of my own world within. For a moment, such birds as soared above the rest might still receive the lustre on their wings, which imparted to their sable plumage the hue and brilliance of deep red gold; at last, that too departed. Twilight came stealing on – the rooks became more quiet – I became more weary, and wished I were going home tomorrow.   (Chapter 22)

As this passage and the previous ones reveal, expression is wholly ruled by what she has to say. The demands of sound, rhythm, or the well-wrought period do not concern her. She does not reject the oddly-used word 'basking', in the second passage; nor does she acknowledge, in the third, that the rhythm of the third sentence concludes at the words 'wooden gate': completeness demands the rather awkwardly attached dependent phrase and clause beginning at 'no doubt communication . . .', and completeness justifies its presence and its form. These sensitive and even lyrical descriptions all belong to Agnes, and bear on her role in the narrative. She is passive and sensitive, a central perception more fine than any other, and so a most accurate measurement of the other characters, though she is not at all the most absorbing interest for the reader.

On its small scale Agnes Grey has much in common with *Mansfield Park*, and Agnes herself with Fanny Price, who is in a similar position, has a rather similar nature, and performs the same functions. Anne Brontë resembles her sisters only where material is concerned (only occasionally do her methods suggest Emily), and resembles the eighteenth century in the type of characterization and the firm morality; the Victorians she suggests are those very different from the Brontës, Mrs Gaskell and Trollope; while a remarkable affinity exists between her and that other modest writer, of deep personal religion, pervadingly humble subjects, and a deceptively simple, literal style – Mark Rutherford.

THE TENANT OF WILDFELL HALL

'Consult your own understanding, your own sense of the probable, your own observation of what is passing around you – Does our education prepare us for such atrocities? Do our laws connive at them? Could they be perpetrated without being known, in a country like this, where social and literary intercourse is on such a footing; where every man is surrounded by a neighbourhood of voluntary spies, and where roads and newspapers lay everything open?'

(*Northanger Abbey*, Vol. II, Chapter 9)

Anne Brontë, whose temperament inclines her to agree with Henry Tilney and his creator about the answer to these rhetorical questions, undertakes in *The Tenant of Wildfell Hall* to reveal what happens when the answer to all but the first of them is not the expected 'no', but 'yes'. Her second novel is necessarily very unlike *Agnes Grey*[1]. A rake's progress is certainly no usual topic for a domestic novel. *The Tenant of Wildfell Hall* contains much that is unusual, uncongenial to readers in 1848, and unpleasant by any standards. It is Anne Brontë's business to be unusual, uncongenial, and unpleasant. She never shrinks from it by euphemisms of expression or presentation, by contriving her characters, or even by following acknowledged conventions of the novel. She is like her sister Emily in being apparently unaware that she is often shocking, when she takes as a matter of course things usually

---

[1] Charlotte Brontë considered that:

'the choice of subject in that work is a mistake: it was too little consonant with the character, tastes, and ideas of the gentle, retiring, inexperienced writer.' (Letter to W. S. Williams, Sept. 5, 1850)

arousing strong reaction.[1] While knowing that the subject of her novel is dreadful, she never considers that she herself may be thought shocking for undertaking it;[2] her attitude is thus much less self-aware than Charlotte's. She sees for instance only one thing to prevent Helen from leaving her husband – even though he controls all her fortune, and though she has no right to a divorce: that she cannot legally take, or hope to be given the care of, the son for whose sake she wants to go. Nor, on an earlier occasion, does Anne Brontë find it at all remarkable for Helen to refuse her husband his marital rights (Chapter 33).

Despite material so much more lurid than *Agnes Grey's*, Anne Brontë keeps resolutely to the normal as far as she can. She keeps melodrama from her methods and hysteria from her voice. Her purpose is a didactic one, again not so much to instruct, as to lay bare candidly that by which the reader may instruct himself. Though the story is fiction, it is told like fact, and documented wherever possible by what the reader may recognize as fact.

The author's intention is thus much clearer than in most novels: Anne Brontë is determined that it shall be plain, and there is no suggestion of preoccupations other than what the writer wittingly devises. Self-effacing as Anne Brontë is, we have no sense that she is hiding herself from her reader. She is the most candid of writers, despite her first-person narrative. Though both the impulse and the foundation of *The Tenant of Wildfell Hall* are Anne's own experiences with her brother Branwell, she never uses any of her personalities, or their sufferings, to reveal herself and her own. One never feels that Helen is Anne, or that Anne uses her for emotional release. The narrators in *The Tenant of*

[1] A casual example may be taken from Gilbert Markham's opinion of Helen – whom he knows only as the mysterious tenant of Wildfell Hall:

It was evident she loved me – probably, she was tired of Mr Lawrence, and wished to exchange him for me.   (Chapter 15)

[2] She was herself both shocked and upset by adverse reviews: as Charlotte Brontë writes, 'I wish my sister felt the adverse ones less keenly. . . . The fact is, neither she nor any of us expected that view to be taken of the book which has been taken by some critics. That it had faults of execution, faults of art, was obvious, but faults of intention or feeling could be suspected by none who knew the writer.'   (Letter to W. S. Williams, July 31st, 1848.)

Wildfell Hall do not expose their author like *Jane Eyre* or *Lucy Snowe*, nor, conversely, blot out the author from our perceptions like those of *Wuthering Heights*. Gilbert Markham and Helen Huntingdon, the narrators here, are devised in the first place to ensure conviction and a first-hand accuracy. Even though Helen Huntingdon is most deeply involved in the main story, it is always clear that Anne Brontë does not let her harrow up the reader's soul except to good purpose outside herself. Anne Brontë is dissecting, not the agonies of her heroine, but the horrors of drink and debauchery in all their possible private and domestic manifestations. The novel is not solely or mainly the progress of Helen's soul as it suffers retribution for the misguided vanity which made her marry Huntingdon – against all advice – to reform him. The retribution she suffers is far too gross to be thus acceptable. Helen's fate and the other elements together demonstrate her author's purpose to expose the natural consequences of self-indulgence – notably here drink, drugs, and lust – in themselves, on the self-indulgent man, on those nearest to him, and, through them, on domestic life as a whole. Hence the assembly of characters such as Hattersley or Lord Lowborough whose fates are not directly connected with Helen's own. The centre of the novel – the structural pivot of the main story, the moving power of the plot, the embodiment of Anne Brontë's purpose – is Arthur Huntingdon, who, the nadir of self-indulgence, decrees the rest of the characters and events. The story follows him inexorably to his end, from which Anne Brontë does not allow herself to be distracted by even quite legitimate interests. She does not dismiss her narrators to happiness until, as she says of Huntingdon's punishment in after-life, she 'has paid the uttermost farthing' (Chapter 20).

Anne Brontë clears from under her a great many difficulties that find their way into the fabric of her sister's work, leaving herself free to handle more simply what is nearest her heart. She is wise to do so, as she is always an unsophisticated writer, a primitive in the art of the novel, gaining her results by very simple methods, which owe little to the techniques she might have learned from others. She assumes from the beginning that the reader acknowledges and agrees with her standards of right and wrong, and her view of man's duty to society, without having to share the emotional position of the narrator. Just as the reader, to judge rightly, did not have to identify himself with Agnes Grey, still less does he have to with Helen Huntingdon.

There are two narrators, who between them unfold the story and give a perspective: Gilbert Markham, the young farmer who, having met Helen when she is hiding with her son, becomes eventually her second husband; and Helen herself, whose journal of her married life forms the bulk of the novel (thirty out of fifty-three chapters). As far as Anne Brontë's main purpose goes, Gilbert Markham seems superfluous, even though the first fifteen chapters are his. The story began, chronologically, when Helen met and married Huntingdon, and ends when he is dead, Anne Brontë having therein faced all the personal, social, and moral situations that can be perceptible from the standpoint and method she has chosen. One must consider, however, whether the time spent at the beginning and end on Helen's second courtship and happy marriage may also reveal Anne Brontë's purpose, whether it is anything more worthy than submitting to the popular liking for a happy ending. *The Tenant of Wildfell Hall* demonstrates, like *Agnes Grey*, that the writer is conscientiously and earnestly unsentimental. Just as in *Agnes Grey* she clearsightedly traces the disastrous consequences of Rosalie's disastrous marriage, so here she equally clearsightedly recognizes that a handsome, strong-minded young widow of twenty-five does not spend the rest of her days mourning a worthless husband, in retreat from the domestic happiness of which it had been one of his crimes to deprive her. To have her *not* marry again would be the sentimental, conventional ending so uncongenial to Anne Brontë. That there is much in common in Anne Brontë's attitude to her two narrators also reveals her purpose. She allows a young man, clearly no hero, to expose ironically his own small follies and vanities; but when her heroine begins her story she exposes herself in the same way, the method becoming less reserved, but no less detached, as the events become more serious. Furthermore, to make Gilbert's common-place, credible story form the introduction renders Helen's

sensational one more credible also. While wishing to hide nothing
of the horrors she is committed to revealing, the author has no
intention of overplaying her hand, by seeming beyond the bounds
of probability, and so losing the game.[1]

The shape and the plot of *The Tenant of Wildfell Hall*, that of
the tale within a tale, resemble those of *Wuthering Heights*. The
narrative is begun by Gilbert Markham, who in the first fifteen
chapters tells of his growing acquaintance with the mysterious
supposed widow Helen Graham. It continues with her narrative
in journal form of the five previous years of her life. It ends with a
return to Gilbert's story, interspersed with Helen's letters, of her
husband's death and her own remarriage. The plot is essentially a
single one, as simple as that of *Agnes Grey*, taking Helen from her
meeting with her first husband to her marriage with her second.
Such a résumé (like that of *Agnes Grey*) does not accurately suggest
the content of the novel, still less its purpose or flavour. Just as
that novel was more essentially Rosalie's fate than Agnes's, so this
is more concerned with Huntingdon's than Helen's. While there
are a few subordinate interests – the married life of the drunkard
Hattersley and his gentle wife Milicent, or the struggles of Milicent's younger sister Esther to resist an uncongenial match – there
is no sub-plot. It is tempting to say that there is indeed no plot,
only a graded series of events.

Nevertheless the story is the most important single element in
the novel, because the moral is inherent in the events forming
Huntingdon's career, and their consequences to all those around
him. The events dictate the characters who participate in them,
rather than the characters seeming to cause the events, as is usually
the case in any novel worthy of serious consideration.

The material from which Anne Brontë builds up her story and
documents it is, like the story itself, of two sorts, that provided by
Markham's narrative, and that by Helen's. Markham's is all
domestic, rural, and unsensational. The Yorkshire farm and
village life, going no higher up the social scale than the rector and

[1] Where she does fail, as Charlotte Brontë suggests, the causes are quite other
and arise from plain artistic incapacity, never from mistaken purpose or misconceived design.

the gentleman farmer and their families, is assumed to be familiar ground. The events are those of daily occurrence, or of very modest excitement, never rising above a small party for neighbours or a picnic by the sea four miles away. Such an opening section successfully enhances the more socially elevated setting and startling events of Helen's story, and at the same time, by being homely, ensures that the narrative keeps its feet on the ground when its material threatens to raise it to melodrama or fantasy.

The contrast soon established between this indigenous life and society, and the newcomer artist-recluse with no origins or known connections, is a nice use of modest materials for a character whose mystery is itself only a modest one. Anne Brontë's success may be seen by comparing Helen, as a mysterious newcomer, with Jane Eyre during her time as schoolmistress at Morton, where Charlotte Brontë creates nothing at all of the impact so mysterious an arrival must have had on village gossip.

Even this preliminary story is more elaborate than *Agnes Grey*, with more character, more varied settings – the farm, the Rectory, Wildfell Hall, and the fields and moors – and more different kinds of events – private family chats, parties, lovers' quarrels, men's disputes – showing how Anne Brontë has gained both confidence and power.

Helen's narrative (Chapters 16–45) is made as far as possible out of the same stuff of everyday country living. The social level is slightly higher: the society is that of the country house, and the gentry who can afford not to know how to farm their own land. The distresses and neglect of the earlier episodes and the horrors of Helen's later married life are firmly based in domesticity, and revealed through social gatherings of the same kind as those of Markham's story. Helen's embarrassments and distresses spring from immediately intelligible situations: such as having her portfolio rifled against her will (Chapter 18) or having her writing-desk and boxes ransacked and the keys taken away (Chapter 40). Huntingdon's atrocities are all domestic ones: abusing the food and his wife's household management, when his digestion is at fault (Chapter 30), brawling drunkenly in the drawing-room

(Chapter 31), encouraging his son to swear and to get drunk after dinner (Chapter 39), and committing adultery under his own roof with the wife of his friend and guest (Chapter 33). The most horrifying scenes use the same elements: frightening violence is suggested when a man uses a drawing-room candle to burn the hands of the drunkard restraining him (Chapter 31); the depths of drunken sottishness by a man who scoops out half-dissolved sugar lumps from his over-sweetened coffee, and dumps them back in the sugar bowl (ibid.). Society at Grassdale Manor – the outside world and surrounding families – is made of the same stuff as in the opening section; but has changed to alien beings who can only exacerbate private domestic agony. The heartless but harmless fortune-seeking, represented by Jane Wilson, is seen in a new light in the Hargrave family: Mrs Hargrave, wishing for the same worldly success as Jane Wilson, thrusts her elder daughter into marriage with a brutal debauchee, and makes her younger one miserable when she refuses the same fate: her son, through irresponsible sympathy with Helen, becomes yet another torment to her as a would-be seducer. The likeness is driven home when Gilbert, miserable for Helen, is tormented by the gossip and scandal about her. Society – Henry Tilney's 'neighbourhood of voluntary spies' – is rendered comic or horrific by circumstance, not by nature. Hargrave – almost the greatest of Helen's trials – sinks, when Helen's happiness is safe, into comic obscurity and marriage, not to the wealthy widow with whose 'rare long purse' he had hoped to console himself, but with a woman 'not quite as rich – nor as handsome either' (Chapter 52); a fate of the same sort as Jane Wilson's who

> wholly unable to re-capture Mr Lawrence or obtain any partner rich and elegant enough to suit her ideas of what the husband of Jane Wilson ought to be ... took lodgings in —— the county town, where she lived, and still lives, I suppose, in a kind of close fisted, cold, uncomfortable gentility, doing no good to others and but little to herself. (Chapter 48)

With such material and such a society, it is probably unavoidable that Anne Brontë in *The Tenant of Wildfell Hall* should resemble

Richardson, especially when she employs the journal as method, and has a situation that also might have suited him. In Helen's story, there are a number of very characteristic situations – such as Helen mediating between Hattersley and his timid wife Milicent, explaining each to the other and telling both their duty (Chapter 32); or Helen behaving with magnanimity to her rival Annabella – which recall the way Sir Charles Grandison and Harriet Byron are held up to be admired for similar feats. Such scenes generally seem to a modern reader both ill-conceived and tasteless. Since Richardson is almost the only novelist who could offer Anne Brontë any assistance in her task, it is more interesting and significant to see how often she avoids being Richardsonian. Helen, beset on all sides, usually manages to extricate herself by some device that is neither heroism nor sentiment, while Anne Brontë is always quite as concerned with chronicling Huntingdon on his downward path of depravity, as Helen's sufferings during it. He, unlike Lovelace, exists primarily for something other than to test a noble spirit to the uttermost limits of endurance. However extraordinary or sensational the events, Anne Brontë documents constantly and accurately with concrete, vivid, and economical detail, of action, the physical results of action, or of setting. Huntingdon's proposal of marriage is a powerful scene, not only for what is said, but for its accessories. Helen, finding him unendurable,

> made an effort to rise, but he was kneeling on my dress.
>
> (Chapter 19)

the clause vividly realizing the almost unavoidable consequence of proposing to a woman in a crinoline; the language of passion leads to practical, prosaic bodily results:

> 'Then let me add, that I cannot live without you, and if you answer, No, to this last question, you will drive me mad — Will you bestow yourself on me? – You will!' he cried, nearly squeezing me to death in his arms. (ibid.)

Scenes are carefully localized; the library, for instance, is Helen's refuge from her husband and his rowdy friends. Hargrave's advances gain more power when he has invaded it:

> Mr Hargrave followed me thither, under pretence of coming for a
> book; and first, turning to the shelves, he selected a volume; and
> then, quietly, but by no means timidly, approaching me, he stood
> beside me, resting his hand on the back of my chair, and said softly, –
> 'And so you consider yourself free, at last?'   (Chapter 35)

The setting and gesture are as significant as the actual speech. The
unpleasant is documented in the same way, allowing the reader
to build up his response from the evidence, not from a character's
own reaction. After the grotesque scene of drunkenness in the
drawing-room (Chapter 31), Anne Brontë faces the consequences.

> At last he came, slowly and stumblingly, ascending the stairs, sup-
> ported by Grimsby and Hattersley, who neither of them walked
> quite steadily themselves, but were both laughing and joking at him,
> and making noise enough for all the servants to hear. He himself was
> no longer laughing now, but sick and stupid – I will write no more
> about *that*.   (Chapter 31)

Since Anne Brontë has no wish to be either exhaustive or revolting, her handling of the unpleasant always strikes a perfect
balance between truth and decorum: Helen's physical fortitude
in nursing the dying man is perceived by the two or three allusions
she makes to the sick-room atmosphere:

> I did but exchange a few words with them, just outside the portico –
> inhaling the fresh, bracing air as I stood.   (Chapter 49)

> I gently disengaged my hand from his, intending to steal away for a
> breath of fresh air, for I was almost ready to faint.   (ibid.)

as well she might, in a Victorian bedroom with a patient with
gangrene.

Characterization for Anne Brontë is far from being what it
seems so often in the Victorian novel, the over-riding impulse.
Events, situations, and actions take priority. As any competent
novelist must, she reconciles the claims of both plot and personality; but basically *The Tenant of Wildfell Hall* is a story of what
happens as a result of drunkenness and dissoluteness – the qualities
Helen sums up as self-indulgence. The characters are conceived
as, at the centre, those who would either create, or get into, events

such as Anne Brontë is committed to depicting; and at the periphery, those who exemplify all the possible consequences. The author's hand is very strong on her characters, who are, much more even than Thackeray's, puppets on the strings of a superb puppet-master. There is never any chance that one of them may win the kind of independent life that Trollope and Thackeray both admitted theirs did, which let them alter or dictate their fate, according to the nature they had assumed. Anne Brontë ensures that what happens and those who make it happen shall fulfil her purposes; nor does she ever suggest that she herself can be influenced by them, or identify herself with her creations. Her characters have only the semblance of free-will that enables them to fulfil their destiny, and convince, like puppets, according to how well they do so. In *The Tenant of Wildfell Hall*, modest as it is, Anne Brontë might well claim like Milton to justify the ways of God to man; and never invite the hint that she is in the least danger of making a hero of her Satan. Like puppets again, her characters are naïve (in no derogatory sense) in type and presentation. Their personalities and their behaviour – even their crimes and deceits – are straightforward. Easily intelligible causes produce natural consequences. She never deals with good intentions that produce disastrous results,[1] or with doing the right deed for the wrong reason, or even with a simple dilemma of motives: Helen, for instance, does not ponder or hesitate long over whether to leave her husband, and has no doubts, when she does so, that it is for her son's sake rather than her own, as she explains in her letter to her aunt:

> I told her I was sensible of my error: I did not complain of its punishment, and was sorry to trouble my friends with its consequences; but in duty to my son, I must submit no longer; it was absolutely necessary that he should be delivered from his father's corrupting influence. (Chapter 43)

[1] The only possible instance would be of Helen marrying Huntingdon to reform him, but in this case so many warnings are given that the act is seen as folly arising from vanity, and Helen's sufferings as her own fault; while Huntingdon himself goes to the bad at his own chosen speed upon which Helen's act has no influence.

The novel would of course become an over-complex one if such matters were entered into with secondary characters – even George Eliot has to abandon the stance of the impartial narrator to do so – but, even among the major ones, the fairly central question of whether Helen, with unimpeachable motives, may yet herself be creating evil by her effect on her husband, is not one the novel raises; while the whole complex structure of causes and impulses rooted in the individual's personality, but not his to control, such as move *Wuthering Heights*, is simply not in question; nor is Jane Eyre's dreadful dilemma when she leaves Mr Rochester, though recognizing that to do what is morally right may drive him to despair and destruction. By the time Helen leaves her husband, she has lost what little power over him she possessed, and her flight cannot alter him in any way.

Anne Brontë's achievement in making memorable such characters, obviously not deeply observed, who do so little to influence events, is an original one, closer, like *Agnes Grey's*, to Fielding than to any before her, but also a little akin to Scott's in such a work as *Guy Mannering*. But Anne Brontë differs from them because her creations are memorable in groups, rather than separately, and because they depend on action to provoke self-revelation. Annabella Wilmot (the fortune-seeking beauty, Helen's rival, who becomes Lady Lowborough) is a fine instance, in the convincing way she reacts when Helen has found out that she is Huntingdon's mistress. At first angrily disconcerted that Helen has discovered —

> 'Ah, you are suspicious!' cried she, smiling with a gleam of hope – hitherto, there had been a kind of desperation in her hardihood; now she was evidently relieved. (Chapter 34)

she changes to inflated promises, nicely punctured, if Helen agrees not to tell Lord Lowborough:

> 'I shall think you the most generous of mortal beings – and if there is anything in the world I can do for you – anything short of —' she hesitated.
>
> 'Short of renouncing your guilty connection with my husband, I suppose you mean,' said I. (ibid.)

and changes again as her stay draws to its end and her sense of
security re-establishes itself:

> She does not scruple to speak to my husband with affectionate
> familiarity in my presence, when no one else is by, and is particularly
> fond of displaying her interest in his health and welfare, or in any-
> thing that concerns him, as if for the purpose of contrasting her kind
> solicitude with my cold indifference. (Chapter 35)

All of this rings precisely and originally true as the record of how
such a person would behave in such circumstances. Anne Brontë
is equally sure where a mixture of good and bad qualities in one
person must be shown; Ralph Hattersley's insensitive affection
for his wife is thoroughly convincing:

> 'What does it amount to, Ralph? Only to this, that though you
> admire Annabella so much, and for qualities that I don't possess,
> you would still rather have me than her for your wife, which merely
> proves that you don't think it necessary to love your wife: you are
> satisfied if she can keep your house and take care of your child. But
> I'm not cross; I'm only sorry; for,' added she, in a low, tremulous
> accent, withdrawing her hand from his arm, and bending her looks
> on the rug, 'if you don't love me, you don't, and it can't be helped.'
> 'Very true; but who told you I didn't? Did I say I loved Anna-
> bella?'
> 'You said you adored her.'
> 'True, but adoration isn't love. I adore Annabella, but I don't love
> her; and I love thee, Milicent, but I don't adore thee!' In proof of his
> affection, he clutched a handful of her light brown ringlets, and
> appeared to twist them unmercifully. (Chapter 32)

In the novel's two narratives – Gilbert's and Helen's – characters,
though of the same kind, are used to different ends. Those in
Gilbert's narrative are essentially examples and instances of what
is to be encountered in such a place and situation as Gilbert's, who
do little or nothing towards advancing the story. The village-
dwellers are instances of the 'neighbourhood of voluntary spies'
of Henry Tilney's opening paragraph, the purpose of them all
being to show how irresponsible and random behaviour can, in
unusual circumstances, become unjust and even cruel. These

THE BRONTË NOVELS

characters are closer than Helen's to *Agnes Grey*, but they show Anne Brontë more assured and more competent than in that novel: there are more individuals kept in the action, from several contrasting families (the farmer Wilsons, the rector Millwoods, Gilbert's own); there are men, of all ages, from the boy Fergus to the middle-aged rector; and there are middle-aged women, like Mrs Markham and Mrs Wilson; as well as the young girls on whom Anne Brontë concentrated in *Agnes Grey*. The personalities in themselves are more varied. They are – as Rosalie Murray is said to be – 'artful', or they are not faulty, but limited: of the first kind are the two young ladies Jane Wilson and Eliza Millwood, who begins as 'a pretty, playful kitten' (Chapter 1) and concludes as a cat; of the second are Gilbert's sister Rose and his mother, who wisely advises Gilbert not to engage himself to Eliza, who scorns Helen for teaching her son to hate alcohol, and whose idea of marriage is sadly low:

> 'He always said I was a good wife, and did my duty; and he always did his – bless him! – he was steady and punctual, seldom found fault without a reason, always did justice to my good dinners, and hardly ever spoiled my cookery by delay – and that's as much as any woman can expect of any man.' (Chapter 6)

On such straightforward persons Anne Brontë does well; but her chosen topic compels her to tackle what is beyond her, her least adequate character being Mr Lawrence, the landlord of Wildfell Hall and Helen's brother, the essential link between Gilbert's world and Helen's, and the person on whom Gilbert depends for all that concerns him and Helen in the last six chapters covering Huntingdon's death and the year following. The 'morbid feeling of delicacy, and a peculiar diffidence, that he was sensible of, but wanted energy to overcome' (Chapter 4) diagnosed by Gilbert, is too complicated a state for Anne Brontë's simple methods, since they always employ speech and action, the two things in which Lawrence is deficient.

In Helen's narrative the characters justify their existence by their bearing on the moral purpose. All are examples or victims of the varying degrees of self-indulgence. Huntingdon is the

240

utterly corrupt and corrupting, attended by Grimsby who lacks Huntingdon's gusto but not his will, Hattersley who is weak-willed but capable of eventual reform through feeling for his wife and family, and Lowborough who reforms himself through deluded love of a worthless wife. The women are equally exemplary. Helen is the incorruptible and completely desolate, Milicent Hattersley the completely subdued, Annabella the wholly selfish and corrupt, Esther Hargrave the prospective victim. Less neatly classifiable is the third Hargrave, Milicent's brother, who consorts with Huntingdon in order to pay court to Helen. Anne Brontë suggests that he is not wholly vicious – his actions show the self-control the others lack – but here, as with Lawrence, the methods at her disposal are inadequate to reveal the man who can spend four years laying siege to a married woman.

Where characters can be explicit, Anne Brontë rarely fails, even in situations so unlikely as never to have been faced in fiction before. A fine instance is the dialogue (in Chapter 38) between Helen and Lord Lowborough, when he has discovered that his wife is Huntingdon's mistress, and that he is the last to find out. He reproaches Helen for not telling him when she herself found out two years before; the whole conversation is astonishing, the climax excellent:

'It was wrong – it was wrong!' he muttered, at length. 'Nothing can excuse it – nothing can atone for it, – for nothing can recall those years of cursed credulity – nothing obliterate them! – nothing, nothing!' he repeated in a whisper whose despairing bitterness precluded all resentment.

'When I put the case to myself, I own it *was* wrong,' I answered; 'but I can only now regret that I did not see it in this light before, and that, as you say, nothing can recall the past.'

Something in my voice or in the spirit of this answer seemed to alter his mood. Turning towards me, and attentively surveying my face by the dim light, he said in a milder tone than he had yet employed—

'You too have suffered, I suppose.'

'I suffered much, at first.'

'When was that?'

'Two years ago; and two years hence you will be as calm as I am now, – and far, far happier, I trust, for you are a man, and free to act as you please.'

Something like a smile, but a *very* bitter one, crossed his face for a moment.

'You have not been happy lately?' he said, with a kind of effort to regain composure, and a determination to waive the further discussion of his own calamity.

'Happy!' I repeated, almost provoked at such a question — 'Could I be so, with such a husband?'

'I have noticed a change in your appearance since the first years of your marriage,' pursued he: 'I observed it to – to that infernal demon,' he muttered between his teeth – 'and he said it was your own sour temper that was eating away your bloom: it was making you old and ugly before your time, and had already made his fireside as comfortless as a convent cell — You smile, Mrs Huntingdon – nothing moves you. I wish my nature were as calm as yours!'

The exchange covers all views of the situation – the wronged husband fiercely hating his ignorance, the wronged wife's cold bitterness, their gradual acknowledgement of the other's plight and its dues; and it precisely notes the changes of tone and mood possible to Helen at this time of dreadful emotion recollected in an appalling tranquillity. At their best Anne Brontë's characters are like these two, impressive and surprising for the variety, not only between them but within them, and for the quite complicated responses she can produce by such simple means.

The three characters who demand individual attention are the two narrators, Gilbert Markham and Helen Huntingdon, and the evil genius himself, Arthur Huntingdon. Gilbert Markham fails, as a personality, even more obviously than Charlotte Brontë's Crimsworth, because Anne Brontë has nothing to do with idiosyncrasy, but keeps close to life as seen by ordinary people, against which Gilbert's deficiencies are obvious. Yet he proves that she is a conscious, sensitive, and conscientious writer, refusing to repeat the safe success of *Agnes Grey*, working still with the stuff of life, and having no literary model available for the mixture that she creates of sound farmer, spoilt son, and aspirant to the artistic and literary. He is both a more complicated nature than

Agnes Grey, and in a more complicated situation. Whereas Agnes's family are not part of the novel's business, Gilbert's are a considerable element in his dealings with Helen. Helen causes him moral problems – by the evidence, as it seems, of her bad character – and emotional ones. Anne Brontë here keeps a balance between a character no longer, like Agnes, morally unimpeachable and generally detached, and the reader's need for a dependable witness. In her treatment of him she shows herself aware of the likely deficiencies of a woman's male hero. She wisely keeps him mainly in the society of women: his family comprises a widowed mother, a sister, and a brother who is as yet a boy; and she makes him an eligible bachelor, of interest to the young women around him. In his role as commentator she provides him with more women than men to work upon, since, like his author, he understands them better.

Gilbert's purpose as a whole is never forgotten. His opening chapters prepare for his later ones. The good sense and uprightness that make him a dependable narrator naturally make him a proper husband for Helen; the impractical aspirations to be something better than a farmer —

> self-conceit assuring me that, in disregarding [ambition's] voice, I was burying my talent in the earth, and hiding my light under a bushel. (Chapter 1)

– suggest a romantic nature, predisposed to wonder and senti-mentalize over a mysterious young widow; the humorous, intelli-gent detachment he shows in looking at himself here, renders convincing his intelligent summaries of others, while not making him either very sympathetic, or even absorbing. It is not intended that he should be so, when Helen is to be the main concern, and any serious anxiety over his ultimate success would be intolerable when the bulk of the novel is involved with other, much graver, anxieties which concern another narrator, Helen.

Her role is in two parts, as the mysterious Mrs Graham of Gilbert's story, and as the teller of her own. The most notable points about her appearance as Mrs Graham are coolness and lack of romance. Mystery is avoided as far as possible, and pity for her difficult position, and sympathy for her as a lonely widow with a young child are never asked. Her situation is one that in novel terms may call for a sentiment which the presentation does nothing to encourage. Her first appearance is neither soft nor winning

> there was a slight hollowness about her cheeks and eyes, and the lips, though finely formed, were a little too thin, a little too firmly compressed, and had something about them that betokened, I thought, no very soft or amiable temper. (Chapter 1)

this anticipates her role as one who is to resist great suffering.

From Chapter 15 onwards, when she is the narrator, Helen is the only personality who can be said to change. She is the moral barometer of Huntingdon's career. The core of her is honest resolution, able to be orthodox on moral or ethical questions, yet think and act independently, or even flout social convention when this is what the action requires. She is equally the person who could choose to marry Huntingdon. Anne Brontë does not shirk the problem (as she might by beginning her story with Helen already married) but most convincingly makes the obstinacy and overconfidence, which cause the downfall of Helen at eighteen, transmute themselves into the determination and assurance that ultimately rescue her and her son.

She is not, as already said, the all-absorbing heroine, though she is much closer to it than Agnes Grey, since suffering as well as observation is part of her role. She is the means of presenting a dreadful example who is himself an absorbing study. Helen, the person closest to Huntingdon, can best reveal him, by seeing most of him, and by experiencing his dreadful career most acutely. Anne Brontë reveals those aspects of her personality that are relevant to his: she subordinates, for instance, her visits to her aunt, her friendship with Esther and with Milicent, and her growing intimacy with her brother; they are taken into account only when they impinge on Huntingdon or on those, such as Hattersley, who represent his influence.

Her constant function is as the norm of good sense and right thinking, to which her journal-story is very appropriate. She writes for herself only, not for a reader, so that the reader can never suspect hypocrisy or self-consciousness, but only the necessary and desirable self-awareness that keeping a journal presupposes. Helen is honest, feeling, just, and detached. She is most successfully always right, with Huntingdon always at a moral disadvantage, yet is never sanctimonious; always suffering, yet never self-pitying, masochistic, or feeble. One reason is that any possible objections to Helen that may occur to the reader, or improper motives for her conduct, are invariably voiced by Huntingdon himself, from whom they are *ipso facto* unacceptable.

> 'Oh, I see,' said he, with a bitter smile, 'it's an act of Christian charity, whereby you hope to gain a higher seat in heaven for yourself, and scoop a deeper pit in hell for me.'   (Chapter 47)

Another reason is that Helen suffers greatly, and is far from being in saintly elevation above her own trials. She convinces by being able to say, like Jane Eyre, '*I* care for myself.' The reader does not wonder much that she comes to hate Huntingdon, but he receives the shock of unexpected truth when, tempted momentarily to yield herself to Hargrave's advances, she bursts out:

> then I hate [Huntingdon] tenfold more than ever for having brought me to this! – God pardon me for it – and all my sinful thoughts! Instead of being humbled and purified by my afflictions, I feel that they are turning my nature into gall.   (Chapter 35)

As purveyor of the moral lesson Helen is not spokesman but theatrical producer. She reveals scenes, and lets the points make themselves, or she examines her responses, and leaves the reader to draw conclusions:

> I must have a bad disposition, for my misfortunes have soured and embittered me exceedingly.   (Chapter 40)

This, her own comment, leaves it to the reader to indict Huntingdon for having brought her to such bitterness and self-doubt.

Huntingdon is the most important person in the novel – the prince of Denmark in this *Hamlet*. He is the awful warning on whom the moral purpose depends, the initiator or instigator behind all the events, the most original and vividly represented personality. Though we see only what thoughts his actions and speech choose to reveal and Helen can guess, he is a frighteningly convincing and original creation. Doubtless much of him must be drawn from Branwell Brontë – whose potential brilliance and personal charm, over men at least, are witnessed reliably by those outside his own family – from whose downward career much of the convincing detail of the way the dipsomaniac mind works must have been drawn. But while he is lifelike, he is so in the manner of the documentary, not of the author's personal experience. He horrifies the reader by what he does and is, and by the consequences of his actions upon himself and others, not by what either the author or the other characters may be supposed to feel about him. Indeed we abhor and detest him much more strongly than Helen, and feel his charm much less.

He functions uncompromisingly and consistently as the example, not only of what indulgence does to the man himself, but of the – to Anne Brontë quite as serious – evil it creates around him. The latter is the first point made about him, and probably the most damning, when he tells his affianced Helen, as a joke, how he has been the means of preventing Lord Lowborough from reform (Chapter 22). From this point he is clearly very much more than merely the victim of his own weakness, who renders his wife and family miserable. While in fact he cannot alter, only degenerate, Anne Brontë manages to create a sense of development, achieved by letting his character and conduct be more fully seen and known as the novel progresses. From seeming one of a group of roisterers (by whom he may seem to be influenced) he comes to be seen as the leader, and himself the main source of corruption, without whom Lowborough would have reformed sooner and would have kept a chaste wife, and Hattersley would have more readily recognized his duty as a landowner and head of a family. The growing sense of his power counterpoints increasing degeneracy, adding interest to what would otherwise be a straightforward downhill path.

The variety of his misdeeds also preserves interest in him. After he has sickened his wife (and the reader with) the drunken disorder of Chapter 31, he commits a sin in seducing Lady Lowborough, which seems, conversely, to demonstrate his powers of attraction.

This skilful presentation of him never flags: we are never permitted to have a surfeit of him, or to sup too full of horrors. The crime for which Helen leaves him is rightly one repellent in idea only, not in representation: there are no revolting scenes between him and his resident mistress, the governess. Thus the way is properly prepared for his dreadful end, which disgusts in all the possible ways open to Anne Brontë to use.

His death is a fine example to add to the Brontë collection of unforgettable death scenes, devoid of sentimentality, conventional responses, or cant. The toughness in the face of artistic truth that makes Charlotte Brontë's Mrs Reed hate Jane Eyre right to the end, and die with only Jane's

> grating anguish for *her* woes – not *my* loss – and a sombre tearless dismay at the fearfulness of death in such a form.
>
> (*Jane Eyre*, Chapter 21)

for epitaph; makes Anne Brontë's Helen face like truths:

> 'I know you cannot love me as you once did – and I should be very sorry if you were to, for I could not pretend to return it.'
>
> (Chapter 48)

She will have nothing to do with deathbed repentance – even a maudlin one – and uncompromisingly goes on depicting Huntingdon's habit of misconstruing Helen's motives:

> 'I would give my life to serve you, if I might.'
> 'Would you *indeed*? – No!'
> 'Most willingly, I would.'
> 'Ah! that's because you think yourself more fit to die!'
>
> (Chapter 49)

Arthur Huntingdon exemplifies another of Anne Brontë's unobtrusive powers as a novelist: he always exists physically. His attraction for Helen is in physical terms – he is her 'flesh and blood lover' (Chapter 21), his 'luxuriant chestnut locks' are frequently noted (ibid.), and his phrenology is significant

> 'But look here, Helen – what can a man do with such a head as this?'

The head looked right enough, but when he placed my hand on top of it, it sunk in a bed of curls, rather alarmingly low, especially in the middle.

'You see I was not made to be a saint,' said he, laughing.

(Chapter 23)

and he dies emphatically in the body as well as the spirit, of gangrene:

His body will be consigned on Thursday to that dark grave he so much dreaded; but the coffin must be closed as soon as possible.

(Chapter 49)

As a creation of character in the medium of the novel, he must stand high as one of the few delineations of powerful evil, of the vicious man who is also socially popular, who indulges in the more attractive vices – those of drink, food and love – and has to his credit a handsome person, a vigorous nature, and for a time a loving wife, yet who is never felt by the reader to be for one moment enjoyable or sympathetic.

Anne Brontë's ways of constructing and presenting what she has to say, use, like her characterization, very simple and unobtrusive means, for results that are effective and original, and more elaborate than they seem. She continues to rely, as in *Agnes Grey*, on a candid literal narrative, without any but the very simplest and commonplace imagery, and still relies also on dialogue to produce an effect of reality, distinguishing her speakers by the content of what they say, rather than by idiom. *The Tenant of Wildfell Hall* represents an advance on *Agnes Grey* however, by its very much more complicated structure.

Like *Wuthering Heights*, *The Tenant of Wildfell Hall* makes vital use of its very precise time-scheme and its narrators, to explore the complexities inherent in a very simple story, by using narrative within narrative, and different degrees of retrospect. It begins, like *Wuthering Heights*, about a year before its end, with a narrator who is more observer than actor, who has no part in the central happenings of the story, which are told to him in his turn by a teller who, much more involved in what she tells, reaches back into the past. For the first fifteen chapters Gilbert Markham narrates the events of the last months of 1827; Helen's journal – the next thirty-nine chapters – covers the earlier years from the summer of 1821; the novel concludes with eight chapters which are again Gilbert's account of the events of 1828, supplemented by Helen's letters. Gilbert purports to be retelling the whole novel from twenty years later, from the position of the contented middle-aged family man surrounded by his own and Helen's 'promising young scions', in the author's 'present' of 1847. The result is a movement which resembles *Wuthering Heights*, where the most vital and moving sections are at the centre of the novel; the beginning being startling, and mysterious, but arousing curiosity rather than inviting participation; and the end being the necessary resolution of what has gone before. Like *Wuthering Heights*, the end is rapidly brought about, with two short chapters to comprehend Gilbert's courtship and marriage. Yet it would not be safe to say that Anne Brontë has imitated *Wuthering Heights*. Her structure seems the natural and proper outcome of her intentions, not something imposed. The resemblance between the two novels shows a similar way of seeing life and human experience – one that involves seeing life as a whole that is formed by the concept of 'paying the uttermost farthing' – rather than a similar idea of how to construct a novel.

There are considerable differences between the methods and effects of Anne Brontë's two narrators. The first, Gilbert Markham, though not completely realized as a person, is more successful as a structural device; though, since his personality actually influences the story, he cannot, like Lockwood in *Wuthering Heights*, be judged to succeed merely because he fulfils his structural purpose. One of his functions is a means of creating the mystery. Anne Brontë shows the influence of *Jane Eyre* in the movement of the first fifteen chapters, through an unconventional courtship to a proposal of marriage to one who is married already, with the whole accompanied by hints of mystery and concealment. The mysterious circumstances in *The Tenant of Wildfell Hall* are far more commonplace – a widow with no connections who supports herself, who never lets her son out of her sight, who puts false titles on her paintings of local scenes, and possesses portraits of a strange man she refuses to identify – but even so, mystery was a method not hinted at in *Agnes Grey*, which was written before *Jane Eyre*.

The result of Gilbert's narrative, moving steadily through its short time-span (the autumn of 1827) and looking back at it from a point twenty years on, is to rob Helen's sensational story of much of its sensationalism before it begins, and to present mystery with the minimum of suspense. Both effects are necessary, when Anne Brontë is so intent on making her horrors not sensational, but real, and when the solution to her mystery cannot be the rapid one suspense would demand (and *Jane Eyre* supplies), but the whole story of Helen's married life. Gilbert's narrative forms a solid convincing reality against which later outrageous events may be assessed; it gives the chance to see the heroine Helen from the observer's point of view before becoming absorbed in her own history; and to see her for the first time when most of her troubles are over. The reader is, therefore, when hearing Helen's story, free enough from anxiety over the outcome to concentrate on the significance of the events.

Helen's journal brings the reader into much closer proximity to the events it relates. There is no sense of retrospect and proportion as there is in Gilbert's account, or as there was in Agnes Grey's story, written by a happy woman years after the unhappy events. Anne Brontë makes sure that the reader shall perceive the brutalizing effects of debauchery, on the debauchee and all his associates, at close range; otherwise the reader, were he not led like Helen to accept one enormity after another, would not credit Huntingdon's final brutalities. Anne Brontë has all the advantages of Richardson's epistolary method and the claustrophobic closeness it produces, while evading most of the improbabilities it entails. Being literal-minded and realistic she tries very successfully to create something like a genuine journal, without depending on literary convention to extenuate improbabilities. She makes Helen's outpourings in her journal her one relief; her journal is her confidante, and telling her troubles helps her to withstand them:

I have found relief in describing the very circumstances that have destroyed my peace, as well as the little trivial details attendant upon their discovery. No sleep I could have got this night would have done so much towards composing my mind, and preparing me to meet the trials of the day – I fancy so, at least; – and yet, when I cease writing, I find my head aches terribly; and when I look into the glass I am startled at my haggard, worn appearance.

(Chapter 33)

Helen's feats of memory in reporting conversation are not past belief, when compared with what Boswell, for instance, can do; while Anne Brontë's own neutral style, which makes little use of personal idiom for different speakers, makes Helen's reporting even more lifelike.

The journal narrative offers a greater number of different perspectives than either the epistolary mode it resembles – of the letter written just after the event – or the autobiography written some time after the events it narrates, like *Agnes Grey*. At moments of climax such as Chapter 34, in which Helen faces Annabella, the journal entry, of events of the morning, is written the same evening; but when a longer view is needed, such as Helen's assessment of her second year of married life (in Chapters 28–30), the entry that comprises them looks back from almost a year later.

That Anne Brontë knows that this diary-structure is not literary structure is proved by the other scheme she imposes on her novel: the customary one of dividing into the normal chapters of the three-volume novel. The journal entries vary from a few lines to over twenty pages, and often run across the divisions of the chapters. A chapter may contain several short journal entries (Chapters 14–15), or may not contain the whole of a single one. Clearly the journal-division is decided by what the author wishes to do through her narrator, whereas the division into chapters is one of the few direct evidences of the author herself. The chapters mark the passage of time in the normal way, without the change of view of a new journal entry, or mark a sudden complete change of topic as at Chapter 39 where, from a Huntingdon relieved that Annabella has left —

'She was so deuced imperious and exacting,' said he: 'now I shall be my own man again, and feel rather more at my ease.'

—Helen moves on abruptly to fears for her son:

My greatest source of uneasiness, in this time of trial, was my son, whom his father and his father's friends delighted to encourage in all the embryo vices a little child can show.

Anne Brontë is like her sisters in being unique, in being apparently very little influenced by any writer before her, and in writing for ends which the novel had not previously been made to serve. While she is not as great as either of them, she is never a bad or second-rate artist. She seems to do all that is possible by taking pains, by being fully conscious of the end to which she is working, and by directing all her powers towards it. She is not a great novelist, because she has no passion to express, nor any new or original view of human nature to expound. But she is never meretricious or showy, having always a purpose in writing worthy in itself, and fit for a novel. Her two novels are original, because both use new material to illuminate old truths about man in his society, and because both work out their own personal methods. She is not derivative – although she does not hesitate to admit influences where an earlier novelist's effects are similar to her own – since no novelist offers her a model in a similar field; and she has no successors, partly because her achievement is so modest (despite the popular success of *The Tenant of Wildfell Hall*), and partly because her effects are so closely the result of her purpose that they cannot be used for any other. The contemporary who comes closest to *The Tenant of Wildfell Hall* – as Mark Rutherford to *Agnes Grey* – is not a novelist, but a writer, Harriet Martineau, who also found that fiction was at some points the fit and proper medium for a theory, even though the theories of Harriet Martineau were more coherent, philosophical and practical. Both women write robustly and plainly, with the startling truth that comes from the apparently self-evident and unremarkable; though neither can make the claim to the single masterpiece that Emily Brontë makes with *Wuthering Heights*, or the claim to be a major novelist with a corpus of professional writing that Charlotte Brontë's four novels make for her. Few people now dispute Emily's claim. Charlotte's, admitted in her lifetime, later suspect and disallowed, is vindicated by close critical scrutiny. Anne has rarely been thought worth the trial, but yet sustains it with a success that, though modest, is complete.

BIBLIOGRAPHY

So much has been written about the Brontës and their works that any
bibliography must necessarily be selective. I have here included,
besides the writings cited in the foregoing chapters, only those others
which I have found particularly important, whether for their intrinsic
value, or for the profitable disagreement which they provoke.

I WORKS BY THE BRONTËS

The Shakespeare Head Brontë, ed, T. J. Wise and J. A. Symington,
19 vols., Oxford, 1931–8.

The Complete Poems of Emily Jane Brontë, ed. C. W. Hatfield, Oxford,
1941.

II OTHER WORKS

BENTLEY, PHYLLIS, *The Brontës*, Home and Van Thal, 1947.
The Brontë Sisters, Longmans, Green & Co., 1950.

BRADBY, G. F., 'Emily Brontë', *The Nineteenth Century*, CVIII, 1930.

BRONTË SOCIETY TRANSACTIONS, Shipley, Yorks, 1895–.

CECIL, LORD DAVID, *Early Victorian Novelists*, Constable, 1934.

CHRISTIAN REMEMBRANCER, XV, Review of *Jane Eyre*.

COOPER-WILLIS, I., *The Authorship of 'Wuthering Heights'*, Hogarth,
1936.

DELAFIELD, E. M., *The Brontës: their Lives Recorded by their Contemporaries*, Hogarth, 1935.

DIMNET, E., *Les Soeurs Brontë*, Paris, 1910.

DOBELL, S., 'Emily Brontë', *Life and Letters*, I, 1878.

DRY, FLORENCE S., *The Sources of 'Jane Eyre'* and *The Sources of
'Wuthering Heights'*, Heffers, 1940.

ELTON, O., *A Survey of English Literature*, 1830–1888, II, 1924.

EWBANK, INGA-STINA, *Their Proper Sphere*, Arnold, 1966.

FORÇADE, E., Reviews of *Jane Eyre* and *Shirley*, *Revue de Deux Mondes*, XXIV and XL, 1849.

GASKELL, E. C., *Life of Charlotte Brontë*, Smith, Elder & Co., 1857 (first and third editions).

GÉRIN, W., *Anne Brontë*, Nelson, 1959.
    Branwell Brontë, Nelson, 1961.

GOODRIDGE, F. G., *Emily Brontë: 'Wuthering Heights'*, Arnold, 1964.

HARDY, BARBARA, *'Wuthering Heights'*, Blackwell, Oxford, 1963.
    'Jane Eyre', Blackwell, Oxford.

LEAVIS, F. R., *The Great Tradition*, Chatto & Windus, 1948.

LEAVIS, Q. D., *Fiction and the Reading Public*, Chatto & Windus, 1932.

LEWES, G. H., 'Recent Novels; French and English', *Fraser's Magazine* XXXVI, 1847.
    Review of *Jane Eyre* and *Shirley*, *Edinburgh Review*, January 1850.

MILLER, J. H., *The Disappearance of God*, Harvard, 1963.

MARTIN, R. B., *The Accents of Persuasion*, Faber & Faber, 1966.

MOORE, GEORGE, *Conversations in Ebury Street*, Heinemann, 1936.

OLIPHANT, M., *Women Novelists of Queen Victoria's Reign*, Hurst and Blackett, 1897.

OXFORD AND CAMBRIDGE MAGAZINE, I, 1856. 'Charlotte Brontë and Thackeray.'

RALLI, A., 'Emily Brontë: the problem of personality', *Critiques*, Longmans, 1927.

RATCHFORD, F. E., *The Brontës' Web of Childhood*, Columbia, 1941.
    Gondal's Queen, Texas, 1955.

RIGBY, E., '*Jane Eyre* and *Vanity Fair*' in *Famous Reviews*, ed. R. B. Johnson Pitman, 1914.

ROBINSON, A. M. F. (Mme Duclaux), *Emily Brontë*, W. H. Allen, 1883.

SAINTSBURY, G., *A History of Nineteenth Century Literature*, Macmillan, 1896.

S(ANGER), C. P., *The Structure of 'Wuthering Heights'*, Hogarth, 1926.

SCHORER, 'Fiction and the Matrix of Analogy', *Kenyon Review* XI, 1949.

SHORTER, C. K., *The Brontës and their Circle*, Hodder and Stoughton, 1896.
    The Brontës: Life and Letters, Hodder and Stoughton, 1908.

SINCLAIR, MAY, *The Three Brontës*, Hutchinson, 1912.

SPARK, M. and STANFORD, D., *Emily Brontë*, Peter Owen, 1953.

TILLOTSON, KATHLEEN, *Novels of the Eighteen-forties*, Oxford, 1954.

THE TIMES, Review of *Shirley*, 7 December 1849.

TURNELL, MARTIN, 'Wuthering Heights', *Dublin Review*, CCVI, 1940.

VAN GHENT, DOROTHY, *The English Novel: Form and Function*, Harper, 1961.

VISICK, MARY, *The Genesis of 'Wuthering Heights'*, Hong Kong, 1958, Oxford, 1959.

WARING, S. M., 'Charlotte Brontë and Lucy Snowe', *Harper's Magazine*, XXXII, 1865.

WOOLF, VIRGINIA, *The Common Reader*, First Series, Hogarth Press, 1925.

INDEX

The titles of the novels have been abbreviated as follows:

WH *Wuthering Heights*
P   *The Professor*
JE *Jane Eyre*
S   *Shirley*
V   *Villete*
AG *Agnes Grey*
T   *The Tenant of Wildfell Hall*

257

The Professor – contd.

its originality, 51–2; use of place, 66–8; style, 68–9; compared with *Wuthering Heights,* 51

Pryor, Mrs (*S*), 132, 136, 141, 151, 154; her nature and functions, 148–9

Rachel (the original of Vashti), 168, 175, 189

Ratchford, F. E., 5

Redgauntlet, see Scott, Sir Walter

Reed, Eliza (*JE*), 76, 90, 115; her nature and functions, 88

Reed, Georgiana (*JE*), 76, 90, 109, 115; her nature and functions, 88

Reed, John (*JE*), 76, 88, 90, 116, 121; his nature and functions, 89

Reed, Mrs (*JE*), 79–80, 88, 90, 95, 114, 115, 116, 117, 181, 247; her nature and functions, 89

Religion, in Charlotte Brontë, 51, 88–9, 125, 131, 139, 192 n., 197, 198; in Emily, 11

Reuter, Mme (*P*), 48, 50, 56; her nature and function, 63

Reuter, Zoraïde (*P*), 50, 51, 53, 56, 58, 148, 181; her nature and functions, 60–2; her sources, 60

Richardson, Samuel, 72 n., 234–5, 250; *Clarissa*, 105 n., 235; *Sir Charles Grandison*, 101, 235

Rigby, E. (Lady Eastlake), Review of *Jane Eyre*, 96

Rivers, Diana (*JE*), 145; her nature and function, 98–9

Rivers, Mary (*JE*), her nature and function, 98–9

Rivers, St John (*JE*), 36, 54, 59, 87, 98, 104, 106 n., 112, 114, 118; his nature and functions, 99–100

Rob Roy, see Scott, Sir Walter

Robinson, Mrs Elizabeth, 204

Rochester, Edward Fairfax (*JE*), 70–122, 53, 59, 64, 68, 127, 136 n., 154, 164, 167, 171, 176 n., 179, 215, 216 n., 238; his nature and functions, 101–7; 110; his antithesis St John Rivers, 99; as seen in Jane's retrospect, 81–3; as revealed by Adèle, 98; by Bertha Mason, 97; by Grace Poole, 94; by Thornfield, 111–12; by Ferndean, 113

Rosine (*V*), 198

Rutherford, Mark, 227, 252

St Pierre, Zélie de (*V*), 170, 181, 198

Schoolgirls, in *The Professor,* 58; in *Villette*, 168, 172–3, 178

Schoolteachers, in *The Professor,* 62; in *Jane Eyre*, 92, 167; in *Shirley*, 148; in *Villette,* 167

Scott, Joe (*S*), 133

Scott, Sir Walter, 42 n., 52, 68, 124, 194; *Guy Mannering*, 238; *Marmion,* 83; *Old Mortality,* 46 n., 128, 174, 184 n.; *Redgauntlet,* 206; *Rob Roy,* 145; *Tales of my Landlord,* 42 n.; *Waverley,* 46 n., 126, 130

Schorer, Mark, 42 n.

Settings, in Anne Brontë, 225–6, 234–5; in Charlotte, 65–7, 109–13, 152, 192–3; in Emily, 43

Shakespeare, William, 6, 154, 194, 198, 208; *King Lear,* 47